CW00678233

The Arabists of Shemlan

Volume I

MECAS Memoirs 1944-78

THE ARABISTS OF SHEMLAN

Copyright © MECAS Association 2006

Stacey International
128 Kensington Church Street
London W8 4BH
Tel: 020 7221 7166 Fax: 020 7792 9288
website: www.stacey-international.co.uk
e-mail: marketing@stacey-international.co.uk

ISBN: 1-905299-14-1

CIP Data: A catalogue record for this book is available from the British Library

Editor: Paul Tempest

Editorial Panel Sir James Craig, Sir Donald Maitland, Paul Tempest

Design: Kitty Carruthers

Printing & Binding: Cambridge University Press

THE ARABISTS
OF SHEMLAN

VOLUME I

MECAS MEMOIRS 1944-78

Editor
Paul Tempest

Editorial Panel
Sir James Craig, Sir Donald Maitland, Paul Tempest

STACEY INTERNATIONAL

CONTENTS

Part Three: The Middle East Centre for Arab Studies 1958-65

PART FOUR: The Middle East Centre for Arab Studies 1966-78

King Abdul Aziz (Ibn Saud) of Saudi Arabia quoted in
Harold Dickson, *Kuwait and her Neighbours, (1956)*:

'*We are most anxious that the British Government should
send us every eight months or so an experienced officer whom
they trust ... But such a person must be thoroughly conversant
with our language, understanding the wider meaning of our
beautiful tongue which is so full of parables and expressive
phrase ... He should know and understand our Arab
psychology, be conversant if possible with our Arabian
manners and customs and above all should be acquainted
with our Arab pride and our hopes and have read something
of God's holy word as vouchsafed to us in our blessed Quran.*'

PREFACE

The nature and the work of MECAS (the Middle East Centre for Arab Studies) are described in the first two chapters of this book. It was a British Government school which set out, at first in Jerusalem and later in the small Lebanese village of Shemlan, to teach the Arabic language and Arab history and culture to people from outside the Middle East. To begin with, it took only students from Britain and the Commonwealth. But soon it opened its doors to allcomers and during the 34 years of its life something over 3,000 students from a wide range of nationalities passed through its various courses: from Australia in the south to Sweden in the north, from California in the west to Japan in the east.

In 1987, nine years after the school closed, the MECAS Association was set up. It is, so to speak, an old boys' club in a very British tradition, but with a cosmopolitan membership. We have a club tie and a newsletter, and twice a year we meet to eat and drink together and to discover how, after so many years, we have all turned out. Young men (and a very few women) who were once nervous students, idle or sedulous, eager or bored, austere or dissolute, have metamorphosed into politicians, professors, ambassadors, generals, businessmen or, nowadays, into old age pensioners, playing golf, babysitting or collecting for Oxfam. Some of us, poor souls, write angry letter to the press about Mr Blair or Mr Bush.

At these bi-annual gatherings there is always a flow of reminiscence. Most of us (perhaps not all) remember Shemlan with affection and nostalgia: a quiet, old-fashioned, hospitable village and a vibrant academy which provided a mixture of hard intellectual work and, only an hour or so away, the city lights of Beirut and the gaiety of the ski resorts.

So we decided to invite our members to submit their recollections. They flooded in, brief anecdotes and meandering screeds, too much to be included in a single book, or even two.

This volume contains only memories of MECAS itself and life in Shemlan. We hope to produce a sequel which will cover our members' experiences in their later careers when they were often conspicuous figures in momentous events, political, financial, military. All contributions, published and unpublished, will be collected and arranged into a MECAS archive and lodged eventually in a suitable academic repository, to be consulted by future historians.

A final word: for an idea of what Shemlan was like in its last dying days, the village community, the civil war, the horrors, the hilarity, even the romance, take the longest piece here, by Duncan Campbell-Smith: vivid, personal, evocative, poignant, yet in the end happy and fruitful. But indeed you will notice in most of the memoirs an affection for Shemlan and the Lebanon, a nostalgia for a place and a society now irretrievably lost.

For a history of MECAS see *Shemlan: A History of MECAS* by James Craig (Macmillan 1998), in whose Foreword Lord Hurd of Westwell writes:

'Eighteen miles into the mountains which overhang Beirut is perched the village of Shemlan, now deserted, but once a place of solid stone houses, harsh winters, many flowers in the spring and an unmatched view to the sea. Here from 1947 until the Lebanese Civil War forced its closure in 1978 the Foreign Office trained in the Arabic language its own officers and students from private firms and foreign countries.

Legends clustered around this school (MECAS) throughout its life, forming one of the minor myths of Midde-Eastern politics.

To the Israelis MECAS was the place where Britain trained its bright young men to be sentimental about the Arabs and hostile to Zionism. To many Arabs it was simply the "School for Spies", the heart of Britain's postwar strategy of dominating the Middle East through its intelligence agencies...'

LIST OF CONTRIBUTORS

Sir Antony Acland
Sir Mark Allen
Nicholas Armour
Michael Ashmore

Michael Baddeley
Rex Baker
Philip Bowcock

Duncan Campbell-Smith
Lt Col. Antony Cawston
Dr Peter Clark
Sir Terence Clark
Major Peter Clayton
Sir John Coles
Sir Sherard Cowper-Coles
Sir James Craig

Wing Commander John Deverill
John Doble

Sir Stephen Egerton
Mark & Kate Evans

Donald Foster
Professor Benjamin Foster

David Gillespie
The Hon. Sir David Gore-Booth

Ann Hopkins

Alan Jones
Frank Jungers

Shirley Kay

Sir Archie Lamb
John Lansley
Norman Lewis
The Hon Ivor Lucas

Sir Donald Maitland
Tony Milson
David Morphet

Bill Norton

Brian Pridham

Sir Antony Reeve
George Rolleston

Ian Skeet
Brian Stewart
Sir Alec Stirling
Major Ben Strachan
David Summerhayes

Paul Tempest

John Udal

Group Captain Brian Walford
Robert Walmsley
Rosalind Ward Gwynne
Sir Michael Weir
Louis Wesseling
Edric Worsnop
Lord (Patrick) Wright of Richmond

MECAS: AN OVERVIEW

James Craig

MECAS is an acronym for the Middle East Centre for Arab Studies, which was a school set up primarily to teach the Arabic language, but also the background to Arab society: history, religion, politics, economics, and geography. It was founded during the Second World War, at a time when Britain was the dominant power in the Middle East and the British army occupied – and ruled – almost the whole of the Levant. It began as an army idea, a place to train officers from the forces, and most of the people behind the idea were army officers – Brigadier Clayton, head of Intelligence in Cairo, Colonel Altounyan, a wandering Intelligence officer, General Glubb, commander of the Arab Legion in what was then called Transjordan. The only civilian involved in the conception was Edwin Chapman – Andrews, a Foreign Office man attached to the Commander-in-Chief's office in Cairo. A junior officer, Robert Maugham, nephew of the writer Somerset Maugham, has claimed to be the originator of the idea. His claim is exaggerated. The army – and Clayton in particular – had been thinking of something similar a year before Maugham appeared on the scene.

What Maugham suggested in 1942 – when it looked as if Rommel was about to occupy Egypt and the Germans might come down in a pincer movement from the Caucasus into the Fertile Crescent – was to train some officers to stay behind in the Arab lands as resistance fighters to harry the putative German forces of occupation. At that time the authorities were too busy to bother with the idea, and in any case the defeat of Rommel at El Alamein in November 1942 removed the need for it. What had already been germinating was a bigger idea. Britain had discovered, as the boundaries of the war expanded, that it needed people who could speak the more unusual languages: Chinese, Japanese, Turkish, Persian, and, of course Arabic. Emergency courses were set up in Britain at universities and at army centres, but they were slow,

1

specialised and limited in capacity. I myself, for example, began a course in Japanese designed to let us intercept communication between the front line and HQ and therefore to teach us only basic grammar and the names of guns, ammunition, spare parts for vehicles and the like. So we learnt the Japanese for a 75 mm shell but not how to say good morning.

Jerusalem

The army in the Middle East had something bigger in mind. It was assumed that the empire would continue after the war and that we should therefore need a pool of men equipped with a knowledge and an understanding of the people who were going to enjoy the benefit of our rule. If you accept the premise (and of course it was mistaken) the intention was good.

It was this intention that attracted politicians and the Foreign Office to the idea. The proposal was taken up by the Minister of State Resident in Cairo (at the time the Australian Richard Casey) and put to the cabinet in London. The result was that, when the centre opened its doors in Jerusalem in 1944, its administration was soon handed over to the Foreign Office and remained with the Foreign Office to the end of its days. This change meant that, though the students on the first course were all officers from the army and RAF, people from Shell and BOAC were admitted to the Second Course a year later. A Foreign Office diplomat was on the Third Course, and thereafter civilians became and remained the great majority of the student body.

Some of the names I have mentioned as joint founders of MECAS will be familiar. Sir Edwin Chapman-Andrews was ambassador in Beirut from 1951 to 1956. Glubb Pasha achieved international fame. Ernest Altounyan for nearly half a century ran a hospital in Aleppo, which charged high fees to the rich and treated the poor for nothing. His knowledge of the area and its languages enabled him to serve as British Intelligence officer in both wars. Brigadier Clayton was an erudite Intelligence officer whose relative had done a similar job in the First World War and had been the patron and guide of T E Lawrence.

The first director of the centre was Bertram Thomas, a famous

British traveller who in 1931 had made the first crossing of the Empty Quarter. His Principal Instructor was a British army officer, Major Aubrey Eban, who was later to become the Foreign Minister of Israel. Eban resigned after two years to join the Jewish Agency. By then Palestine was a turmoil of bombs and riots and in the autumn of 1947 MECAS was obliged for security reasons to move to the little village of Shemlan in the Lebanon.

The Spy School Allegations

The combination of Eban, army intelligence and the Foreign Office soon gave rise to the story that MECAS was a school for spies. The story was current as early as 1948, when a MECAS student, an officer from a Scottish regiment, walking – for the sake of exercise – from Shemlan to Btaddin, was stopped by the gendarmerie at Deir al Qamar and searched on suspicion of being a Jewish spy. His indignation was increased by their attempt to find pockets in his kilt.

Let me dispose of this story – I was going to say once and for all; but it will never die. Imagine that you are the commander of the famous Secret Intelligence Service. You wish to train your men in the arts of espionage. Would you send them to a foreign country where your government is extremely unpopular? To a tiny mountain village where the movements of every stranger can be constantly observed and reported? Would you staff the school with Palestinian teachers, who believed, not without reason, that your government had recently stolen their country and handed it over to an enemy state? Would you then open the school for employees of 97 different organisations, 51 of them from outside the United Kingdom, governments, oil companies, banks, business firms, and mix them all up side by side with your trainee spies? Would you later invite any journalist, from any nationality, to visit the school without notice? Would you finally invite the representative of your bitterest critic in the Middle East, the Egyptian Ambassador to Lebanon, to come and look round whenever he liked? Would you indeed, In the midst of all the accusations, have appointed James Craig as the Principal Instructor, a man who had never had any contact with the government who had spent his working life teaching grammar at university, who couldn't tell a spy from a sparrow-hawk.

Anyone who did such things would surely have been off his head – unless of course it was a characteristic piece of double bluff by perfidious Albion. Nevertheless, thousands of people, sensible people, educated people, believed the story. Many still do. Heaven help us all.

Life in Shemlan was Spartan

At any rate, almost exactly fifty years ago, MECAS moved into three old buildings at the bottom of Shemlan. There was a house for the Director and two square blocks for the school, with classrooms, a common room and a dining room on the ground floor and bed-sitters for bachelor students upstairs. Married students, who began to arrive a year or two later, rented houses in the village.

The school buildings were in the traditional Lebanese style of fine masonry. They had been put up in the 1920s by a British missionary, Miss Frearson, as an orphanage for Armenian refugees. But they occupied the site of an earlier silk factory established in the middle of the last century by a Mr Scott and later sold to a Beiruti, the Marquis de Freij. Originally those older buildings had been a residence of the Emir Haydar Shehab. The school was handsome to look at and had splendid views down over the coast. But it was not at all comfortable and in the winter it could be grim when the electricity was cut off and there was no hot water. The students for the most part were young and tough and the cold kept them awake for their studies. On the old British university pattern, the mornings were devoted to lessons, the afternoons to recreation and the evenings to homework and private study. The fleshpots of Beirut were too far away to be a temptation, except at weekends.

At first the teaching was unsystematic, even chaotic, and some of the students were less than enthusiastic. Two army officers who arrived for the 1947 course left after one night when they had seen the conditions. They were particularly incensed by the absence of a bar. Whether you succeeded or failed in those early years depended often on personal initiative and application.

Academic Reform

But the arrival of Donald Maitland as Director in 1956 saw the beginning of a period of reform. He and I worked as a team – the soft cop and the hard cop. I leave you to speculate which was which. The famous MECAS Word List was produced and applied to all the branches of teaching. New textbooks were written, a new curriculum devised, a new spirit imbued. The language break, a month in the middle of the year when the students went off to practise what they had learnt, was tightened up. They no longer rambled aimlessly round the Levant but were sent to live with families or in small country inns or even in a monastery. The main emphasis was placed on the acquisition of language. Lectures on background subjects continued but less time was devoted to them. Students were expected to read up those things for themselves. MECAS was no longer a holiday. But I think it was still fun.

The most visible change in those years was to move the school to a new site. The old buildings were inconvenient and inefficient. Expectations of comfort were rising. We looked at other villages – at Suq el Gharb and Brummana, for example – but without satisfaction. Finally, a son of Shemlan came to our rescue. The late and much loved Eddy Hitti agreed to build us a new school at the top of the village and offered generous terms. The 16th Course started in October 1959 in the new buildings, designed to our own specifications, not so beautiful, not so traditional, not so Lebanese as the old school, but much easier to run. That is the way of the world nowadays.

Growth and Expansion

This was a time not only of reform and removal but also of expansion. The 1947 course had accepted only 20 students. The numbers steadily increased until in the sixties 60 or more were passing through our school each year. Of these sixty, more and more were non-British. The Japanese began to come in large numbers, both from the Diplomatic Service and from business firms. American universities organised a programme, supervised by Professor Bayly Winder of Princeton the son-in-law of Philip Hitti, a distinguished Lebanese-American scholar, to send their students

5

of Arabic for a year at Shemlan in the middle of their undergraduate course. The Swiss came, the Germans, Pakistanis, Swedes, a Cuban and even an Omani diplomat. Even officers from the Quai d'Orsay in Paris, came to study Arabic at a British institution through the medium of English. This was a real feather in our cap.

In addition, Maitland introduced the Background Course, a week of lectures and discussions on politics, history, economics, and religion designed for expatriate businessmen and officials (and their wives) who were working all over the Middle East and came to Shemlan to learn about the society they were living in. The first course was in 1959 with thirty applicants. It proved so popular that soon there were two courses a year with sixty attending from a wide variety of nationalities. MECAS was thus carrying out a higher mission: to spread an understanding of the East among more or less ignorant westerners.

Teaching Arabic

Teaching the Arabic language remained, nevertheless, the main task. Arabic poses particular problems. First, there is the deep split between literary Arabic, the language of the media and formality, and the colloquial, the language of everyday intercourse. Which should we teach? Answer: both. Our students would need to read and also to talk and listen. Fine, but then, which colloquial do we teach? Our students at the end of their course would be going to all parts of the Arabic world: to Cairo, Morocco, the Yemen. Answer: we teach a modified colloquial, the dialect of the Levant with the extreme local peculiarities removed. But that, you will say, is not proper Arabic at all. No, but it will provide a base on which the student can build when he gets to his first new post. It was of course an artificial, factitious solution. Critics said that before the foundation of MECAS there were 18 dialects of Arabic; afterwards there were 19. Yet another black mark on the record of British imperialism.

In fact the linguistic standards reached by the ablest students were very high indeed. After ten months they moved on to the Advanced Course and then they began to toy with the language, to make puns, to deploy alliteration, to search dictionaries for obscure and amusing words. Playing a word game with me one day, one of them produced two words which I did not know after 13 years of Arabic studies. Yet another found a word meaning 'having six fingers on each hand.' Yet another claimed to have discovered a verb which meant 'he fell down the well and died of thirst.' The rest of us never found it.

Financial Constraints

The progress of MECAS was never smooth. There were always problems, some of them local, some of them originating in London. One of the home-made obstacles was money. The Treasury, i.e. the British Ministry of Finance, which like all paymasters never believes in spending a pound if a penny will do, was hostile to the very idea of MECAS. In their view it was not the business of the government to teach languages. If the Foreign Office wanted their officers to speak Arabic they should recruit people who spoke it already. If they had to teach them, they should do the job in London where it would be cheaper. And why should it take a year? Any intelligent man could pick up a language in evening classes after a good day's work at their proper job. But if there had to be a MECAS, then it must pay its way. It must charge the foreigners and non-government British such fees as would cover the cost of teaching the official students. The Foreign Office, for its part, feared that raising the fees for the outsiders would drive customers away. The result, inevitably, was a compromise: timid increases from time to time, achieved only after agonising debate; and never enough investment in new equipment and techniques or in better salaries for teachers with higher qualifications.

Propaganda Politics

The spy school myth was one of the local handicaps. One might have expected that Arabs proud of their heritage would be pleased that a leading Western power was taking such trouble to spread a knowledge of the Arabic language and Arab achievements to a wider audience. But no, nationalist politicians, were convinced or pretended to be convinced that the presence of MECAS on

Lebanese soil was a danger to the Arab cause, an instrument of lingering imperialism. From time to time they would mount a campaign for closure, sometimes on straight political grounds, sometimes using the Lebanese legal system. MECAS, they argued, was a private school. Therefore it was subject to the Private Schools Law of 1956, which laid down rigid rules for curriculums, inspections, teachers' pay and working hours. The strict application of these rules would have made it impossible to run MECAS. We should have been obliged to move elsewhere – to Jordan perhaps, or Tunisia. But that would have been a serious blow to the economy of Shemlan and its neighbouring villages, whose people worked at the Centre or sold us groceries and leased their houses. The debate went on for several years. It was largely an argument between Lebanese, with occasional interventions by the British Embassy. In the end a compromise solution was reached. It was based on that common-sense pragmatism which is one of the characteristics shared by the Lebanese and British peoples.

Arab opposition to MECAS was counter-balanced, exasperatingly, by Zionist criticism. The Israelis and their supporters in Britain regarded the Foreign Office as incorrigibly pro-Arab and attributed the blame for that to the presence in the British Diplomatic Service of a mafia of Arabists whose breeding ground was Shemlan. Pressure was applied sporadically to Foreign Secretaries to correct the alleged pro-Arab bias. It achieved a minor and not unreasonable success during the Labour Government of 1974-76, when the Foreign Secretary, James Callaghan, ruled that all Foreign Office graduates of MECAS should, soon after their graduation, pay a visit to Israel to see, as it were, the other side of the hill.

Security Risks

But the biggest problem that faced MECAS continually throughout its life was security. The main reason why the Lebanon was chosen as the new home for the Centre in 1947 when Jerusalem became impossible was Lebanese stability. As we all know now, that stability proved to be precarious and temporary. In all the troubles that followed over the years

8

Shemlan was in a very sensitive position. It was a Maronite Christian village on the border of the Druze homeland. It was always on the front line. One night during the Suez affair of 1956 my office was blown up. No-one was seriously hurt. During the civil war of 1958 MECAS had to close for a time and move the students and their families down the mountain to Beirut. Again during the Six-Day War of 1967 evacuation proved necessary. This time it lasted longer and temporary arrangements had to be made for the teaching to continue in England. The arrival of the PLO in the Lebanon after Black September in 1970 caused further problems. A bomb was discovered beside the Director's house. It was disarmed safely, but from then on security became increasingly fragile and in 1975 the civil war started. Skirmishes between rival militias, ubiquitous road blocks and the inability of the teachers to reach Shemlan from their homes eventually made life impossible and the centre was closed in 1976. This time the closure lasted a year

After much debate between London and Beirut and with many misgivings MECAS reopened in 1977. But the end came in October 1978. The teachers were paid off and the lease terminated. Since then there has been no MECAS and I do not think there ever will be again. The decision to close was taken precipitately; in my view too precipitately. I was ambassador in Damascus at the time and was indignant that I had not been consulted. But it was bound to come, if not at that particular time, then very soon afterwards. The Lebanon was in turmoil, lives were at stake and the responsibility on ministers in London was heavy. Because of the bombs MECAS ended with a bang, not a whimper. But it was a melancholy end to 34 years of honourable and successful work and achievement.

Achievements

Do those words exaggerate? Let me give some statistics. It is impossible to be exact, but about 1,100 students learnt Arabic at MECAS and over 2,000 attended the Background Courses. Those 1,100 language students came from 97 different organisations, of which 46 were from the United Kingdom, and 51 from elsewhere. 33 of those 97 organisations were governmental bodies. Fifteen were banks. Seven were oil companies. Twenty were commercial companies. Twenty-two were universities or other academic institutions. Between 1966 and 1997, 103 British ambassadorial appointments to the Arab world were MECAS graduates. (That does not mean 103 men: some of them served more than one post.) During the Kuwait crisis of 1990-91 every British ambassador in the Arab countries involved was a graduate of Shemlan. In 1997 the three senior officers in the Foreign and Commonwealth Office in London (that is, the Permanent Under Secretary, the Political Director and the Chief Clerk) the Head of the Secret Intelligence Service (MI6), and the director-general of the Middle East Association were all sons of MECAS. So were the British Ambassadors in 12 Arab countries. So, for example, were the American Ambassador in Damascus and the Japanese Ambassadors in Cairo and Kuwait. MECAS graduates have also been British ambassadors to the USA, the United Nations in New York, the European Union, Germany, Australia, India, South Africa, Pakistan, Iran, Spain, Singapore, Ireland, and the OECD. Two have even been the Governors of the Falkland Islands. One has been the Deputy Secretary General to the United Nations and another has been Commander-in-Chief of Allied Forces in Northern Europe. Not a bad record for a small school in a tiny village in the Lebanese mountains. In the process the name of that village has become famous throughout the world.

Enough of trumpet-blowing. But before I stop I must say a word of thanks – and I am sure I speak for the Foreign Office as a whole as well as for all those *khawajas* who studied or taught at Shemlan. First we owe a great debt to the Arab teachers who served at the Centre over the years. I have counted 36 in all, (20 Palestinians and 16 Lebanese) though I may have missed some who were only there temporarily or part-time. I mention five by name because of the length and dedication of their service: Taufiq Farah, Wadi' Khoury, Qustantin Theodory, Farid Tabib, and Tal'at Dajani. To them I add the long-serving British principal instructor, Leslie McLoughlin. Their names are cherished by generations of Mecasians.

I do not forget, either, some teachers who were only names to us, but names who dominated our lives at Shemlan : The Reverend

George Thatcher, whose grammar book, at first the original but later modified by our own recension, was for long the foundation of our studies and whose name was sacrilegiously given to the students' club; the German professor, Hans Wehr, whose Arabic-English dictionary, published too late for the earlier students, came to be an indispensable and scholarly resource; and Wehr's predecessor, the Lebanese Jesuit Father J G Hava, whose dictionary was in the early years the students' main support and, with its sometimes hilarious mistranslations from the French original, a welcome source of comic relief. Thatcher, Wehr and Hava, God bless them all.

The villagers of Shemlan, with its five main families – Muqaddim, Hitti, Tabib, Jabbour and Farajallah – gave us a home for 31 years and joined enthusiastically in our endeavours. Many of them who could speak English (George Hitti the taxi-driver for example) pretended not to, at our request, so as to oblige the students to use their halting Arabic. But the students learnt more from them than their language: they learnt Arab hospitality, Arab tradition, Arab life. I particularly record our debt to Eddie Hitti and his wife, true friends indeed.

Above all, we express our gratitude to the Lebanese people and their governments who welcomed us to their country and gave us shelter and support over so many years. I hope they will consider that our conduct in Shemlan and the success of our graduates have justified their kindness and their generosity. I hope too that the friendship which grew between us during our long association will last for many generations.

Sir James Craig GCMG graduated in Oriental languages (Arabic and Persian) at Oxford and became Lecturer in Arabic at Durham University for seven years. In 1948-55 he was seconded to the Foreign Office as Principal Instructor at the Middle East Centre for Arab Studies (MECAS) in Shemlan, Lebanon. He joined the Foreign Office substantively in 1956, serving as HM Political Agent in the Trucial States (1961-1964), First Secretary, Beirut (1964-1967), Counsellor and Head of Chancery, Jeddah (1967-1970), Head of Near East and North Africa Department, Foreign and Commonwealth Office, London, 1971-1975. He was appointed Ambasador to Syria (1976-1979) and to Saudi Arabia (1979-1984).

On retirement he became Visiting Professor in Arabic at Oxford, Director-General and then President of the Middle East Association (MEA), President of the British Society for Middle East Studies (BRISMES), Chairman of the Anglo-Arab Association, and several other committees and conferences connected with the Middle East. He also held several banking and commercial directorships and other academic appointments.

In 1998 he published Shemlan, A History of the Middle East Centre for Arab Studies, *(Macmillan, St Antony's series).*

FROM COLONIALISM TO FRIENDSHIP IN THE MIDDLE EAST

Donald Maitland

Human history has shown that great changes, whether political, social or economic, often followed in the wake of some cataclysm – a destructive war or some overwhelming natural disaster. We have had proof of this theory more than once during the twentieth century.

Of course the depth and pace of change will vary according to circumstances. The months I spent in the Indian sub-continent during the Second World War persuaded me that any continuation of British rule once the fighting was over would be unjustified. In this respect, when the allies debated the principles on which the post-war world order would be based, I was on Roosevelt's side not Churchill's. The emergence of India and Pakistan as independent states within two years of the end of the war inspired freedom movements throughout the world.

I was less sure about South East Asia. The Japanese claimed that they were rescuing the peoples of the countries they had overrun from western imperialism. This argument seduced even the best people including, for example, Aung San in Burma. In truth the Japanese were merely replacing one imperialism with another under the guise of the cynically named 'Greater East Asia Co-Prosperity Sphere'. It seemed unlikely that when the Japanese were removed after the war these peoples would willingly accept a return to their previous status. In any case, there would be many local scores to settle. So far as the Middle East was concerned, the future course of events seemed even more difficult to foresee. Anyone hoping to unravel the complexities to that region would face a long and steep learning curve.

Like many of my generation, I had my first glimpse of the Middle East from the deck of a troopship. The bare mountains on the north shore of the Strait of Hormuz looked forbidding, the date gardens along the banks of the Shatt al-Arab seemed artificially green and the refinery at Abadan underlined my reason for arrival to join what was known as Persia and Iraq Force. Stalingrad was under siege and I was curious to see the land which would become a major battlefield if the German 6th Army broke through the Russian defences and descended on the oilfields of Iraq and Persia.

The troopship which had brought me and my companions from Bombay to Basra had followed a much travelled route. Kaiser Wilhelm's ambition to build a railway from Berlin to Baghdad and on to Basra – the critical element in his 'Drang nach Osten', the 'Drive to the East' – had been seen in London and Delhi as a threat to the Jewel in the Crown. In 1912 the Government of India had prepared some plans to occupy Basra in the event of war and had undertaken the support of the well-disposed Sheikh of Muhammara against both the Ottoman Sultan and the Shah. The resulting campaign in Mesopotamia shattered the Kaiser's dream, ended four centuries of indifferent Ottoman rule in the land of the twin rivers, and led to the creation of the kingdom of Iraq.

In the early 1940s history was doing its best to repeat itself. The German threat was obvious and the reverses the British suffered in the Mediterranean seemed to present the Iraqi Prime Minister with the opportunity to seize power on behalf of their patrons in Berlin and Rome. By the end of May 1941 their venture had failed. Sir Kinahan Cornwallis, a well-known figure in Iraq, took over the British Embassy. Under the terms of the existing Anglo-Iraqi Treaty, the new Iraqi government agreed to the deployment of a military force of sufficient strength at least to prevent further subversion. Meanwhile, Riza Shah's tolerance of the activities of Axis agents led to the invasion of Persia by British and Russian forces. The Persia and Iraq force was created. For a time this included the Polish Division, which was to distinguish itself at Monte Cassino in 1944. While in Persia opinion remained sympathetic to the Axis cause, relations between the troops and the civilian population in Iraq were on the whole free from acrimony.

When I disembarked at Basra on Christmas Eve in 1942, the question uppermost in my mind was how the Indian battalion I was to join would fare in the event of a German victory at Stalingrad. I had no idea then that I was about to set foot in a region of the world in which I would spend a major part of my career, in which I would witness great events, see societies and relationships between peoples transformed, and learn that the virtues of friendship and generosity have dimensions I had not imagined.

* * *

In the reinforcement camp in the desert at al-Zubair no more than a sheet of canvas protected us from the piercing cold. Five months later I fell victim to heatstroke near Kirkuk. In the meantime, I had tried and failed to relate the majestic Tigris, the shining domes, the bustling traffic, the coffee houses and the clamour of the great *suq* in Baghdad to the glories of the Abbasids, the sumptuous life-style of Haroun al-Rachid and that most accomplished of confidence-tricksters, the story-teller Semiramis.

Wisely the brigade to which my battalion belonged kept its distance from towns and villages. To deceive German intelligence agents as to our real strength, we moved at frequent but irregular intervals from one site to another and, though we saw much of the country in both Iraq and Persia (as we still called Iran in those days), we had few contacts with the inhabitants. We were instructed to respect local susceptibilities. For instance, when we camped in the hills overlooking the city of Qum, we were warned not in any circumstances to approach the great mosque. On one of our exercises a member of the signal platoon which I commanded, a Muslim from the Punjab who spoke Arabic, approached me in an agitated state. A camel belonging to one of the nearby bedu had been injured; could I help? It transpired that the camel had been caught in one of our field telephone lines, and being frightened, had bolted. As it did so, the line had all but severed its foreleg. Its distressed owner indicated that he wanted me to put it out of its misery. I took my orderly's rifle and did so. When I gave the owner a note explaining what had happened and told him where to go to obtain compensation, he grabbed my hand. Out poured a torrent of words. My signalman said he was probably thanking me. Years later I realised that the old

15

man was probably asking God to give me good health, to prolong my life and to increase my well being. But at that moment his resilience impressed me. I moved up another centimetre on the learning curve.

In the autumn of 1943 I returned to India and was in South East Asia when the war ended. In 1946 I had my next glimpse of the Arab world – and not this time in the Middle East. The Mediterranean coast of Morocco provided relief from the confined environment of Gibraltar, where I had joined the staff of the Fortress Commander. Tangier's international status at the time attracted members of the cafe society. The restaurant patronised by Barbara Hutton, the notoriously wealthy Woolworth heiress, was on the list of tourist attractions. The port of Cueta was a curiosity. Scarcely any Moroccans were to be seen; one might have been in Andalucia. Tetuan was another world. As the horsemen of the Khalifa's guard in their sumptuous flowing cloaks clattered and jingled their way through the narrow streets, past whitewashed houses with green shutters, past the coffee shops and the open-school rooms, young boys being taught to recite the Quran, I admired the scrupulous way in which the fabric and traditions of a glorious inheritance were being preserved. Meanwhile, back at the War Office in London, a friendly colonel was hatching a plot. In September of that year I arrived in Jerusalem to spend a year learning Arabic at the Middle East Centre for Arab Studies

MECAS in Jerusalem, 1946

The serenity of the Austrian Hospice, at the junction of the Damascus road and the Via Dolorosa and only a short step from the Sixth Station of the Cross, was in sharp contrast to the situation beyond the walls of the Old City. The background to this unfolding tragedy was explained to us by our principal instructor, the historian George Kirk. He had succeeded a major in the British Army named Aubrey Eban, who was to achieve world renown as Abba Eban, the eloquent foreign minister of Israel. Kirk had almost completed work on his *Short History of the Middle East*, and his head was full of facts and considered judgements. From him we learned of the rivalry among the colonial powers for dominance in the Arab world, the deals of dubious wisdom struck by the victorious allies after the two world wars, the growth of Arab nationalism and the steady rise of Zionist influence in Palestine.

The last of these was in the forefront of our minds. A few weeks before our course assembled in Jerusalem, some ninety occupants of the King David Hotel had been killed by a bomb planted by the Irgun Zvai Leumi, the more active of the two Jewish terrorist groups in Palestine. The students at the Centre, most of whom, like me, were still serving officers in the armed forces, were required to wear civilian clothes, walk about in pairs, and later to carry at least one concealed pistol. A bomb in the Street of the Prophets not long after a group of us had taken tea there with one of our Arab instructors underlined the need for these precautions.

Although preoccupied with our studies, we could not fail to recognise the intractable nature of the problem facing our government in London. The facts emerging about the scale of the holocaust in occupied Europe and the determination of the survivors to make a new life in what they regarded as their 'Promised Land' steadily undermined Britain's position as mandatory power. It was already clear that the attitude of the United States administration would have a crucial impact on events and that this in turn was susceptible to the pressure of public opinion. We read with concern that Ben Hecht, a noted New York playwright and film producer, had said that his heart leapt every time he heard of the death of a British soldier in Palestine. Not long after this, President Truman pressed for the admission into Palestine of the hundreds of Jewish refugees crowded on to ships arriving unannounced into Haifa.

The situation deteriorated rapidly and at the end of January 1947 the High Commissioner decided that all non-essential personnel should leave Palestine. The Centre was closed. The students were dispersed throughout the region until temporary accommodation was found several weeks later in a tented camp in Zerqa in what was then Transjordan. I spent the intervening weeks in southern Iraq and joined the Foreign Service soon after completing the course in the autumn of 1947.

The Egyptian Department of the Foreign Office handled Britain's relations with Egypt, what was still the Anglo-Egyptian Sudan, and

Ethiopia. The department was also involved in the negotiations to determine the future status of the former Italian colonies. As the junior secretary dealing with Egypt and the Sudan, I saw all the papers relating to the future of Palestine and could sense the burden this problem placed on the shoulders of the Foreign Secretary, Ernest Bevin. The choice he and his principal colleagues faced was agonising and they were not helped by the behaviour of Richard Crossman and other leading figures sympathetic to the Zionist cause. Those of us in the Middle East departments of the Foreign Office feared the consequences for our British relations with the rest of the Arab world when, as was inevitable, the British mandate came to an end and the United Nations established the state of Israel.

I had a chance to see another side of Ernest Bevin's character. He was an ardent de-coloniser. But he recognised that the countries emerging from their colonial past into a world recovering from wartime deprivation could not achieve true independence unless they developed economically and socially. He gave strong support to the American inspired Point Four programme and was one of the principal architects of the Colombo Plan for economic assistance to the poorer members of the Commonwealth.

One of my tasks was to pursue a scheme for exploitation of the waters of the Nile. This great project envisaged regulating the flow of water from the Great Lakes in Central Africa and Ethiopia, the prevention of flooding, and the great generation of power. Talks with the Egyptian Ambassador in London and with the ministries concerned in Cairo led to a limited agreement which allowed for the construction of the Owen Falls dam in Uganda. This would regulate the outflow from Lake Victoria into the White Nile and generate electricity for the new industries to be established in the area. For Ernest Bevin this was an appropriate way of bringing the colonial era to an end. His only regret was that neither King Farouk nor the government in Addis Ababa had appreciated the immense benefits that a comprehensive scheme for more effective use of the waters of the Nile would bring to the peoples of the region. He recognised that the others involved had different preoccupations and consoled himself with the knowledge that a start had been made.

Iraq 1949-53

Towards the end of 1949 I received my first overseas posting. Having spent some months in Iraq during the war and later when studying Arabic, I at least knew how to find Amara on the map. I was to replace a former political agent who had ended his career there as Consul. Amara, I was led to understand, was an important listening post, but I was not told what I should expect to hear.

My arrival in this agreeable town on the Tigris was greeted with courtesy and understandable lack of enthusiasm by the *mutasarrif* of Amara province and his senior colleagues. In contrast, many of the tribal leaders in the area assumed that I had come to turn back the clock. It took two weeks of patient explanation to persuade my visitors that I was not in a position to intervene with anyone in Baghdad on their behalf. If, in the light of this, they wondered what purpose my presence in Amara was serving, they would have been surprised to learn that I was equally unsure. Any doubts they had did not diminish their courtesy to the guest in their country and over the months I learned much about their way of life, their alliances and their feuds and about the contribution senior members of the British administration had made to the creation of the modern state of Iraq. They spoke with reverence of such figures as Percy Cox, Henry Dobbs, Kinahan Cornwallis and the redoubtable Gertrude Bell. In his masterly work *The Arab Awakening*, George Antonius was right to acknowledge their contribution to the reconstruction of the country after the First World War.

In the summer of 1950 I was transferred to the Embassy in Baghdad where I took up the post of Oriental Secretary. My immediate chief was the Oriental Counsellor. These somewhat patronising titles implicitly, if not explicitly, evoked a former era. For nearly four years I was immersed in the political life of Iraq. In those days many senior Iraqis spoke no English and, for the foreign diplomat, knowledge of Arabic was a passport to their opinions. Fortunately, none of the current problems in Anglo-Iraqi relations gave cause for serious concern. Saleh Jabr's attempt to revise the Treaty had failed. The RAF retained their base at Habbaniya. The British Embassy continued to offer advice over the recruitment of experts to help with economic development. The long-standing Iraqi aspiration to acquire Kuwait was pursued with more rhetoric than vigour and the establishment of the state of Israel had not caused the disturbance which had been expected. Even the overthrow of the monarchy in Egypt in 1952 and the emergence of an able, ambitious and charismatic leader in the person of Gamal Abdul Nasser were accepted with little obvious enthusiasm. The Nile Valley seemed far removed from the Twin Rivers.

I soon discovered that it was not the only the *shuyukh* of Amara province and the *Muntafiq* who were reluctant to accept that the days of the British mandate were over. Faruq Samarrai, the indefatigable editor of the opposition newspaper *al-Istiqlal*, showed remarkable ingenuity in attributing every misfortune to the machinations of the British. Many others, with no similar axe to grind, were inclined to believe that the British, and the Embassy in particular, still wielded important influence not merely in regard to Iraq's foreign policy but also over the country's domestic affairs.

To be saddled with responsibility without corresponding power is never comfortable. But there was a more serious consideration. From our contacts with the moderate opposition leaders who had no illusions about the limited extent of our influence we were able to form a picture about the aspirations of the new generation. Their resentment at being persistently excluded from the centres of power was understandable. Nuri Said, who had played a distinguished role in the Arab revolt against the Turks, was still the dominant political figure. His fault was not his belief that Iraq's interests were best served by close relations with Britain, but rather his indifference to the need to delegate authority. He dismissed the occasional ugly disturbances in the streets as provocations inspired by Iraq's enemies. Sir John Troutbeck, the wise and sensitive ambassador, did his best to convey the need for reform both to the Regent and to Nuri Said, but to little effect. His reports to London and his carefully argued advice were noted, but the need for effective defence in the region to counter Soviet ambitions was a prime consideration, and London gave Nuri Said the benefit of the doubt.

During our years in Iraq my wife and I visited every corner of the country. We enjoyed our life among a most hospitable people in a land of many delights. The Tigris flowed past our house. We awakened in the crisp summer mornings to the call of the doves. It was in Iraq that our son was born; as all our friends said: 'This is what God willed.' When we left for home at the end of 1953, we were apprehensive. We feared that domestic discontent could undermine the fabric of the state the British had created a generation earlier, and that the consequences would be felt well beyond Iraq's borders.

Anthony Eden 1955-56

For most of the next two years I was involved in wider issues - the negotiations to end the wars in Korea and Indo-China, collective security arrangements in South East Asia and aid to developing countries. From the sidelines I followed Anthony Eden's efforts to promote peace in the Middle East. Since becoming Foreign Secretary in 1951 he had been active on the international stage. His successes in securing a settlement of the Trieste problem, in master-minding the Austrian State Treaty and steering the Geneva Conference on Korea and Indo-China to a reasonable conclusion encouraged him to seek yet another diplomatic triumph. This would secure his place in history as a great peacemaker. Against the better judgement of his close advisers, he turned his attention to the Middle East.

In his first public speech as Prime Minister Eden signalled his sympathy for the Arab cause. However, almost immediately his initiative ran into difficulties. Despite the successful conclusion the previous year of the negotiations to end the Anglo-Egyptian Treaty, President Nasser announced that Egypt was to purchase arms from the Soviet Bloc countries. Confusion followed on a western loan for the construction of the new Aswan Dam. However, this did not justify Eden's violent reaction to Nasser's nationalisation of the Suez Canal Company in July 1956. The most charitable verdict on Eden's conduct must be that at the time he was a sick man.

Many commentators on international diplomacy are enamoured of the 'conspiracy theory', whereas practitioners prefer the 'cock-up'. The unique feature of the Suez episode is that it was both. The one redeeming feature of this affair, which finally ended any lingering aspiration in Britain to play a world role, was the outrage at the actions of the Government expressed in Parliament and by sections of the press. I felt sympathy for those of my collegues in the small unit in Whitehall formed to handle the crisis who were obliged to carry out ministerial instructions. Lord Reading, the minister of state for whom I worked at the time, warned the Foreign Secretary of the consequences for our relations with the Commonwealth and the developing world of any military action against Egypt. For his pains his ministerial career was brought to a premature end.

I became involved after the hostilities had begun. A few days after arriving with my family in Shemlan to take up my new post as Director of the Middle East Centre for Arab Studies, I was instructed at once to go to Cyprus to take charge of the Near East Broadcasting Station whose staff, not surprisingly, had walked out in protest at the Anglo-French military intervention in Egypt. The task I was given was both distasteful and futile and it was a relief when I was permitted after a few weeks to return to Shemlan. When Peter Mansfield, one of the Foreign Service students at the Centre, told me that he could not work for a government capable of such action, and intended to resign, I suggested an alternative – to remain in the service, to seek to repair the damage and to ensure such folly was never repeated. This was the course I intended to follow. Peter Mansfield stood by his decision, and in a different way contributed brilliantly over the years to the same objectives. His tragic death in 1996 was a severe loss to a noble cause.

John Henniker-Major – A Significant Rule
Great benefits can flow when a person in authority has the wit and ability to put a good idea into practice. As head of the Personnel Department of the Foreign Office for seven years in the 1950's, John Henniker-Major, later Lord Henniker, played a critical role in creating a British Foreign Service fitted for the tasks of the post-war world. He had no doubt about the importance of Britain's relations with the countries of the Middle East. He also understood the special importance the people of the region attached to their language. Proficiency in Arabic among the members of the pre-war Levant Service was uneven and, in any case, they were given few opportunities to widen their horizons by service elsewhere in the

world. John Henniker's aim was to improve instruction in Arabic and to persuade new recruits that acquiring this specialism would not exclude them from other work, nor from the higher posts in the service.

With meticulous care, Sir James Craig, with whom I enjoyed the closest collaboration in Shemlan, has compiled a history of the Middle East Centre for Arab Studies from its establishment in the Old City of Jerusalem in the latter days of the Second World War, though its halcyon years in Lebanon until its enforced closure in the worst days of the tragic civil war. As Sir James's story shows, John Henniker's ambitions were fulfilled.

The programme launched by John Henniker had a greater significance. Britain's interests in the region had not diminished. On the contrary. But the nature of our relationship with governments in the Middle East was steadily being transformed and with the new circumstances demanded a new style of diplomacy. When Sir James and I had completed the work on the word list of modern literary Arabic, we looked for an appropriate motto which we could inscribe on the title page. In the end we settled for these words: 'To increase understanding among nations.' This expressed our determination to contribute through our work at the Centre to a new relationship with the peoples of the Middle East.

The Civil War in Lebanon in 1958

The activities of the Centre had to be suspended for some months in 1958 at the time of the first civil war in Lebanon. This sad event highlighted the difficulty of balancing that country's strong links with Europe and the United States with the need to remain in harmony with Arab nationalism. In Iraq, the violent overthrow of the monarchy had wider implications. For one thing it ended the country's long-standing special relationship with Britain; for another it introduced into the region an element of unpredictability. In Egypt other moves of significance were being made. However, the various alliances proposed by President Nasser, which were intended to enhance the international influence of the Arab world under his leadership, foundered not only because of personal rivalries but also because the platform of common interest was too narrow.

During the two years I spent in what was still the United Arab Republic in the early 1960s, I watched a revolution lose momentum. President Nasser acknowledged that the success of the revolution to which he had made the crucial contribution would depend on the leadership's understanding of the conditions they faced. Their original ambitions were admirably clear and clearly admirable. They sought the regeneration of their country within the framework of a re-awakening Arab world. They attributed the parlous state of Egypt, the unequal distribution of wealth, the incompetence of the military and the widespread corruption to the alliance between the monarchy, the land-owning class and the imperialists, by which they meant the British. They chose their moments to deal with each of these cancers in turn. In some instances they seemed not to be in a hurry. It was not until ten years after the revolution that they revealed their social programme.

For the Free Officers 1956 was a critical year. The defeat they feared over the Suez issue turned into victory. Overnight their leader became not only a popular hero in the Arab world but also a world figure of consequence. This may have persuaded Nasser and his colleagues that other governments in the Middle East, the Muslim world in general and Africa shared their wider aspirations. But this proved not to be so. Early on Nasser had correctly identified the key to the success of the revolution. But, in the event, the Free Officers misread the conditions they faced.

Repercussions of the Suez Crisis
The Suez crisis had repercussions in the Red Sea and the Gulf. The disastrous civil war in the Yemen, Kuwait's advance to independence, the British withdrawal from South Arabia, the closing down of the Political Residency based in Bahrain, the process of modernisation in Saudi Arabia and the rapid growth of the oil industry along the shores of the Gulf – all these marked the emergence of a new Arabia.

Meanwhile, in western capitals governments were coming to terms with the new realities in the Middle East. Attempts to concert reactions were often frustrated by commercial rivalries and, more serious, by the different approaches of the United States and the Europeans to the Arab-Israel dispute. In 1967 an opportunity arose to demonstrate a desire for partnership. George Brown, the British Foreign Secretary at the time, realised that the disasters that had befallen the armed forces of Egypt and other Arab states in the Six Day War offered the possibility of a fresh approach to peace. I accompanied him to the scores of meetings he held with other foreign ministers during the special debate in the General Assembly of the United Nations in New York. He was indefatigable. He pressed them all to accept the simple proposition – 'Arab recognition of Israel in exchange for the territory seized by Israel'. This was, of course, the essence of resolution number 242 adopted by the Security Council later in the year which has been the basis of such progress as has been made since then.

Libya under Qaddafi

There remained some relics of the past. Libya had emerged from under the wing of the United Nations to become an independent state in December 1951. Treaties permitted Britain and the United States to retain their bases in Cyrenaica and Tripolitania respectively. Oil was discovered in 1955 and, over the next three years, more than half of the land area was allocated to fourteen oil companies for purposes of exploration. The western, and especially the British, presence was strong and influential.

The head of state, King Idris, was a benevolent ruler, but insensitive to the transformation taking place elsewhere. His entourage had their own reasons for keeping things more or less as they were. However, in 1969, with one exception, they and the royal family made the mistake of taking their normal vacation in August and awoke on the first of September to discover that, after a bloodless revolution, Libya was now in the hands of twelve anonymous junior army officers.

I presented my credentials as British ambassador to the newly identified leader, Colonel Qaddafi, on 9 October. He wore his twenty-seven years with confidence and, throughout my time in Libya, he treated me with courtesy and consideration. For him and his young colleagues Nasser was a heroic figure and the world was as had been portrayed throughout their formative years by the *'Voice of the Arabs'*. They confessed to me later that they had been convinced that the British would invade Libya the day after their revolution to restore monarchy.

In the negotiations that led to the evacuation of the British bases at El Adem and Tobruk there were few moments of drama. Although the demands of the new regime were reasonable, it took me some time to persuade London, and the Chiefs of Staff in particular, to accept the inevitable. The formula that I put to Abdul Salam Jallud, who headed the Libyan team, envisaged a new relationship after the British withdrawal. Across the negotiating table he steadfastly refused to accept this proposition, But when our talks ended and we jointly addressed the media, he spoke eloquently about the basis which had been established for a new era in Anglo-Libyan relations. Of course, what the new regime meant by this remained to be seen.

The Euro-Arab Dialogue

Similar negotiations having led to the evacuation of the United States base outside Tripoli, the Libyan government turned their attention to the oil industry. They saw no reason why the price of oil should be set unilaterally by the companies and they cut back the production of those which did not accept their demands for a bigger share. Anti-trust legislation in the United States prevented the companies from concerting their responses. This Libyan initiative opened the way for the price increases which led to the oil crisis three years later.

I was still finding my way around the United Nations in New York when Egypt and Syria mounted their joint assault on Israel in October 1973. An early morning telephone conversation with Henry Kissinger persuaded me that concerting our response with the Americans might not be easy. So it proved. However, from the outset, my French colleague and I found ourselves in total agreement. We kept our European Community colleagues informed of our discussions with the Egyptians and the non-aligned members of the Security Council. Over the weeks the scope of these talks widened. The other European Community representatives joined us and we laid the foundation of the Euro-Arab Dialogue – a new and rewarding exercise in partnership.

The emerging relationship survived the oil crisis. When Soviet forces invaded Afghanistan on Christmas Day 1979, the response in London was swift. I accompanied Lord Carrington, the Foreign Secretary, when, in eight days in January 1980, he conveyed a message of reassurance and support to governments in Ankara, Muscat, Riyadh, Islamabad and New Delhi. This gesture was appreciated in every capital. A decade later, in the most tragic of circumstances, the emerging partnership was sealed with blood in the Gulf War.

If in 1945 it was difficult to foresee the future course of events in the Middle East, the question arises: is the crystal ball any clearer today? Threats to the stability of the region remain. Prospects for peace between Israelis and Palestinians are uncertain. The people of Iraq await the return to more tolerable government. In the name of religion, extremist movements set their own rules, which are not those of the Muslim world as a whole. But today there is an important difference. Europe and the Middle East have derived much benefit from the friendship, based on common interest and common perceptions, which has replaced the old colonialism. Surely this new strength can be deployed to influence the course of events. There can be no harm in trying.

Sir Donald Maitland GCMG OBE is a graduate of Edinburgh University. He served with the Royal Scots and Rajputana Rifles in 1941-47 in India, the Middle East and Burma. He joined the Foreign Service in 1947 with overseas appointments in Amara, Baghdad, Lebanon and Cairo. He was Director of MECAS 1956-60, Private Secretary to the Foreign Secretary 1967-69, Ambassador to Libya 1969-70, Chief Press Secretary 10 Downing Street 1970-73, UK Permanent Representative to the UN 1973-74, Ambassador to the EEC 1975-79, Permanent Under-Secretary of State, Department of Energy 1980-82. From 1996 to 2000 he was Pro-Chancellor of Bath University where he is now a Visiting Professor. His autobiography Diverse Times, Sundry Places was published in 1996 and his collected essays and lectures appeared in 2000 under the title The Running Tide. This text is based on a talk given to the Anglo-Arab Association in London, on 3 June 1997.

Part One

1944-54

JERUSALEM WITH
SPITFIRES
1944-45

Brian Walford

Whilst I was serving as Chief Instructor at the RAF Fighter Reconnaissance Operational Training Unit, my Station Commander sent for me to say that he had had a general signal from the Air Ministry inviting volunteers to attend a course at the new Middle East Centre for Arab Studies in Jerusalem. Fancying himself as a bit of a Middle-East buff, he recommended putting my name down as he thought it would be a good career move especially for anyone such as myself on a Short Service Commission since 1937, who hoped to be taken on permanently after the war.

To my astonishment I found myself selected, and not long after en route to Cairo in a cargo-carrying Dakota alongside Peter McMillan, whose academic ability soon became apparent as studies eventually began under the tutelage of Bertram Thomas and Aubrey Eban (later Israeli Foreign Minister!) at the Austrian Hospice in the old city of Jerusalem.

Surprisingly, I was retained as a student, lurking around the bottom of the class, but having a thoroughly pleasant time. My seniority, and Thomas's reluctance to offend the RAF might have had something to do with it, especially after the C-in-C RAF Middle East, Sir John Slessor, had visited the Centre and arranged for a couple of Spitfires to be established nearby for us to keep our hand in. My priorities were soon established, to the detriment of my ability to speak Arabic. The year passed agreeably enough with the RAF's reputation being well sustained by the scholarship and zeal of Peter McMillan and John Mould.

I emerged in the spring of 1945, to find myself posted to the Air Headquarters Levant outside the Damascus Gate as the Chief Intelligence Officer, working with, but far behind, Martin Charteris the GSO1 Intelligence at the Army HQ. The AOC unaccountably offered me accommodation in his official residence, which I was flattered to accept. At the closing stages of the war there was a fairly constant flow of VIPs from the UK 'swanning' out to the Middle East and beyond, and Jerusalem was always a popular attraction; my kind host deluded himself into thinking that a brand-new graduate from the Centre in his house would enhance his ability to entertain his guests and offer some authoritative views on the local scene. Although receiving no specific complaints on the quality of my duties in this respect, I managed successfully to pour out the drinks and to marry his lovely WAAF secretary.

Group Captain Brian Walford OBE attended the first MECAS course in 1944-45. He had a rich variety of postings in Britain, Antarctica, Paris, Norway and Germany before returning to the Middle East in the late 1950s as Commander RAF Persian Gulf and as the British Air Attaché in Cairo and Jeddah.

JERUSALEM IN
1945-46

David Summerhayes

Before recounting briefly some of my own experiences on the Second Course in Jerusalem, I think it worth turning back the pages of the history of MECAS to pre-war days in the Levant Consular Service. One of the regulations of the Levant Service was that new entrants should learn Arabic, Turkish or Persian to a competent standard before becoming established. You were sent to Beirut as Probationer Vice Consul until you could pass the higher standard Arabic exam. I remember meeting the then Probationers when I spent two days in Beirut in September 1939. Geoffrey Jackson was my kind host at his house in Aley, and Geoffrey Furlonge was the Consul.

Then came the war and, after the French had been evicted from Lebanon and Syria in 1941, Geoffrey Furlonge returned to Beirut as Political Officer and Consul General under the Spears Mission. At the same time my father, Christopher Summerhayes, was appointed Political Officer for the Spears Mission in Aleppo. Also prominent at that time in Aleppo was Colonel Ernest Altounyan, who became a close friend of my father. As recounted in Chapter I, page 1 of James Craig's *Shemlan*, it was Altounyan who gave Robin Maugham the impetus that got him started on the MECAS idea in mid-1942.

But it was the Levant Consular Service thinking on the vital importance of speaking Arabic with a thorough knowledge of the Arab world that inspired Maugham. He had several discussions with my father in Aleppo in 1942 and also with Furlonge in Beirut. Edwin Chapman-Andrews later gave his backing from Cairo. All these men had worked together in the Levant Consular Service and their experience pointed the way for MECAS.

Selected for MECAS, June 1945

My own first step towards joining MECAS was taken on the beach at Salerno, Italy. Assembled there to be interviewed in June 1945 came a large gathering of officers from all over the Mediterranean theatre, who had applied to become students of Arabic in Jerusalem. I had driven down there from Austria, where my wartime campaigning as a Gunner Officer had ended. I had started on the Italian campaign less than two years before from near Salerno and thus completed a circle.

The selection board sat for two full days and by the end some 60 applicants had been reduced to fewer than 10, so I considered myself very fortunate still to be on the final list. After a short and much enjoyed post-war leave at home in England, I made my way out to Jerusalem, and in October 1945 walked through the imposing arched gateway of the Austrian Hospice, deep in the Arab quarter of the Old City. I found myself part of a mixed group of 40 from all three Services, including four civilians – two from Shell and two from BOAC – all with a wide variety of experience. To me, coming from the grind of war in Italy, Palestine seemed a marvellous change. We were comfortably housed and most kindly catered for by the Austrian nuns, whose normal flow of devout pilgrims had been cut off by war. We had a competent teaching staff under George Kirk, for history, and Aubrey Eban, for Arabic, with three Palestinian Arabs – Messrs Farah, Haddad and Sa'ad – to coach us in the complication of a new and difficult language. Bertram Thomas, the Director, was good at inviting distinguished speakers from all over the Middle East to give us an insight into the problems of the day. 'BT', as we called him, was otherwise a somewhat aloof figure who did no teaching and showed little personal interest in our lives.

For me, it was George Kirk's lectures and background papers on Middle Eastern history that have left the most lasting impression. His style was dry, but his genuine enthusiasm in exploring the endless complexities of the religious and political differences in the Levant was admirable.

Palestine at that time was living out the final years of the British Mandate, which had started so promisingly in 1920. The evil consequences of Hitler's war and the holocaust were being increasingly felt, with mounting pressure on HMG to allow more immigrants to flood into the already established Jewish areas of Palestine. The ambiguities of the Balfour Declaration were being ruthlessly exploited by militant Zionism against the interests of the indigenous Moslem and Christian Arabs. British soldiers, who longed to get home after the war, were being kept on duty in Palestine and given the unpopular task of fending off illegal shipments of suffering Jewish refugees. Meanwhile, there was a growing threat from Jewish terrorists against anyone in British uniform – I was an eyewitness later to the bombing of the King David Hotel.

All this, however, did not prevent us from travelling widely in Palestine and beyond. Near at hand, we had the Old City and the ever-beautiful gilded Dome of the Rock. Outside the City, there were endless possibilities for weekend visits to biblical and other ancient sites. Some of us went over to Transjordan at the invitation of Brigadier Glubb Pasha of the Arab Legion. He also came to talk to us at MECAS and was most inspiring. Alec Kirkbride, who at that time was the other most influential figure in Amman, also gave a memorable lecture.

Probably because Aubrey (Abba) Eban was already preparing to transfer his allegiance to the Jewish Agency – as a prelude to eventually becoming Foreign Minister of Israel – he did nothing to help us in making the contacts we would have welcomed with leading Arab Palestinians. Some of us made up for this with help from well-known local notables like Mrs Katy Antonius, who introduced us to Albert Hourani and his scholarly family, and to Lulie Abul-Huda, who had worked closely with Freya Stark as a leader of the Ikhwan Al-Hurriya. Freya herself came to Jerusalem in 1946 and I was happy to see her again, having first known her when she stayed with my parents at the Hamadan Consulate in 1931, on her way to Alamut and the Valley of the Assassins. Robin Maugham himself came later to visit the Centre and told some of us of his regrets that the training at MECAS had not turned out as he had originally planned. We contested this.

The Bombing of the King David Hotel

During that summer of 1946 our studies were sometimes interrupted by the outbreak of Jewish terrorism against the restrictions imposed on the tide of attempted Jewish illegal immigration into Palestine. British forces had the thankless task of trying to prevent illegal landings in excess of the permitted quota and any British uniform could risk a bullet from Irgun terrorists in key areas of the City. This made our travels more complicated. From our windows in the Hospice we looked directly across the huddled rooftops of the Old City to the imposing stone façade of the King David Hotel. One evening as I looked out on the familiar scene, there was a rumbling explosion and the east wing of the hotel collapsed before my eyes, having been car-bombed by an Irgun team; they killed more than 20 people, two of them Army friends of ours. At the end of July we sat our final exam and were then sent off to practise our Arabic for the next month anywhere we chose to travel. Much ingenuity was applied in finding congenial and original destinations somewhere in the Arab world. I got myself an invitation to stay for two weeks with the Atiyah family in the delightful Lebanese village of Beinou, north of Beirut. They were immensely hospitable and kind, taking me for tours to the picturesque villages perched high in the Lebanese mountains. Every evening I was invited to sit with the menfolk in their *nadi* or club, where tric-trac and chess were played endlessly.

St Catherine's Monastery

For the second fortnight I joined Tony Simonds who, through a friend in the Arab Legion, had arranged a camel party to meet us at Aqaba. From there we set out to cross the Sinai desert and mountains to visit St Catherine's Monastery, which was then still a remote and inaccessible place where visitors were extremely rare. Our small party consisted of a mounted policeman, who was also our guide, a local camel-man with his young son, who was expected to walk all the way, and their Saluki dog, which ran all day through the desert chasing hares and mice (it was given no other kind of food). Tony Simonds knew all about camels – and mules – having spent several months accompanying the Emperor Haile Selassie through the Ethiopian mountains to regain his kingdom in 1941. I knew nothing about camel riding but soon learned the commands. We spent ten days riding and camping out under the stars. One night there was a spectacular thunderstorm a few miles to the north of us, and early next morning the dry river bed just in front of us filled with muddy water. A river ran for ten minutes and then just as quickly dried up. We reached the ancient St Catherine's Monastery late of an evening. Tony and I were hauled up by basket to greet the black-robed Greek Orthodox monks inside (there being no gate) while our camel party camped outside. We were taken to simple, spotlessly clean guest rooms and then entertained to supper in the Refectory. After that we took coffee with the venerable old librarian, who showed us some of the treasures of the monastery library, with many dusty volumes collected since earliest Christian days. He opened for us the famous Sinai Codex, with the earliest known version of the gospels. Time seemed to have stood still as he read some of the words of St Luke's Gospel to us.

Early next morning one of the monks came and offered to take us up the pilgrim's path to the top of Mount Sinai. It is a rough and stony climb, which some of the devout climb on their knees. The view northwards from the top was impressive and we could follow part of our route through the barren mountains beside the Gulf of Aqaba.

That trip concluded a memorable year in Jerusalem and it is very sad to reflect on the travails that the now permanently divided city has endured since 1946. The choice of the Old City as the initial home of MECAS had been an inspired one. To live for a year beside the Via Dolorosa was a unique and moving experience with the weight of history all around. It seems to me that when the Centre had to be removed to Zerka and then to Shemlan an important element was lost.

David M Summerhayes CMG served in the Royal Artillery (Captain) in 1939-45. He attended the Second Course at MECAS in 1945-46 and pursued a diplomatic career leading to Head of Arms Control and Disarmament Department, FCO 1970-74, and Ambassador and Leader of the UK Delegation to the Committee on Disarmament, Geneva 1979-82.

FROM THE AUSTRIAN HOSPICE TO ZERQA AND SHEMLAN 1947

Donald Maitland

The Austrian Hospice

The Austrian Hospice which housed the centre was a substantial building in the Old City of Jerusalem at the junction of the Via Dolorosa and the Damascus Road. On the opposite side of the Via was a small coffee house from which, for eighteen out of twenty-four hours, arose an aroma of Arabica and a steady murmur of conversation. Nearby was the Sixth Station of the Cross, where Veronica wiped the face of Jesus. At regular intervals groups of tourists would stop there while their guide pointed them in the right direction and said: 'Kodachrome; a fiftieth at f eleven.' My room looked down on to a cluster of small houses where mothers with small children seemed interminably engaged in washing and drying clothes. The Austrian nuns were still in residence and looked after us with quiet efficiency and loving concern for our well-being. I was elected mess secretary for the first term of the course and had daily dealings with Sister Liliosor, a latter-day angel who was in charge of the kitchen. What could have been a chore was unalloyed pleasure.

By the time everyone had reached Jerusalem we totalled twenty-three students, of whom the majority were still in the armed forces. Four had recently joined the Sudan Political Service, one was a new entrant to the Foreign Service and others came from the British Council, the Colonial Service and BOAC. The Director of the Centre was Colonel Bertram Thomas, who made his name in 1930 by completing a courageous journey across the Empty Quarter of Arabia – the first European to do so. He had subsequently served as *Wazir* to the Sultan of Oman. During the first two courses at the Centre the Principal Instructor had been Major Aubrey Eban, who later achieved international distinction as Abba Eban, the immensely articulate foreign minister of Israel. His successor was an academic historian, George Kirk, an authority on recent Middle Eastern history, who however did not know Arabic.

Responsibility for language instruction was delegated to a handful of Palestinian Christians, some of them with experience as schoolteachers. They were in their element teaching us Arabic script and the fundamentals of grammar. But some of them found it hard to respond to our demand at a later stage for instruction in the kind of Arabic we expected to use in our future work. Storybooks for young Arab children were of limited appeal and even less use. 'Would that I Were a Cat!' was not an ambition I was ever called upon to express in several years living and working with Arabs.

While we felt reasonably secure in the Old City, we had to be on our guard when we wanted to penetrate the New City. A few weeks before our arrival in Jerusalem the Irgun Zwai Leumi had bombed the King David Hotel, killing over ninety of the occupants. Public buildings were protected with barbed wire and sandbags. We were requested to move about in civilian clothes and in pairs and later at least one of us had to carry a concealed pistol. Nonetheless social life continued. With a fellow student I called by invitation on Mrs. Vester, described by Sir Ronald Storrs as 'that charming and great-hearted leader of the American Colony'. She had lived for over sixty years in Jerusalem. Jemal Pasha, Allenby and Storrs himself had been among her friends and she had been hostess to almost all those who had left their mark on the Near East. We did not discover what had brought her father to Jerusalem in the first place, whether it was proselytising or commercial mission. The ungenerous said that the Vesters came to Jerusalem to do good and did very well. Whatever the facts, we spent an agreeable and instructive hour or so at her feet.

A notice was posted in the Centre advertising a Voigtländer camera for five pounds. The name of the advertiser was Petrie. I responded and was invited to tea. My hostess was Lady Flinders Petrie, widow of the archaeologist. She explained that she was in the middle of packing up to return to England and had been sorting out her late husband's belongings. She did not need the camera herself and would be pleased if it could be put to good use somewhere in the Middle East. I was privileged to be shown a selection of archaeological photographs dating back many years. Among them was a picture of a lunch party at a dig. I thought I recognised the face of one of T.E. Lawrence. 'Quite right,' she said 'the best-read and most interesting young man I have ever met.'

Bertram Thomas, who took little interest in our studies, called on members of his wide circle of contacts to come to the Centre to lecture. In this way our horizons were undoubtedly widened and over drinks and dinner we were able to talk with a number of personalities who had hitherto been no more than names. The Patriarch of the American Orthodox Church explained the roles of the various churches in protecting Christian holy places; we were glad to have an authoritative guide to help us through this particular maze. We had expected a panegyric about the Arabs from Glubb Pasha and were surprised not only by his objectivity, but also by his well-researched assessment of the prospects for the entire region. This unassuming man, held in high esteem in many parts of the Arab world, invited us to call on him should we ever need assistance or advice.

My good fortune lay in the friends I made. John Rae was at that time a recruit to the British Council. Peter Tripp had joined the Sudan Political Service. Both had served as Royal Marines during the war. What brought us together was a common desire to take full advantage of the opportunities the Centre offered. In the late afternoon one or the other would knock on the door: 'Up and down the Mount of Olives before tea?' 'Of course'. And we went further afield – to Bethlehem, Hebron, Haifa and Acre, Nazareth, the Dead Sea and spent an unforgettable weekend in a monastery overlooking the north-western shore of Lake Tiberias. It was not difficult to imagine those muscular Galilean fishermen unloading their drafts of fish on that same shore many centuries earlier. All these were rewarding experiences; the dictum was proving to be true that no one can leave the Holy Land unaffected.

Zerqa, Jordan

Meanwhile Bertram Thomas had re-established the Middle East Centre in a corner of the camp of the Transjordan Frontier Force at Zerqa, north of Amman. Each student had a ridge tent of the type known in India as EPIP – Eight Person Indian Pattern. Two of these were erected side by side to serve as mess. The teaching routine was the same as in Jerusalem, except that a degree of specialisation was introduced to cater for our different future requirements.

I arrived about a week late for the start of the new term to a sympathetic welcome from John Rae and Peter Tripp. They had both incidentally been pressing their suits and were both on the point of becoming engaged. At our encampment at Zerqa there was of course no 'up and down the Mount of Olives before tea.' Instead, the three of us met each evening after completing our studies to talk over cups of Turkish coffee. The final examinations were on our mind as well as our future prospects.

A Mistaken Identity in Egypt

In the middle of July I received a curious request to go to Cairo for an interview with a representative of the Civil Service Commission. Ronald Searight of the Anglo – Egyptian Oilfields, who happened to be in Transjordan at the time, offered to fly me to Egypt. Breakfasting on the terrace of the Continental Savoy Hotel in Cairo, I recognised St. John Philby at another table. In 1930 he had crossed the Empty Quarter a few months after Bertram Thomas, and in the opposite direction. I introduced myself. He was most interested in the Middle East Centre of which he was only vaguely aware. But what impressed me was that he spoke charitably about all his fellow orientalists and modestly about his own achievements.

John Rae had asked me to deliver a letter to his beloved Nonie, who worked in the British Embassy. There I was introduced to Mary Grepe in the ambassador's office – an encounter which was to prove of great significance. We arranged to dine together. After cocktails on the terrace of the Continental Savoy, I called a taxi. At this point a policeman on duty at the hotel stepped forward and insisted on travelling with us to the restaurant. Throughout the dinner he remained in view and again sat in the front of the taxi as I delivered Mary to the House of the Palm and then returned to the hotel. When I asked for an explanation he said, with what he no doubt intended to be a knowing look, that it was the duty of the police to protect Colonel Lawrence whenever he visited Egypt.

CROSSING THE RUB' AL-KHALI

Donald Maitland

He had to go and cross the Rub' al-Khali.
    He wouldn't take the Sultan's good advice.
There aren't so many chaps today who've crossed it,
    And none of them has ever crossed it twice.

He had to go and cross the Rub' al-Khali.
    Some people thought it something of a shame.
But no one really ever saw him do it;
    They only knew he'd done it when he came.

He had to go and join the Athenaeum,
    And hob-nob with the Bishops in the Club.
He really is so frightfully distinguished
For having been and gone and crossed the Rub'.

He had to found a school for Arab studies
    To add a little lustre to his name.
He rarely ever visited his students;
    But he's twice the fellow since the Daimler came.

'Now gentlemen, we're really very honoured
    To have with us another one as bright.
He's come to talk about the laws of England:
    That fourth at bridge and leading Irish Knight ...'

He had to go and cross the Rub' al-Khali.
    He did it on his favourite camel's back.
When he reached the other end
    He'd gone completely round the bend,
And he said he'd been and crossed the Rub' al-Khali.

Zerqa, 1947

FROM LEBANON
WITH LOVE 1948

Donald Foster

A Long Walk to Beirut

Yesterday I walked to Beirut – the first of us to do so, although Dennison had done it from Beirut upwards. It's about eleven miles across country, or rather by hill paths and village road. I set off at nine, a glorious morning warm and dry, not a cloud, everything brilliant after the heavy rains of the past week. Beirut was bright against the sea below, and Sannin – smooth under new snow – white and cool up above. First, down the looping road to Ain Ainoub, through the village, saying good morning (in Arabic) to everyone – they know by now of the 'Ingleez' at Shemlan. The road ran along the side of the hill, over bridges under which streams were full, water everywhere, its music filling all the morning, a cheerful noise, a dozen impromptu waterfalls among the rocks. A hillside covered in fruit trees all in blossom – no leaves, so the bare branches made a mauve-coloured haze on which the white and pink flowers floated like spray. Through small pine woods, the road dappled in light and shade. Past a shepherd-boy with a new-born kid, still wet and sticky from birth. Dust already on the roads after two days of sun. Down and down, with the sea horizon rising to meet me, and Sannin always towering behind. Through villages noisy with activity – stone-masons chipping, carpenters banging, animals being driven, cows, goats, sheep and the long painful bray of donkeys. Down, while the sun climbed and the air grew warmer and less rare, until I came to the level at the foot of the hills, on the Haifa road, where a bridge spans a shallow and stony river bed. I rested here, and smoked a cigarette, my legs dangling over the water. On one side the river ran down to the sea, a mile or two off, between low banks of grey olives, through the orange-red dunes (they look quite high from here, but from Shemlan are just a red smear outside the city). A youth passed, with a gun and a dozen dead birds, mostly blackcaps and goldfinches. I suppose that the birds do eat the olives but it seemed a shame on such a fine morning.

From there on, it was not so interesting, the road at first among the olives, then the outskirts of town, orchards of oranges and lemons (such a picture, trees laden with lemons and under them masses of red poppies). It was warm and my feet were sore, but having got so far, I was resolved not to take a lift and plodded on the whole way, past the Greek Catholic Patriarchate, where bearded old gentlemen in funny hats slowly paced the garden, past the Ministry of War where soldiers in British battledress dyed blue are on guard (in a very casual fashion) and into town. There I saw a little girl carrying a huge altar candle, bigger than herself, for today's Palm Sunday celebrations, I suppose. Such a solemn little girl she was, too, weighed down both literally and spiritually with the weight of such a big candle. I hope the saints hear her intercessions.

Editor's Note:
From Lebanon With Love 1947-48 published privately in 1996 consisting of 56 letters to his fiancé and 14 watercolour sketches of Shemlan and other parts of the Arab World.

Donald Foster attended MECAS in 1947-48. With Indian Independence in 1947, he was posted from the Indian to the British army, serving in Nigeria, Aden and Thailand.

BY TAXI WITH A BEAR 1948-55

Norman Lewis

In the summer of 1948 I was appointed Principal Instructor at
MECAS: Bertram Thomas, the then director, had told me and
the travel department at the Foreign Office that I should get to
Shemlan as quickly as possible and so I went to the department to
discuss ways and means.

When I turned up, they suggested that it might be best for me to
go by boat (I think they believed it would be cheaper). Unfortunately
there was no boat to Beirut (or no berths) in the immediate future but
they said they could get me a berth to Istanbul in a few days. They
could ask the Consulate-General in Istanbul to book me on a train
from there to Aleppo or even to Beirut; would this be acceptable? I
was delighted; I had never been to Istanbul or travelled on what
remained of the old Berlin-Baghdad railway and I looked forward to
getting back to Syria, a country I knew well. I replied that if no
Damascus flight were available (at which they murmured negatively)
I thought the Istanbul suggestion would be acceptable and I would be
grateful if they would make arrangements accordingly.

A Misunderstanding in Istanbul

All went well and after a pleasant enough Mediterranean cruise ending with the famous view of Istanbul from shipboard I prepared to disembark and to find my way to the Consulate-General. Before I could reach the gangplank however a charming young man introduced himself as one of the staff of the Consulate-General and ushered me to a waiting car. My query about Customs was brushed aside and porters deposited my baggage in the boot of the car. My 'minder' suggested that I might like to go to meet the Consul-General. I concurred, we were driven to what was evidently the smartest hotel in the city where my shabby luggage, including tea chest, was deposited in a splendid room, and were then whisked off to the Consulate-General.

The Consul-General looked a little startled as I was shown into his office. After we had exchanged a few conventional remarks he asked me if I intended to work while I was in Istanbul. I replied to the effect that I would of course make use of this opportunity to see all that I could of the city. ' So you will be inspecting us while you are here?' he asked, and then added 'Perhaps you would like to read this' and handed me a sheet of paper. It was the telegram from the Foreign Office informing him of my movements and asking him to facilitate them. I was described as Mr N N Lewis, Principal Inspector, proceeding to MECAS, Shemlan, Lebanon. I commented that it should have read 'Principal Instructor' not 'Principal Inspector'. He laughed and asked if I had any idea what an Inspector from the FO might be expected to do and went on to explain that an official inspection was an important and often rather nerve-racking affair. He had been somewhat worried by the message because it was unusual for a visit by an Inspector to be announced in this fashion at short notice and because the title 'Principal Inspector' as distinct from, say, 'Chief Inspector', was unfamiliar (I wondered, but did not ask, why he had not sought clarification of the message.) He was frankly delighted that I was not an Inspector, allowed me to keep my hotel room and arranged for someone to show me the city. I thoroughly enjoyed the next few days.

By Train from Istanbul to Beirut

I remember very little about the long railway journey, which followed, but I have retained a vivid memory of one incident. As the train approached the Syrian frontier a large, dour, uniformed armed Turk appeared in the doorway of the carriage in which at that time I was the only passenger and made signs which I interpreted to mean that he wanted to examine my luggage. Making 'help yourself' gestures I helped him open my bags and scatter my things about. Then he seemed to want to know what was in the tea chest standing in the corridor; 'books' said I, and aped someone reading. This didn't help, and nor did 'Kutub' or 'Livres'. He insisted, in mime, that I open the box and harangued me more and more vehemently, in Turkish – he had an enormously loud voice. 'Can't you see I can't open it without tools' I mimed and shouted in English. He went red in the face, stamped and developed a pretty good line in menacing gestures. I was getting desperate but suddenly noticed a sort of heavenly vision: strapped to the side of the carriage was a large axe (along with a fire bucket etc.). I lunged forward, unstrapped the axe (astonished that he let me do so) and took two huge swings at the top of the tea chest. Against all the probabilities I didn't injure myself or him and sliced enough off the top of the tea chest to make it possible to get the books out. He took one look, said nothing, shook my hand and continued on his way.

A day and a night later I reached Beirut and made for St George's Club where I was greeted by a group of cheerful young men who soon discovered who I was; they were members of the fourth course, then dispersing. That was the beginning of several long-lasting friendships for me. The next day I went up to Shemlan.

By Taxi with a Bear

One of the more surprising experiences which Rosemary and I had early in our Shemlan years was sharing a taxi with a dancing bear. We were on our way back from Damascus in a 'taxi-service', on the Syrian side of the border, when we saw the bear and his keeper by the roadside. The taxi was a big roomy old Chevrolet; Rosemary and I were in the front with the driver and there were two other passengers in the back. The bear's keeper offered to pay for himself and the bear and the driver agreed to take them despite the objections of the people in the back because, he said, there was room there for two more passengers. The bear and his man sat down side by side and we started off. Within minutes, however, the objections of the other passengers reached a crescendo; they were, they complained, overrun with fleas. They threatened to report the driver and after a good old shouting match the driver stopped and the poor, mangy old bear and his keeper were ejected. The driver and the rear seat passengers argued about it all the way to Beirut. We said not a word and enjoyed a shower as soon as we got home.

Norman Lewis MBE went up to Cambridge in 1938 to read Geography. In January 1940, he joined the Friends' Ambulance Unit. Training was followed by work in hospitals, air raid shelters and rest centres during the London Blitz and after that in casualty clearing stations and mobile hospitals in the Western Desert of Egypt and Libya. After the fall of Tripoli and the end of the desert campaigns he was transferred to Syria. In 1948, just before leaving Cambridge (with a first), he saw an advertisement in The Times, *saying that a 'Principal Instructor, non-linguistic' was required at MECAS, Shemlan, Lebanon. Soon after leaving MECAS he joined the Government Agreements Department of Gulf Eastern Co. in November 1955 and stayed with the company for a quarter of a century.*

FIRST IMPRESSIONS OF
SHEMLAN 1948-49

John Deverill

I was allocated a room, facing uphill, with a view on to a street with one or two shops of Shemlan, especially the butcher's shop, which was right opposite my window. The butcher killed a sheep every few days by the bloody *halal* process, the Arab equivalent of the Jewish *shechita*, which ensures that no blood is left in the animal before it is cut up into joints, cutlets etc., a wise precaution in a hot climate. No black pudding in Semitic societies!

Further to the right along the same street was the post office, grocer and bar (a few tables and chairs) run by Bahij. After supper at the school a number of us often went to have an arak in the bar (arak is an aniseed alcoholic drink similar to Pernod, *zibib* and ouzo, usually taken with water which turns it milky). Arak is the native drink in the Lebanon, almost always served with a plate of *mezze*, small cubes of goat cheese, and other bits and pieces on the same lines as peanuts but more substantial. Among other things available from the bar was hashish (Arabic for grass), more commonly cannabis, of which Bahij kept 25kg hessian sacks. Hashish was smoked in the hubble-bubble, the Turkish water-pipe. I only knew one of our students who smoked it, possibly for the effect on us rather than on himself. He was Flight Lieutenant Folkard whom I replaced many years later as Senior Intelligence Officer HQBFAP. Folkard had only one arm; he had lost the other during the war either on operations or in an accident. He was not a very good student of the Arabic, and seemed to have a cruel streak. A favourite trick of his was to grip one's arm (preferably a girl's) with the forceps of his artificial hand and tighten the fingers, as with a vice, smiling broadly of course.

The Civilians

Apart from the armed service contingents, our course was made up to 24 with eight 'civilians'. Two were from the South African Ministry of Foreign Affairs, three from the Sudan Police, one from our own Foreign Office, one from the British Council and one from the Iraq Petroleum Company. Initially we consorted in three 'social' groups; the RAF kept largely to themselves; the Navy, Army and Sudan Police formed another group; the Foreign Office, South African MFA, British Council and oil company students made the third group. The third group were the 'intellectuals' and looked down upon the other two (not without reason). The RAF and the Army groups were much of a muchness but kept apart by their service traditions, attitudes to authority, etc. Later there was more mixing as academic prowess started to sort the men from the boys.

The Scholastic Day

The scholastic day at Shemlan ran from 0830 to 1300 with a break for elevenses, and after lunch further work in one's room or in the Library until another class, usually a plenary lecture, at 1700 followed by supper. Glubb Pasha had been very definite that students should learn about the Arab countries and how their people live, rather than having fluency in the language as top priority. Lecturers, often from the universities in Beirut, came to speak about a great variety of topics bearing on Arab life, the history of Arabic speaking countries, their problems – economic, social, religious. This made the course especially interesting.

In November it became so cold that it was as much as I could do to use a pen to write Arabic and my letters home, and rain penetrated the roof and walls of the room so that there were puddles inches deep on the floor. Fortunately I had a service camp bed with legs which kept me above the water. Apart from wrapping up well in all the warm clothes we had (and I was badly off having joined the course from Singapore), wearing knitted mittens and scarves, there was not much we could do. Billy Butts used to howl with laughter to see my white tropical Mess Dress hanging neatly in the corner of my room. And the food was not really of the quality to keep grown men warm. We had an Armenian housekeeper who was responsible for turning the rations into meals, for which we paid quite a bit.

There was no choice; you had to eat what was cooked, or nothing. The poor woman, who had a tragic history, was always being criticised by the students who disliked her choice of meals, the quality of the meat, vegetables, fruit etc. Some students eventually opted out of the Centre meals and went to restaurants. At the end of the course, when I revisited Shemlan, I found the Suggestions Book lying around the ining Room and pocketed it. It makes interesting reading. On one page of the exercise book was stapled a slice of meat with a caption criticising its toughness. On another, two small envelopes, one containing cinnamon, and the other pepper, to demonstrate the difference to the housekeeper. Most of the suggestions and criticisms were made by the 'civilian' students. The servicemen were probably inured to dodgy cuisine.

Cricket

At the Centre the cricket season had now started. The yard between the two main buildings was almost exactly the length of a cricket pitch. The wicket was improvised in one of the doorways so that there would be room for the wicket keeper in the hall behind him. The bowler ran up the opposite corridor and the crease was the threshold. The bat was a length of 2" x 1" wood and the ball a tennis ball.

Although a tennis ball is soft compared to a cricket ball, it can still do some damage if hit hard. In early February one ball went clean through the Centre office window, and another through the fanlight over the bowler's head. There were penalties for hitting the ball over the west wall and down the terraced hillside.

Wing Commander John Deverill attended MECAS in 1948-49. These extracts are taken from a 45 page memoir, which includes detailed descriptions of Shemlan with many anecdotes and an account of his language break working with Palestine Arab refugees.

EASTER IN
JERUSALEM 1950

Philip Bowcock

From April there was a fortnight's break for Easter spent mostly in Jerusalem. We went there via Damascus and Amman, then over the Allenby Bridge which crossed the Jordan and past Jericho to Jerusalem. Michael, whose father was an Anglican priest and former naval chaplain, fixed up for us to stay at St. George's Hostel, attached to the Anglican Cathedral, while Bryan and Ralph found a pension. The hostel was perfect, comfortable and decent in the Anglican way with some interesting guests – archaeologists and redoubtable ladies of the British Empire. At the time the Old City was under Jordanian control and the New City was Israeli and could not be visited unless one had a second passport. We saw all the holy sites, the Holy Sepulchre Church, Bethlehem, the Dome of the Rock, an Armenian service, Orthodox feet-washing on Maundy Thursday, a service in Gethsemane, the Via Dolorosa, an Ethiopian service, and drove to Ramallah to meet the family of Mr. Theodory one of our Arab instructors. Fortunately the western and eastern Easters coincided that year and the high point was the Orthodox ceremony of the Holy Fire at midnight on Easter eve in the church of the Holy Sepulchre. The round medieval church is packed and the people of all nations stand with their candles ready.

Then the fire appears in the middle and is spread to all the candles with astonishing speed, all shouting 'Christ has risen' in their own tongues.

On Easter day after Holy Communion and the Anglican Bishop's At Home we walked up the Mount of Olives to the Russian Convent and then over to Bethany. In the following days we visited Nablus, stopping at Jacob's Well on the way, and the pool of Bethesda. On the way back to Shemlan we bathed in the Dead Sea, wearing trilby hats to demonstrate the buoyancy of the very salty water. The final stop was to see Jerash, north of Amman one of the Roman cities of the Decapolis. I wrote in my diary: 'A wonderful end to the holiday. The country was lovely, quite well wooded, flowers in profusion. Jerash magnificent, extremely well preserved, showing just what the Roman Empire meant. Needed all of four hours there to see it.' We had the site almost to ourselves.

Philip Bowcock attended MECAS in 1950. His memoir goes on to recount travels round Lebanon, Syria and Jordan.

A LANGUAGE
BREAK IN NORTH
AFRICA 1951

Michael Weir

The MECAS intake from the Foreign Office for 1950-51 comprised three new entrants, John Thomson, Johnny Graham, and myself, and two existing members of the Service, Martin Buckmaster and Robert MacGregor. None of us new boys volunteered for Arabic as far as I know, though the other two may have. But Johnny had done army service in Palestine, John Thomson was writing a book on Crusader castles, and I had done RAF service in the Middle East as well as a wartime SOAS course in Persian. According to Foreign Office logic that made us natural candidates for Arabic, and that was that. But we did not see ourselves as serious scholars. The teaching regime of Pastor Nielsen, and the four Palestinian instructors was fairly rudimentary and undemanding, and it was not too difficult to keep pace while leaving plenty of time for extra-curricular activity. In between hitting the Beirut night-spots and ski-ing weekends at the Cedars, Johnny Graham and I, along with two other Johns (Udal and Haggar, both of the Sudan Civil Service), made frequent trips farther afield in a battered Ford V8 we had bought. It took us to most of the crusader castles in the Levant, to Palmyra and the immortal Hotel Zenobia, Damascus, Amman and Jerusalem; we spent one night under arrest by the Syrian Army for camping in an (undeclared) prohibited area at the mouth of the Orontes, and another climbing Mount Hermon in order to enjoy the view over Palestine at dawn.

When the time came for the language break Johnny Graham and I chose to go west, rather than immerse ourselves in the approved Arab family milieu in neighbouring territory. The Director, Terry Brennan, had received a letter from Stewart Perowne, then an Adviser with the UN Administration in Cyrenaica (whom I had known in 1946 as the flamboyant Oriental Counsellor in the Baghdad Embassy, just before his ill-fated marriage to Freya Stark) inviting him to send a couple of his students to Cyrenaica for their language break: he would arrange tuition, accommodation, etc. We jumped at the invitation. Getting there was more fun than arriving. Johnny flew direct to Benghazi, but I hankered after travelling overland and flew only to Alexandria, where I was entertained by Willie Morris of the Cairo Embassy (and the 1947 MECAS course), who were enjoying what proved to be their penultimate annual sojourn at the summer capital of the Farouk regime. From there I took an antiquated Egyptian Railways train – a far cry from the wartime Pullman that carried the officer class between Alexandria and Cairo – to the end of the line at Mersa Matruh, where the wife of Alastair Maitland of the Embassy (Donald's elder brother), who was aestivating there with her children, kindly put up the unexpected and self-invited guest. The town was still largely derelict from war damage, but the limpid blue waters of the bay were a delight I never forgot, and was pleased to find almost unblemished – unlike the incredible building rash that now disfigures the entire Egyptian coastline. For the rest of the journey I hitched a ride on a Shell oil tanker, along a road still littered with the carcasses of German and British tanks and aircraft of the Desert War; the scrap metal merchants who created Libya's and their own pre-oil prosperity had not yet got into their stride.

Libya and Tunisia

When Johnny and I met up in Benghazi we found that Stewart Perowne had disappeared on a desert trip and no arrangements for us had been made. We were taken in hand by a colleague of his in the Administration, who arranged for us to stay at a school in a village on the *jebel* inland from Benghazi, which was empty for the summer holidays, in the hope that the schoolmaster would be able to give us some lessons in colloquial Arabic. The schoolroom provided was empty in every sense, including furniture, so that we slept on the floor, and we never tracked down the schoolmaster. We were however able to hire a local bedu to do some primitive cooking and cleaning. His Arabic was unintelligible, but he had a rich fund of English obscenities, which he would produce, for effect, pronounced in the broadest Australian accent – another relic of the war. As an immersion, or even an introduction to colloquial Arabic the experience was virtually useless, but we took full advantage of other cultural opportunities, notably the Greco-Roman sites at Cyrene, Apollonia, Sabratha and Leptis Magna. We also had the unexpected bonus of a meeting with King Idris, thanks to the chief administrator of Cyrenaica, Eric de Candole, who took us along with him when he came to call at the royal residence in Beidha. De Candole, who was seconded from the Sudan Civil Service, conducted the discussion in Arabic; I don't think that either of us presumed to utter a word.

After a fortnight marooned on the *jebel* we returned to Benghazi and continued by slow and painful bus to Tripoli, where we were looked after by Brigadier Blackley, de Candole's opposite number in Tripolitania. Staying at the British Army officers' club Johnny learned from the barman the only useful addition he remembers from the trip to his Arabic vocabulary: *Kaman wahid* (Same again). From Tripoli Johnny and I made our separate ways overland to Tunis. I hitched a ride with a British Army officer to the delightful island of Djerba off southern Tunisia, spent a night in the newly established Club Mediterranee, and visited the ancient synagogue, said to have been founded by Jews fleeing the sack of the temple in Jerusalem in AD 70; the synagogue itself was the victim of a bloody terrorist attack in the late 90s. I completed this unashamedly tourist itinerary by bus to a French hill station set in spectacular woods of cork trees above the northern coastline, and finally by air to Athens to visit the antiquities I had never managed to see before. The Foreign Office reluctantly paid my travel claim, but I believe may have taken steps to ensure that future language breaks were less ambitious geographically and more so academically. If so I offer my apologies half-a-century late to any colleagues on succeeding courses who found themselves unduly constrained.

Sir Michael Weir KCMG attended MECAS in 1951 His diplomatic appointments included Political Agent to the Trucial States 1952-54, Deputy Political Resident, Persian Gulf 1968-71, Assistant Under-Secretary of State, Foreign Office, 1974-79 and Ambassador to Egypt 1979-85.

FLEAS IN A SYRIAN VILLAGE 1951

John Udal

The country between Palmyra and Aleppo is desert inhabited by Bedouin, until you get to the more fertile strip to the west, the country of pleasant villages. The tracks were even worse than those between Damascus and Palmyra, but by late afternoon we reached a village called Muffakar es Sharq, near the Ismaili stronghold of Salamiya. Lewis the Chief Instructor, knew the Mukhtar so we stopped to call, with half an eye, it must be confessed, to staying the night! Sure enough the invitation was readily forthcoming and after polite protestation we accepted the offer. They were all most friendly, but as none could speak English, and only appeared latterly speaking difficult French, and as the lamb slain in our honour was not forthcoming for some four hours, I think we earned our keep endeavouring to stoke up conversation in extremely broken Arabic to an audience that was never less than six. Exhausted we slept fitfully but well, only alas to find that we had by our departure reduced the flea population of the village somewhat.

John Udal attended MECAS in 1951. This extract is taken from a collection of manuscript letters to his parents and others which are now lodged at Durham University.

INTO THE MARSHES OF SOUTHERN IRAQ

A LANGUAGE BREAK IN 1952

Ivor Lucas

Thanks to the offer of accommodation from a friend of a friend, I chose Basra as my base. After driving with John Moberly as far as Baghdad I proceeded to Basra by a comfortable overnight train and in the agreeable company of one Salman Juwaideh, the Assistant Director-General of the Iraqi Date Association. There, the combination of heat and humidity in July and August was so appalling that one was compelled to get out and about for fear of spending the entire time lying under a ceiling fan.

My particular antidotes to this danger were three. The first was a Muslim weekend spent in Suwaib, a charming village of reed huts built among a cluster of date palms on the banks of a tributary of the Shatt al Arab north of Basra. I had an introduction to Sheikh Chiad, who accommodated me in his reed hut *madhif*, or guest house, though at night I slept on a special bed under the stars, swaying palms and a mosquito net. He and his friends conversed animatedly about politics and, more reticently, about religion.

In Nasriyah, the principal town of the Muntafiq district 130 miles north-west of Basra, where I next ventured, Iraqis were less inhibited about expressing their views on Islam. Indeed I nearly precipitated a local version of the Thirty Years War when I initiated an after-dinner debate between an official and a merchant on the Quran's relevance to the contemporary world.

My Muntafiq journey was undertaken in the often exhilarating company of three Iraqis who operated the British Consulate's touring cinema van: Hadi, the cinema operator, Muhammad, the commentator and Salman, the driver. The value of the exercise from HMG's point of view struck me as dubious. Our audiences in the small towns and rural areas we visited were less than receptive to the mixture of entertainment, information and propaganda we purveyed. But for me it was an excellent education. For ten days I spoke nothing but Arabic, lived comparatively rough and learned something of the Iraqi life-style and thought - processes.

My third foray was to the Marshes. This was a fascinating and primitive area lying north of Basra between the Tigris and the Euphrates near the point where the great twin rivers join to form the Shatt al Arab waterway. It was about to be made better known to the outside world through the writings of a number of intrepid British travellers, pre-eminent among them Wilfred Thesiger. I cannot claim to have emulated any of their exploits. After four days my internal economy collapsed and obliged me to return to the relative comforts of the city.

Once again, I had an introduction to the local shaikh. To reach him involved first of all a taxi ride to Al Madina, near Qurna, the confluence of the two rivers 40 miles from Basra. There I hired a motor launch of ancient vintage which chugged along the Euphrates for two and a half hours until it brought me to Chubaish, the self-styled 'capital' of the marshes. It was a long, straggling village of reed huts with an imitation 'corniche'. My intended host proved to be out of town, but in no time at all I was being warmly welcomed by his nephew, Habib al Faris al Kheyun, and comfortably installed in the family's reed house, with no questions asked.

From there Habib's 13-year-old son, three boatmen and I set off on an eight hour voyage by *mashuf* – a kind of canoe – to Saiqal, in the very heart of the marshes. We punted and paddled up streams which wound their way through the reeds, barely giving room to pass in places, and across spacious tranquil lakes. Buffaloes were everywhere, snorting through the water and sharing huts with the inhabitants. Against the sun, my companions erected an ingenious canopy of reed and rags, making me feel like Old Bones of the River. We fed on fish speared from the water and cooked, with skilful improvisation, by burning a long bundle of reeds. Bread was made on the spot the same way. Eventually, through the gloom of dust and dusk, there appeared a larger island of the now familiar reed huts with an occasional *madhif* standing out like some strange cathedral.

As we drew nearer, the island proved to be several islets, each with its complement of men, women, children, buffaloes and cows. As the waters rose, so the occupants had to move to higher ground. Communication between the tiny floating colonies was by *mashuf*, so that the vast marsh area looked something like an unglorified cross between Venice and the Norfolk Broads. The main occupations were growing rice and breeding buffaloes. Illiteracy was as near 100 per cent as makes no difference, and there were no medical or sanitary arrangements of any kind. One pathetic old man, no doubt accustomed to the tender ministrations of Thesiger, came up to ask if I had any medicine for his son, who had been ill for a fortnight with malaria. He picked up an almost empty bottle labelled 'hydrogen peroxide' and plaintively asked if that was any good.

Forty years later the oppressive regime of Saddam Hussain drained the marshes, ostensibly for economic but in fact political reasons: the region was the centre of the Shi'a opposition to Saddam. A traditional way of life was destroyed – despite the well-meaning efforts of the redoubtable Emma Nicholson to save it. But she may have taken a somewhat rosy view of both the way of life itself – which may have been idyllic in the 'noble savage, golden age' sense but was certainly primitive and poverty-stricken – and of the desire of many inhabitants to return to it.

The Hon Ivor Lucas CMG attended MECAS in 1952. His archive contribution goes on to describe in detail life in Sharjah and other assignments in the Arab world. His diplomatic service appointments included Head of Middle East Department, Foreign Office 1975-79 and Ambassador to Oman 1979-81 and to Syria 1982-84.

BRINGING CINEMA TO SOUTHERN IRAQ 1952

Alec Stirling

Accompanying the Cinema Van on my Language Break

At 8 o'clock sharp on 4 August, the cinema van rattled to a stop outside the house. Leon shouldered his way up the path to collect my luggage and I was met by a straight-backed little man with a pleasant anxious smile who gave me a semi-salute and said 'Mejid, commentator'. In the background, Mesjin was bobbing and grinning. My kit was stowed in the body of the van with their great comfortable bedding rolls. Mejid settled himself among them. Leon had a small makeshift chair in front of the cinema generator and behind the engine, which meant he had the enormous gear lever jutting between his knees.

At first sight I thought the vehicle was a disgrace. Drab green paint that no washing could make look clean; an air of dilapidation throughout and no door or window fitted properly. Its metal fittings and bucket seats hardly promised comfort. Yet some of the best times of the trip were spent bowling along in that travelling tin trunk. Besides, after I'd had fourteen days of first-hand experience of Iraqi travelling conditions, I was certain that if roads, rocks and small boys' graffiti which their vehicle endured in that time were a fair sample, then the van was anything but a disgrace. It was, rather, a miracle. Austin's can be proud of the simple fact that the van was still in existence.

We left Baghdad at a steady 30mph and came out on to one of the better (*i.e.* no worse than frightful) Iraqi main roads. The scenery was deadly. Flat plains, very dusty, hardly a tree in sight. After an hour and a half we came to a sort of halfway house, a village where we climbed out and had drinks. Here we started the *daftar* system by which Mejid paid for everything and I gave him a dinar from time to time – hardly more than ID6 for the whole tour. Another hour brought us to Mussayib, where the children flocked into the streets clapping their hands and shouting 'Cinema! Cinema!'. Five miles further, through palm trees, we came to Hindiyah Barrage. A village of little more than a long road, ankle deep in dust, and a few short side streets flanking it. I followed Mejid into the *mudir's* office. Where we sat on hard, straight-backed settees and spread out the half dozen sentences we had to say over nearly an hour and several Pepsi Colas. The *mudir* was a young man who wasn't terribly sure what to do with me. However I gathered that I was invited to lunch and the afternoon was siesta. I managed to convey my thanks. At this stage my Iraqi Arabic was futile. We retired to the 'club' a three-roomed square building on the riverbank and I watched Mesjin and Leon play tric trac on the verandah.

Lunch in the *mudir's* austerely furnished dining room was a large and simple meal of chicken and melon set out by a silent, black-clad woman whom I took to be his wife. After it the *mudir* accompanied me to a side room where two mattresses had been unrolled on the floor and a ceiling fan whupped slowly round. We rested for a couple of hours, had mint tea and then I rejoined the cinema crew, who were getting ready for the evening performance. There was a cleared stretch of beaten earth under palm trees near the river bank, probably used for other occasions. The van was parked at one end, facing the river, and the screen set up near the other end with a loudspeaker below it. Wires ran from the van's huge generator to the speaker, to the projector just outside the van and to a powerful light, which was hung from a convenient tree. Children gathered as soon as the preparations began and the older ones bought magazines which the crew sold for a few *fils*, standing in the back of the van because they got mobbed if they stayed on the ground. Sensible not to give the magazines – *Britain Today* and the like – away because, having been paid for, they were actually read. People packed in to watch, sitting on the ground round the edges and the babble of voices died away as soon as the light was switched off and the show started. Only appreciative murmurs during the films, though in some places (not Hindiyah) there were catcalls at the end when Abdullah, the Regent, was shown with young King Faisal while the national anthem was played.

Under Attack in Nejef

The Nejef incident was the only bit of excitement I had in the whole week. The crew were as jumpy as frogs with St Vitus' dance when we got ready for the show in the new part of town. The operator was grinning nervously – usually he worked with an abstracted frown. The commentator was fooling around with the screen – he had selected an old one – and sending kids off on vague errands. However everyone was friendly, we had sold a lot of magazines and drew our largest crowd – between 1,000 and 1,500 people. The show started without incident. Then, after ten minutes, a whistle blew.

Instantly there was the most appalling racket as a shower of rocks and half bricks crashed against the metal van. The crowd panicked. The square was almost completely emptied in one wild surge. The projector, some distance from the van, was smashed flat, the operator was swept away; women and children. especially the babies, were knocked down. The square looked like a battlefield as men had kicked off their sandals and thrown aside cloaks and *keffiyehs* to flee faster. Several people had been trampled by the crowd and were still lying there; tiny children, always a large proportion of our audiences, were wandering weeping through the wreckage. I turned to the van to see how our escort of six armed police was protecting it: I was just in time to see their putteed legs twinkling into the surrounding darkness.

The commentator, who had been beside me, had vanished; the driver whipped the loudspeaker off the roof of the van and bolted with incredible speed; I found I had a solitary companion – the village idiot, who gibbered at me till I told him rather curtly to take himself away. Meanwhile someone had trained the headlights of a car on the van, so that I felt uncommonly conspicuous. The half-bricks kept sailing out of the darkness and I was hit twice. The police evidently considered that the time had not yet come to stage a rescue.

I stayed where I was in the hope that the sight of a large angry man might dissuade the stone-throwers from trying to fire the van (as had happened on the previous visit). Eventually fewer missiles came over, though I saw one old lady come into the circle of light to hurl a stone from close quarters. She missed. The police rallied and came across the square in a fine skirmishing line. They cleared it quickly – chiefly of small boys who were gleaning handfuls of discarded clothing – as the last stones rattled down. I was ordered into the van for my safety's sake. I was glad to go as the policemen's rifles looked dangerous. One man tried to fire his in the air but it went to half-cock and he couldn't get it out again.

When the place was quite empty, a jeep with a machine gun was brought round and I was whisked off to the police station. There I was patted all over to make sure I wasn't hurt. I, incoherent with rage, tried to tell them what I thought of them in inadequate Arabic.

A brief and ineffectual enquiry was held on the spot. No arrests had been made, nobody had seen anybody throwing stones. A youth was brought in with blood spattered all over his clothing; he had been standing near the van. There were others, apparently, similarly hurt and all were taken to hospital. I was rushed back to the school, where I was staying and they tried to make me stay on the roof the whole time in case I should be assaulted on the way to the bathroom. I drew a line at that, but they insisted that two policemen should sleep at the foot of my bed. We were moved from there to a fine old house with a wind tower, like a campanile with built-in vanes where bells would have been. These caught any breath of air and channelled it down to a spacious underground room, keeping it far cooler than anywhere else in the building.

Next morning I made a formal statement to the police officers. They had been in civvies and smiling when we had first arrived, now they were wearing uniforms and worried frowns for my benefit. We hadn't suffered much damage. The projector was out of action and the van was badly dented, but miraculously no windows were broken. I reported back to the Embassy by telephone (which took only five minutes) and I was told I might have a word with the Kaimakam in Kufa on the way back to Baghdad. This I did. I said blisteringly that my escorts had run like rabbits. He actually sat up at that, but not because of his men's poltroonery: '*Aranib*', he repeated after me, savouring the word, '*Aranib* ... very good expression!'. I got Leon to translate the rest of my demarche. When the Kaimakam heard that I considered his officers incompetent and his security arrangements worse than useless, he spread his hands and blandly agreed ' I have no control in this district, *wallahi*!' This was the actual truth. Nejef is a hotbed of trouble and roughnecks calling themselves communists have the whiphand. The identity of the ringleaders is known but no-one dares give evidence against them. All have been in prison but could never be held for longer than a month or so. Only 20 or 30 people out of all that crowd were involved in the stone throwing, but the remainder would never think of pointing out the culprits. A police officer was murdered in a crowded square under the eyes of men about three months ago. Nobody was arrested, let alone convicted.

Sir Alexander (Alec) Stirling KBE CMG attended MECAS in 1952 The extracts quoted here are taken from a detailed memoir covering the journey to Iraq and a succession of adventures on his language break. He was British Political Agent in Bahrain (1969-71), Ambassador to Bahrain (1971-72), Iraq (1977-80), Tunisia (1981-84) and the Sudan (1984-86).

THE LEBANESE
ARMY 1952-53

Ben Strachan

A Taste for Good Living

Our MECAS course numbered 20: 6 Foreign Service, 6 Army, 3 RAF, 1 Australian Foreign Service, 1 New Zealand Army, and 3 (British) civilians from the Iraq Petroleum Co (IPC). Age divided us naturally into two groups: The Foreign Service men, newly joined graduates in their early twenties, and the rest of us, old sweats, aged around thirty, with one exception.

The exception was a genial 50 year old from the IPC. He was nicknamed 'Pop', not because he was the father of the course but because in appearance (short, rotund and bald-headed), he looked like Pop, the hero of the comic strip in one of the popular newspapers. Pop had a taste for good living in the fleshpots of Beirut. The rest of us had to make do with more modest pleasures.

Two incidents still live in my memory. I was walking in the mountains when a man shouted at me from a distance and hurried towards me. I walked towards him rehearsing the Arabic for my apology for trespassing on his land. No need. He had come to present me with a bunch of wild flowers hastily picked as a gesture of welcome to a visitor to his land.

Another occasion. We held a party on our balcony. Booze had

flowed freely and our sing-song had lasted far into the night. I woke late, made the usual vows which a hangover enjoins, and hastened down to my next door neighbour, the village blacksmith, to apologise for disturbing him with our noisy party. Before I could do so, he told me that he had told his children to keep quiet that morning because he knew we would be tired. Where in the world could you find such a gentle and considerate neighbour? Sixteen years later, during Lebanon's terrible civil war, I visited Shemlan and enquired of my gentle blacksmith. He had been taken hostage and murdered two months before.

Language Break with the Lebanese Army

The time had come for us to plan our 'language break' in the summer. For this, MECAS would arrange for each of us to spend six weeks immersed in an Arabic speaking environment, usually with an Arab family in Syria, Iraq or Jordan. I asked whether I could spend it with the Lebanese army. This had never been done before and MECAS were sure the Lebanese government would veto it. However, our Embassy put my request to them and were astonished when it was approved. So I found myself an honorary member of the Officers' Mess of an armoured car battalion in the barracks near Zahle, principal town in the beautiful fertile Bekaa valley. I was very impressed by the fitness and training of the battalion. Its CO insisted that I played a full part in all activities, though I firmly declined to join my brother officers at early morning PT at 6 a.m! Most days we went out on manoeuvres. The CO made me travel with him and we discussed tactics as we went along. We were both keen professionals: I had always loved armoured car work and I think that the CO found it useful to consult me for my experiences in the France and Germany campaign and in Malaya. Amongst the battalion's officers I met nothing but good will and the high morale of a good unit.

About a month after I had returned to Shemlan, I was told that the Military Attache at our Embassy wanted to see me. I had always kept as far away from senior officers as possible, so I wondered which particular misdemeanour had been brought to the MA's attention: was it perhaps my fondness for tap-dancing on

Lebanese bars? In the event, the MA was affable but baffled: The Lebanese Government had formally approached the Embassy to ask whether I could be attached to the Lebanese Army as an adviser for two years as soon as my course was over. I was pleasantly surprised but could not understand the Embassy's total astonishment. It was then explained to me that Arab nationalism and anti-imperialism were becoming more and more strident, so that it was quite inexplicable that the Lebanese Government should ask for an officer of an imperial army to formally infiltrate its army. I simply said that I had got on well with the Lebanese officers and would be enthusiastic to accept. Alas, my masters in London said 'no', I know not whether for financial or political reasons.

Major Ben Strachan CMG attended MECAS from 1952-53. He retired from the army and joined the Diplomatic Service in 1951, becoming Ambassador to the Yemen Arab Republic in 1977-78, to the Lebanon in 1979-81 and to Algeria 1981-84. These extracts are taken from a thirteen-page memoir of his time at MECAS.

UNDER ARREST IN SYRIA 1953

Peter Clayton

Life in Shemlan, 1953

John and I together with Major Dick Gammon (Black Watch) and Philip Giles (FO) were lodged in 'Khartoum Castle', a two storey stone building up the hill from the school complex that had been a silk mill. Right next to our place was Elias's little shop and beside that was a garage to let for my little car. It was still mid-winter and the rain fell and the ancient electricity supply failed regularly but we had our paraffin stoves for heating and Aladdin lamps for light to do our homework by. It was back to school with a vengeance for us non-academic bunch of soldiers but the language instruction was gauged to our progress. As a bachelor with a car I was, of course, very popular, until I got fed up with being a taxi service and others bought cars. When the world warmed up enough for sea bathing from the St. George's Club one or two of us took up schnorkel skin-diving and spear fishing for our supper. Later we found the Normandie Restaurant that served splendid meals and became my 'Saturday Lunch Club' venue.

Coronation Weekend, Syria

With Colin Brant (FO) I planned to tour Syria from Damascus, out as far as Palmyra ('Tadmur) and Aleppo (Haleb) before returning to Beirut through the Bekka valley in time for the Embassy cocktail party in Beirut. I had designed and had made a single pole five-panel windproof tent in time for this trip. It was high enough for me to stand up inside and very quick to erect once the one metre radius ground plan had been pegged out. The main guy line over the entrance could be tied to the open boot lid of the car which became the work surface for cooking etc. We did not stop at Damascus and headed off across the desert northeastwards to the old Roman dam. Before we got to Palmyra we followed the single tyre track of a motor cycle, which led all the way up to Palmyra Hotel, our destination. There we caught up with Major Dick Gammon. The hotel was fully booked by a group from the American University of Beirut but we found space in the attic with their driver. We explored the sights of Palmyra and fell in with the friendly Syrian Security Officer. We drove him around the local desert and made friends. We wanted to go directly to Aleppo on the local desert track by Saba'a Biar and were assured by the officer that there was no restriction. We camped one night on the way and it was a clear sky with all the stars at work and the far away barking of a dog in a bedu encampment. Gerbils came over to our circle of light in search of crumbs and the spell of the desert fell upon Colin.

Under Arrest

We called in on the Police camp at Saba'a Biar and the Corporal in Charge asked to see our passports, which we handed over. Too late we realised that he could not read them and by then he indicated that we were under arrest. In vain we explained that the Captain in Palmyra had told us that the route was open. We were told to go to the Military HQ on the main road far to the south of Aleppo with an armed soldier in the back of the car. Off we went with a very nervous young soldier with his rifle loaded sitting behind us. After some time he relaxed and told us his name was Ahmed. On the desert edge there was a typical Syrian mud-built 'beehive' village to which Ahmed directed us because that was where his family were. We met his parents, drank coffee and went on our way. This was remarkable at that time for the Syrian authorities discouraged foreigners from visiting such 'backward places'. Ahmed was now our friend, having forgotten that we were dangerous English spies.

Major Peter Clayton MBE attended MECAS in 1953. These two abstracts are taken from a detailed account of his trip to Shemlan by Morris Minor, life in Shemlan and his breaks in Egypt, Jordan and Syria.

A RUNAWAY CAMEL
1953-55

Antony Cawston

It is no exaggeration to say that MECAS affected the whole course of my life. I applied and was accepted. This meant an initial three months stint at the School of Oriental and Asian Studies to assess one's aptitude for learning languages and then the posting to MECAS where the course assembled in December 1953. The course lasted for the whole of 1954 and the military people then took the 2nd class military interpretership exam. If they did well enough they stayed on another three months to take the 1st class exam. The FCO people took similar exams and liked to think that the standard of those was higher than the military exams. In fact, having done a number of previous papers of both sorts for practice, I can vouch for the fact that the standards were the same. In fact when I took the 1st class paper it contained a word none of the MECAS instructors had ever heard of!

It was a thoroughly enjoyable course and the discipline was very lax. One could work as hard as one liked and received every encouragement, but one could also get away with doing virtually nothing. This was under the auspices of the then Director, Alan Trott, a charming Foreign Office man who had been ambassador in Saudi Arabia at one time. He used to take us once a week on the

Quran and could not resist telling us all the various meanings associated with the triliteral or quadriliteral root of some word that caught his attention. He used to scrawl these in chalk on his metal filing cabinet and as every Arabic root in the language has several meanings, two of which will be diametrical opposites and one of which will have a sexual connotation, the filing cabinet door used to present a fascinating spectacle towards the end of a lesson. At that stage, as often as not, the Director's charming Lebanese secretary would come in and tell him he was late for something or other. At which he would move himself hastily towards the filing cabinet door and endeavour to erase the offending graffiti by leaning his back against the door and moving surreptitiously from side to side!

From time to time during the MECAS course there were breaks when we were encouraged to go off somewhere to practise some colloquial. On such an occasion I went off to Jordan to spend two weeks in one of the Desert Patrol's frontier forts, where none of the residents spoke any English at all. There was a sergeant and about a dozen soldiers and a dozen camels. Their duty was to patrol the Jordan frontier along to the next post and back every two weeks or so. Each post was a four-square mud brick fort and there must have been about twenty of these along the northern, eastern, and southern frontiers of the country.

My people in the fort I was allocated to at H4 on the pipeline to Iraq were very friendly and we got on well, although I was surprised to find how much the soldiers' sex lives dominated their conversation. I don't know why I was surprised, but I had somehow thought that the noble bedouin of the desert thought more about higher things. However I learnt a lot of new words that could well be of use in military service in the area, but were no good to me at all in my later diplomatic postings.

I had one exciting incident during my stay. One of the soldiers told me that they had been invited to a local wedding in a nearby village and asked me if I would like to come too. This seemed a good thing to do, so the next day I found myself being taught how to mount a couched camel for a ride across the desert to a village whose palm tree tops were just visible behind a sand dune on the horizon. The motion when the camel rose to its feet nearly unseated me, but after that I felt fairly comfortable, although I sorely missed a proper saddle and proper reins. In fact I was sitting side saddle and in my hands held only a rope attached somehow to the animal's mouth, but with no bit. We set off, I in front, followed by three of my new friends on their camels behind me. They said 'That's fine, just head for those palm trees in the distance. You can't go wrong'. So we proceeded tranquilly across the desert. After a time I heard some giggling behind me which was quickly surpressed, but when I glanced round at another snigger, I was just in time to see one of my companions with his camel stick stretched out at the end of his arm delivering a rapier like lunge with it up the tenderest part of my animal's backside. This resulted in a peculiar strangled cry from the camel and an immediate surge into a mad gallop. I was horrified to see when I looked down at the ground that it seemed far away but going past at a frightening speed, with the animal's legs appearing to be all over the place and quite uncontrolled. I frantically pulled on the rope which was the only substitute for reins, but, there being no bit, the only result was that the animal's head was pulled round at the end of its long neck until it faced me, crouched on its back. There was this great head facing backwards towards me with its lips dribbling froth while it continued to gallop forwards with its legs seemingly floundering about in all directions. I knew how to control a runaway horse, but I was completely defeated by this runaway camel. All I could do was hang onto its rump while it continued its mad gallop, ending up in the middle of the village where the wedding was. There it stopped in the middle of the village square and sank exhausted to its knees enabling me to slide off onto the ground with a sigh of relief. Everyone thought the whole thing uproarious and once my feet were again on the ground I had to acknowledge that it had been funny. On the way back to the fort I was allowed a comfortable ride.

Lt Colonel Antony Cawston attended MECAS in 1953-55. His memoir also includes a detailed account of how the rebels were dislodged from the Jabal Akhdar in Oman in January 1959.

ALAN TROTT –
AN ECCENTRIC
DIRECTOR 1954

Antony Acland

It is a sobering thought that fifty years have passed since I first arrived at MECAS. But half a century cannot dim the memory of the view from the paved area between the two buildings at Shemlan, where we slept and where we struggled to learn the Arabic language. The lights of Beirut shone and beckoned from the darkness thousands of feet below. I remember thinking that if one did a good throw, a stone would fall straight into the sea, lapping lazily on the shores at the foot of the mountain.

Arabic we certainly learnt, together with insights into Arab history and culture, but MECAS was not in 1954 the intensive language laboratory it was to become. The school was directed by Norman Lewis and presided over by Alan Trott. The latter had spent much of his career in Persia and was a good Persian scholar. His last post, however, before coming to MECAS, was in Saudi Arabia where he had picked up a good smattering of Arabic, being as he was a proficient linguist, but he took no part that I can remember in the day to day teaching of the school. Curiously his current hobby and enthusiasm was the trapping, skinning and stuffing (taxidermy I suppose you would call it) of small birds (Arabic – *asfur*, plural *asafir*). Before the process of restoring the birds to their natural shape, their limp skins were for some reason rolled up in a number of pages of the overseas version of the Times – that thin, crinkly paper which resembled in texture the old fashioned Bronco or Bromo lavatory paper. The rolls were secured by two or more elastic bands.

Alan Trott and his wife were hospitable hosts and enjoyed inviting the smart French-speaking Lebanese ladies and their husbands up for dinner from Beirut. The latter seemed to find it a novelty to drive up to the remote village of Shemlan, and responded enthusiastically. After dinner, Trott's party trick was to ask the ladies, not whether they would like to see his etchings but whether they would enjoy inspecting the birds he was stuffing. This unusual enquiry invariably generated affirmative interest, so he would casually toss into the ladies' satin laps the little rolls of the international Times done up with elastic bands. Bejewelled fingers took a little time to unroll the packages, which eventually revealed a mangle of skin and congealed blood. Shrieks followed of *'Quelle horreur'* and *'Oh c'est horrible',* and it took a considerable time for the ladies to regain their composure. The inspection of the birds usually led to a hurried departure, which may have been Trott's motive. Not all the ladies, I fear, risked a second visit to the eccentric retired British diplomat.

Mrs Trott played no part in the taxidermy. She concentrated on the logistics of the meal and was more interested in entertaining the students. She was, if my memory is right, daughter of an Anglican Bishop in Tehran. She was certainly skilled at organising fetes, sewing groups and jolly evenings. Proficient on the piano, she coralled the students, diplomatic and military alike, whether musical or not, to evenings of part song practice. We sang, to the best of our ability and to a rousing volume, rounds, catches and snatches, indeed all sorts of musical variety, and were rewarded with beer and cake. It always struck me throughout my diplomatic career as extraordinary that in the remotest of places and in the hottest of climates, the British enthusiasm for party games, part songs and Scottish dancing ran riot. At Shemlan in the heat of summer, and even in our mountain fastness it could indeed be hot, yet reel parties were often organised. I think, however, that we were spared the hottest of hot curries, which were the Sunday pleasure during my subsequent posting to Kuwait.

During my time at Shemlan, my mother and father paid a visit and we went off together for a week's trip to Syria. I suppose that it was 'half term'. My parents were experienced travellers in the Middle East. They both spoke Arabic, of the Egyptian variety, having served in the Sudan. As we set out from Shemlan, they asked if I had furnished myself with what they considered to be the most useful piece of travelling equipment. This turned out to be an all-purpose plug for bath and basin. And how right they were. In Damascus, in Aleppo, in Homs and in Hama, not a plug did we see. It led me to reflect on the illogicality of the situation. If all travellers only left plugs where they were, nobody would be inconvenienced, and no one need take the precaution of bringing plugs with them. But perhaps plug makers and suppliers would lose some revenue.

The region was happily tranquil in those far off days, and though one was faced with the usual complications, misunderstandings and delays when crossing the frontier (particularly into Syria), travel was easy. During the summer break when we sent off to practise our Arabic, I drove down to Jordan. My first attachment was with the Jordanian Ministry of Agriculture. We rode out on horses to villages near Amman under a scheme to delineate property boundaries. The officials from the Ministry and I tethered our horses and sat under a prominent tree to listen to the complicated claims and counter claims of the inhabitants. As voices became more raised and gestures more uninhibited, I frequently lost the thread of the arguments, but it was good training, and I greatly admired the judgements of Solomon which were handed down. I then went on to Bir Zeit, the Biblical village of Emmaus, and stayed for some days in the monastery there. Finally I lived with a charming family in Jerusalem, sharing meals with them, and going out in the evenings with their two attractive daughters in addition to seeing all the historic and religious sites on the Arab side of that then divided city. Split though it was into two distinct parts with little contact one with the other, it was at least peaceful and without violence, unlike today.

Remembering all those happy days in Shemlan and in the region, my only prayer and hope is that in spite of all the negative signs at the moment, it can somehow return to the calm and tranquillity which I and my colleagues were able to enjoy fifty years ago.

Sir Antony Acland KG GCMG GCVO attended MECAS in 1954. His appointments included Head of Arabian Department, Foreign Office 1970-72, Ambassador to Luxembourg 1975-77, to Spain, 1977-79, Permanent Under-Secretary of State FCO and Ambassador to Washington 1986-91. From 1991 to 2000, he was Provost of Eton.

Peter Trott, son of Alan Trott writes:

My elder brother and I visited Shemlan for the Christmas holidays in 1954. Indeed I had my 21st birthday there which was celebrated with a dinner in Beirut. We stayed with my parents who were in the Director's house and had a wonderful time seeing the country and going to Baalbek, as well as all the local sites elsewhere. The Director's house had a wonderful view all over the southern end of Beirut including the airport and indeed on a clear day, with a bit of imagination, you could see the eastern end of Cyprus.

Around Christmas all the students and other admin staff were invited to the director's house for a Christmas party. I can remember Scottish dancing and other energetic activities as well as singing songs round the piano. My father was very keen on games and we were all summoned into the sitting room, perhaps forty people, and given pencils and paper. My father then announced that we had to write down everything beginning with a certain letter that we would need on a desert island. My father then opened the Bible and selected the letter 'M'. Of course to win the game you had to write down the things that no one else had thought of and it was pretty useless to think of matches, marmalade and even motor cars and if I remember rightly two people wrote down 'machete'. An army officer who was resentful at being called away from my father's whisky which was freely available, only wrote the two words 'Marilyn Monroe' which nobody else thought of. His resentment at having to play the game was obvious to everybody and my father was visibly irritated when he was announced the winner.

My father suffered badly from headache and eye problems as a result of high blood pressure for which in those days there was no effective medication. I remember him as a 'man's man' full of applause for one's activity with lots of jokes, some of them rather obscure. He died in September 1959.

Part Two
1955-58

THE SUEZ CRISIS 1956

Archie Lamb

At the end of 1955, we travelled to Beirut to become students at the Middle East Centre for Arab Studies in the village of Shemlan in the mountains above Beirut with a breathtaking view to the west across the Mediterranean. The sunsets were spectacular. We had still not travelled by air, the 1950's version of 'post chaise and fast packet' being the Golden Arrow Pullman train from Victoria Station to Paris, and express train from Paris to Genoa (or Venice) and a passenger ship (the *Esperia* or *Enotria* of the Adriatica Line) from Italy to the Levant. These were beautifully found ships with high quality Italian crews for whom the passengers'needs never appeared to cause problems. The four days we spent on the cruise from Genoa to Beirut were idyllic and as good a holiday as could be found anywhere.

After arriving in Shemlan we stayed for a while in the local tourist hotel, Mulberry Lodge, before moving into one of four flats in a new block built for the purpose of accommodating students at the Centre. The landlord was Shukri Hitti who, in the fashion of Yasser Arafat of the Palestine Liberation Organisation (PLO), always had a growth of beard suggesting that he had not shaved for three days. He and his wife were friendly and sympathetic landlords who valued what they considered to be a secure contract with the Centre. Shemlan was a Christian village although the so-called shaikh was a Druze. Everybody had a gun and at a village wedding the men continually fired *feux de joie*. Shukri Hitti told me on more than one occasion that there were guns stored in every

85

house and that one day they would have to be used against the Muslims. A sad prophecy which has come true and destroyed a country.

The Centre was housed in a former silk factory that had once been fed by the activities of silkworms on local mulberry trees (hence the name of the local hotel). Its Director when we arrived was Mr. Alan Trott, a distinguished orientalist who had served as Ambassador to Saudi Arabia. He was a dedicated naturalist, who was given to keeping the bodies of birds he wished to study in the refrigerator in his kitchen. He was one of those men who are too brilliant at their own speciality to be able to pass it on successfully to others. He used to take my class for readings of the Quran when we had no real knowledge of Arabic or understanding of Islam. But he derived much enjoyment for himself from reading the Quran. James Craig was already the Chief Instructor at the Centre when I joined it and Alan Trott was soon succeeded by Donald Maitland, also a distinguished Foreign Office Arabist, but still on his way up to the highest echelons of the Diplomatic Service and eventually to the post of Permanent Under Secretary at the Department of Energy before his retirement as Sir Donald. Our studies prospered under the guidance of these distinguished Arabic scholars and I was pleased to pass out third in the order of merit in the final Foreign Service Higher Standard Arabic Examination (equivalent to Honours Degree standard) in March 1957, behind Patrick Wright, later the Permanent Under Secretary of the Foreign Office and Head of the Diplomatic Service, and Terry Clark, later Her Majesty's Ambassador to Iraq and Oman, both of whom were more than ten years my junior. My major problem in learning Arabic at the age of 35 was the absorption of vocabulary and pronunciation. I had less difficulty with the structure of the language but getting Arabic words to stay in my head was a problem. We used visiting cards, on one side of which we wrote the English word and on the other the Arabic, and carried these cards with us everywhere, turning them over and muttering the Arabic to ourselves. Reading the English-Arabic or Arabic-English dictionary was also a help. The fifteen months I was at MECAS was a hard but eventually worthwhile slog. Christina also studied Arabic, having said, when I told her of my Middle East ambitions, that if I was going to be an Arabist she too had better learn Arabic.

The Suez Crisis of 1956

While we were at MECAS there took place an international confrontation which has been seen as the last gasp of British imperialism in the Middle East. The Suez adventure was seen as disastrous for British interests in the Middle East and, more narrowly, making the task of Foreign Office Arabists more demanding. Those *en poste* and in the Foreign Office were unanimously against the misguided adventure; and the corridor outside the Personnel Department was lined with members of the Service queuing up to resign. Fortunately, most of them were persuaded to stand by to retrieve British fortunes in the Middle East. One Foreign Office student at MECAS did resign, but his value was not lost since he became a well-informed and distinguished journalist specialising in Arab affairs. The British debacle at Suez did not discourage the rest of us; and neither did an Arab terrorist bomb attack against the Centre. Terry Clark was slightly injured but little damage was done to the fabric of the Centre or to its ability to teach. In the Middle East the Centre had acquired a false reputation as a 'school for spies' and for British Imperialists at that. It was also a soft target for the perpetrators of the terrorist attack since at night the only occupants of the unguarded, security-free Centre were the unmarried students who lived in. The Army officers who were studying Arabic at the Centre, at the time of the Suez crisis, were recalled to their units, but only one of them saw any action; the rest would have been better employed at their books in Shemlan.

Sir Archie Lamb KBE CMG DFC joined the Foreign Office as a Clerical Officer in 1938, served with the Royal Air Force as a Hurricane and Typhoon fighter-bomber pilot during the Second World War, and returned to the Foreign Office in 1946. He was British Political Agent in Abu Dhabi 1965-68, Inspector of the Diplomatic Service 1968-74, Ambassador to Kuwait 1974-77 and to Norway 1978-80. He retired in 1981. His Memoirs, A Long Way *from Swansea,* from which these extracts are taken, and Abu Dhabi 1965-1968 *were published in 2003.* The Last Voyage of SS Oronsay, *published in 2004, describes the sinking of the* Oronsay *by a German U-boat in the South Atlantic and his survival after nine days in a lifeboat.*

MY BLACK BOX,
A SYMBOL 1955

Ian Skeet

Attending MECAS was like going back to school, except that they paid you; and was there any other school at which you could sit on the wall with your homework and watch from on high the sun setting over the Mediterranean? Moreover, under the auspices of Shell I had my own house, beside the road that led down to the school, opposite the village fountain. The walls were hardly weatherproof, but we could sit on my balcony, drink beer and listen to Sibelius 2 as the evening darkness took over. That was played on my Black Box, a symbol of new financial independence that had been bought in London before my departure for Jordan a year earlier.

The usual MECAS months passed, full of word lists and grammar, interspersed with hectic trips in service taxis up and down the mountain to and from Beirut. In the Easter break I meant to get to Dura Europus, but, having reached Deir-ez-Zur, lost heart and took the bus back to Aleppo, returning to visit the crusader castles that Robin Fedden's book on Syria had inspired us to visit. For some reason Shell, which had decided with foresight to send one of its management trainees to MECAS every year, legislated that six months was enough. This meant that Shell students left before the language break gave us the theoretical chance to practise what we'd learned. Instead, I was sent off to Cairo where, of course, the dialect of Arabic spoken bore little relation to what we'd been taught in Lebanon. Never mind, for in career terms it was a good move. When, a year later, Eden invaded Suez and expatriates were all forbidden to leave Egypt I was the only person in the company who could fill up the forms and tell my superiors how to get out when we were finally ejected from the country.

As part of the MECAS course we used to get background lectures on the Arab world. I well remember hearing for the first time about a place called Muscat and Oman in which there was, maybe only rumoured to be, an unapproachable Green Mountain on which green vines and apricots grew – a sort of Shangri La it sounded to my distinctly hazy idea of the Arabian desert, rising out of the scorched sands. Little did I imagine that a few years later I would be sent to the Gulf by Shell, that I would end up by writing two books on Oman and that I would have eaten the grapes of Jebel Akhdar somewhere near its summit.

Ian Skeet attended MECAS in 1955. He retired from Shell International in 1985. In addition to his two books on Oman, he is the author of OPEC, the First 25 Years 1960-1985

STORMS, AN
EARTHQUAKE AND
BOMBS 1956

Patrick Wright

The Selection Process

I suppose it all started with my call on the Personnel Department, during my first week in the Foreign Service in late August or early September 1955. I had already been advised, by the only member of the Service whom I knew at that time (the late Peter Mennell), that I would be well advised not to volunteer for a hard language, since it was likely to restrict my career to one place or, at best, to one region of the world.

When I was asked by Personnel Department (in what classicists would recognise as a *nonne* question) whether I would like to learn a hard language, I rather naively replied that I had received strong advice not to do so. This received the predictable *dementi* , with the encouraging prospect of a glittering career, outstripping all those who had boringly opted for the chancelleries of Europe. So when I was presented with a choice of five languages, I opted for Arabic, on the (illogical) grounds that, since it was spoken in some 15 posts, it would give me a more varied career. I say illogical because, had I opted for, say, Burmese I doubt if I would have had more than three postings to

Burma, and the rest of my career would have ranged from Iceland to Indonesia. As it turned out, I had no less than five Arab postings, in addition to my spell as the Middle East Member of Chancery in Washington and the Head of Middle East Department in the Office.

But Arabic it was, and at that time Arabist new entrants started their Arabic studies (after a laughably brief Introductory Training Course) at the School of Oriental and African Studies, learning little more than the alphabet and basic grammar. Peter Mansfield and Ramsay Melhuish (the latter to be my best man when I married Virginia three years later) were learning Arabic with me, and after a course of about six weeks Ramsay and I travelled together across Europe and by ship to Alexandria and Beirut, to reach MECAS by the New Year (each of us the proud owner of half a Morris Minor). Incidentally, one of the reasons why I have always admired Ramsay (apart from his many gifts as a diplomat) is that he was, I think, the only one of the 15 or so Fast Stream Entrants in 1955 who did *not* appear at the Introductory Course with the traditional bowler hat and furled umbrella.

Others of our entry were directed towards Persian, Chinese and other 'hard languages'. I remember complaining to one of my colleagues that I had been slogging away at Arabic for a month and still had learnt only 300 words, to which he exclaimed: '300 words! I still have some difficulty with 25 Characters'.

Storms, an Earthquake and Bombs
So we arrived at MECAS in the early days of January by sea – having tried to keep as tactfully out of the way as possible of Malcolm and Pam Holding, who were on their honeymoon. I can't remember who (if anyone) met us on arrival at Beirut; but we must have been driven – perhaps Ramsay and I each drove our half share of the Morris Minor? – up the hill to Shemlan. Our rooms were either side of the courtyard of the old silk mill, below the village of Shemlan – a charming Turkish-style building, but whose roof leaked so badly that a storm (and they were quite frequent in the early spring) produced about two inches of water on the floor of one's room. The water took some time to dry out, since the only form of heating was a very smelly Primus stove.

The Director was Alan Trott, a remarkable Islamic scholar, whose reading of the Quran was as near inspirational as an irreverent young diplomat could hope for. I think that his main language had been Persian, and the only specific linguistic advice I can remember from him was that the House of Saud was, if one was correct, the House of Su'ud – a theory ignored by Hava, and contradicted by Hans Wehr. Having much later become Ambassador to Saudi Arabia, I am bound to say that I never found one Su'udi who was aware of this.

Perhaps because we shared a car, Ramsay and I were (at least) twice invited together to the Director's house for dinner during our time at MECAS. The first occasion coincided with the terrible Lebanese earthquake of 1956, and I remember the *sang froid* of Alan Trott, who calmly told us to get under the dining table, and continued to fulfil his hostly duties by passing the bread from the table above him to those sitting underneath. Later that year, after Donald and Jean Maitland had succeeded the Trotts, Ramsay and I were again invited to the Director's house for dinner. Donald was away but Jean had been looking at the Director's Guest Book and was just remarking that the entry for our previous dinner had received a marginal note of 'Earthquake!', when there was a shattering explosion. This turned out to be what would nowadays be called a terrorist attack against the School (no doubt in response to Suez – see below), but which would almost certainly have killed Terry Clark or Dick Giddens, had they been in their rooms, situated immediately above the explosion.

We were also, as students, occasionally invited to receptions by members of the Embassy in Beirut. I remember one occasion when the Head of Chancery, the late Ian Scott, very kindly invited a number of us to one of his cocktail parties. A group of Lebanese men were deep in Arabic conversation in the corner of the room; so, emboldened by what I thought was by then an adequate control of social Arabic, I approached the group and said, '*Masa'al khair*' (good evening) – to which, as one man, they replied, '*Bon soir*', and turned away – my first experience of the linguistic snobbery of a certain class of Lebanese, which still, to some extent, persists today. I was happy to discover, later in my career, that this particular form of snobbery hardly applied in either of the two Arab countries in which I was Ambassador: Syria and Saudi Arabia.

An Abiding Fascination

When I arrived at MECAS, James Craig had recently taken over as Principal Instructor, and he certainly instilled in me (if not in all our colleagues) an abiding fascination with the Arabic langauge. (I later succeeded him twice, as Ambassador to both Syria and Saudi Arabia, and had to endure frequent comment on how brilliantly my predecessor had spoken Arabic). Just as Alan Trott had recited the Quran to us, James would recite, or read, pre-Islamic poetry – my first introduction to one secret of the Arabic language which I was later to experience in Egypt when I listened with an Egyptian friend to a rousing (and probably anti-British) speech by President Gamal Abdul Nasser. I asked my friend what a certain phrase meant. He replied, 'I haven't the faintest idea; but isn't it wonderful Arabic?' I am bound to say that our attempts to translate pre-Islamic poetry word by word from Hava's Dictionary, produced some grotesque gibberish.

But I count myself extremely fortunate to have spent most of my time at MECAS under the supervision of James Craig and Donald Maitland, who together did a fantastic job in modernising the techniques of Arabic instruction through their work in producing the MECAS Grammar and Word List.

Work and play were hard. We were kept at our studies, not only by James Craig but also by the Arab instructors, who happily fell in with James's discipline of Word Cards. I particularly remember the Palestinian triad of Messrs Khoury, Farah and Theodory – the latter cruelly teased by the students when we discovered that he was editing a book of English proverbs, for which we provided him with bogus examples, many of which can still be found in his published book.

Play consisted of skiing at the Cedars in winter, dancing at the Elephant Noir in Beirut, and swimming or picnicking on the Damour river in spring. We went for tea or drinks at the St George's Club, and occasional parties at the Goslings – where two of the prettiest English girls were constantly wooed by MECAS students. And there was also Scottish dancing at MECAS itself, where many of us (including myself) found our future brides among the 'girls' from the Embassy.

In the summer of 1956, Terry Clark and I were seconded to Damascus, to interpret for the British Stand at the Damascus International Fair. I don't remember very much about the Fair itself, other than a very proud Syrian, who told us that 'this little man who stands before you' had been elected to be doyen of the Consular Corps in Manchester. But I do remember where we stayed – in the old British Embassy building (now collapsed) near the Hejaz Railway Station, with a wonderful grand piano in the main reception room – a piano which I tried unsuccesfully to track down as Ambassador some 23 years later. As we were not in diplomatic relations with Syria at the time, I suppose Terry and I represented the British Diplomatic Presence.

One of my main memories of the school (apart from the leaking roof) is of us students sitting on the wall overlooking one of the most magical views of the Mediterranean, Word Cards in hand and mouthing feverishly in the hope that the other side of the card would actually turn out to be the right word.

But there were also lessons in Persian Gulf Law from Judge Haines, who had no doubt been a distinguished jurist, but who, I fear, received scant respect from us. As it happened, I was not posted to the Gulf for another 15 years, and then had no judicial responsibilities as the last Deputy Political Resident. I wonder how my colleagues, who had more immediate practical experience of the Persian Gulf Courts, found their grounding of the law at the feet of Judge Haines.

And then there were the Language Breaks: in my case, two weeks with a Palestinian schoolmaster in Ramallah; two weeks with a Lebanese schoolmaster in the high Lebanese mountains at Kefr Aaqaab (whose daughter was still pining for a naval predecessor of mine); followed by two weeks in Kurdistan. I understand that our Language Break Reports have disappeared (not perhaps surprisingly). But I wish I could re-read my report on a magical two weeks in Kurdistan – travelling with John Burgess from the Information Office in Mosul; camping overnight and riding with the Iraqi Army (who insisted on putting arak into the infidel's Coca Cola) through Rawanduz; and being taken across the Iranian border at Hajji Umran and Diana, to find that the Iranian border guards spoke nothing but Turkic.

The Voice of Britain

Then came Suez, and the extraordinary period when, in the company of Dick Fyjis-Walker, Bertie Saunders, Philip McKearney and others, I was summoned to sit at Donald Maitland's feet, at Zyghi in Cyprus, to help run a covert broadcasting station, called Saut Britannia (*'al mahattat allati tuqaddim anbaa al-aalam, li aalam al-aalimin'*), directed against Nasser's Egypt, in place of the excellent, and popular, Near East Arab Broadcasting Station which the British Government had nationalised. We were there for several weeks, at the height of the EOKA terrorist campaign, armed with loaded revolvers for which we were given no training whatsoever.

Suez also brought what was, I believe, the only official (as opposed to ministerial) resignation from the Service, by Peter Mansfield. The Service certainly lost a brilliant and witty diplomat, but the literary world was the gainer, since Peter went on to write definitive works on the Arabs, on President Nasser and on Egypt.

Then, one day, one of those Staff in Confidence letters arrived, telling me that I had been posted to Jeddah, as soon as diplomatic relations had been restored, and that meanwhile, I should go to the Residency in Bahrain. But hepatitis, and Dr Dragatsi (unbribed) intervened, and I took my final exams in the American University Hospital in Beirut (the oral administered by Mahmoud Akhal). I was asked to remain at MECAS, and to teach some of the next course – from which I stake my claim to have taught Hooky Walker – probably the best Arabist of his generation – and Chris Willy, who has remained a good friend ever since.

MECAS remains a fond memory, and it saddens me that our Arabist successors nowadays have not had the experience which we enjoyed.

Baron Wright of Richmond GCMG attended MECAS in 1956-57. He served as Head of Middle East Department FCO (1972-74), Private Secretary (Overseas Affairs) to the Prime Minister (1974-77) and Ambassador to Luxembourg (1977-79), Syria (1979-81) and Saudi Arabia (1984-86). From 1986 to 1991, he was Permanent Under-Secretary of State in the Foreign and Commonwealth Office and Head of the Diplomatic Service.

GAMESMANSHIP
1956-57

Terence Clark

As was the practice at the time, I made my way to MECAS by the Simplon Orient Express to Venice, then by a Greek Line cruise ship, the *Agamemnon*, to Beirut and finally by road to Shemlan. I travelled with some of my course colleagues, viz. Malcolm Holding and his wife, Pam, Peter Mansfield, Ramsey Melhuish, and Patrick Wright. We were joined in Shemlan by Dick Giddens and Archie and Christina Lamb from the Foreign Service and a number of other students from the armed forces and oil companies. We left Venice in high spirits as it was New Year's Eve 1955 and the town was in festive mood. The Italians were tossing empty bottles from their windows, making our somewhat unsteady path to the ship even more hazardous.

Our course overlapped with a small group of students completing the long course for the Higher Arabic examination. One of them was Claude Rocquet from the Canadian Foreign Service who was a brilliant Arabist but was matched by Lt. Robert Irving RN. They completely demoralised us newcomers by learning Elias' dictionary and testing each other on it. At least that is how it appeared to us but as they were both inclined to practical jokes we were not sure whether they were doing it merely to impress us.

Our own course later demoralised other newcomers by playing an Arabic version of Lexicon, devised by James Craig. We became rather good at learning abstruse words from Hava's dictionary, which tended to become more and more outrageous as the evening wore on and the circulating bottle of arak was consumed. Some of these expensive words, as we called them, have remained with me ever since, such as *a'nash*, meaning to have six fingers. A group of us were having lunch in a restaurant when we noticed that the waiter serving the soup had six fingers. We all roared *a'nash* to the poor man's complete amazement, for like so many of our expensive words 'it was not being much used', as Ustadh Theodory would say. I had occasion to use it again years later in Baghdad when I met a doctor with six fingers. I think it was Peter Mansfield who found the most expensive word which meant 'to fall down a well and die of thirst' but, alas, I can no longer remember it – no doubt for lack of use!

A Large Bomb In Shemlan

It was in the winter of 1956, shortly after the start of the Suez campaign with the bombing of Cairo by Israeli aircraft that the peace of our existence at Shemlan was rudely shattered by an incident that I shall never forget. It was a stormy night with thunder, lightning and pouring rain. I was in my room after dinner, sitting in a high-backed armchair with the polished wooden headboard from my bed stretched out across the arms as a makeshift table, on which I had set out my piles of Arabic word cards. Suddenly there was an almighty bang, the lights went out and the air was filled with dust. My initial thought was that we had been struck by lightning. Then through the door came Dick Giddens, who lived across the corridor from me. He grabbed me by the arm and said that we must get out, as there had been a bomb. He was an ex-Palestine policeman and knew all about bombs. So I followed him through the darkness of the library to the outside stairs that gave onto a courtyard below. At the foot was Nimr, the night watchman, screaming at the top of his voice 'sharmouta', which I later learned was the Arabic for prostitute. It was only when we came out into the fresh night air that I realised that there was blood trickling down my neck from a wound in my scalp. James Craig, Principal Instructor, came down from dinner at the Director's house, and drove me to the nearest doctor in Souq al-Gharb. The doctor cleaned the wound and dressed it with a bandage wound around my head like a Druze turban.

It was only when visiting the school next morning that I realised how lucky I had been. The bomb, apparently several kilos of explosives, had been stuffed into a gap in the outside wall of the Principal Instructor's office, which was on the ground floor. The main force of the explosion had fortunately been absorbed by the massive stone built walls or had been deflected outwards. My room above was a shambles, with shattered glass and word cards strewn everywhere. The armchair in which I had sat still backed towards the side window and looked more like a pincushion, with slivers of glass protruding from it. On the door facing it more slivers outlined the shape of the armchair like a knifethrower's knives at the circus. I had had a very lucky escape. My Vespa, which had been parked under the outside staircase leading up to my room, was not so lucky. I had been conscious at the time of the bang of a bright light in the sky but I had not realised then that it was my burning machine that had been propelled by the blast down the mountainside like a Roman candle. The school wall was blackened and all the windows on that side had lost their glass, as had the veranda roof its tiles. But overall the damage was remarkably light – a tribute to the solid construction of the building.

Some while later I had an unexpected and extremely awkward reminder of the bomb. After Suez an official British radio station was set up in Cyprus and began broadcasting in Arabic under the name of *Sawt Britanya* (the Voice of Britain) to put across the British view of events and to counteract the hostile broadcasting from Arabic stations in the area. Donald Maitland was called in to run it. It was not easy in those circumstances to recruit Arabs to broadcast for us and he resorted to MECAS for help. Patrick Wright was sent over for a few weeks to read the news and I was selected to succeed him. However shortly before my departure a slight bang to the back of the neck brought up a large swelling. On investigation it was found to contain a further sliver of glass, which had to be removed. By the time this was done the requirement for MECAS students in Cyprus was over and I never went.

Our Tutors

We worked under the tutorship of Constantine Theodory, Wadi'
Khoury, Tawfiq Farah, Khalil Khoury, Shamma', the Rev. Maqdisi
and Yusef al- Khadra. Theodory was the butt of many practical
jokes. We were always inventing words and expressions in English
and asking him the Arabic equivalents. He was never sure whether
we were pulling his leg but would equally never admit that he did
not know the answer. The result was often some hilarious
translation, which he would solemnly say he would put in the
dictionary that he was forever writing.

Tawfiq Farah was a lovely old man with a dry sense of humour.
Wadi' Khoury was a pedant who insisted that we got every vowel
(*fatha*, *kasra* and *dhamma)* absolutely right. But even he was
reduced to tears of laughter with the rest of us when Malcolm
Holding translated the signature Farid al-Najjar to a letter in our
reading book as Fred Carpenter!

One instance of the effective use of a limited knowledge of
Arabic was when one of the Army officers, Peter Bartlett, was
accosted in Arabic by a policeman for illegally parking near the St.
George's Club in Beirut. Peter, showing great presence of mind,
replied in the best traditions of the Raj: '*Ma'lish ana Inglizi!*' (never
mind, I'm English). He walked off leaving a flabbergasted and
acquiescent policeman.

During the 15 months of otherwise intensive tuition at MECAS
we gradually became aware that, with greater or lesser competence
depending on individual linguistic aptitude, each one of us was
slowly turning from an ignoramus into an increasingly fluent
Arabist. The fact that all but one of the Foreign Service students on
my course reached the Higher Standard reflected the more
structured teaching methods introduced in our time as well as on the
selection of volunteers. Good though the examination results
suggested we were, I believe we were all humbled to find on going
out into the real Arab world that in such a rich and varied language,
especially in its spoken forms, we were only just beginning.

A NEW
CURRICULUM AND
NEW PREMISES
1956-60

Donald Maitland

Appointment as Director

One day in the summer of 1956, as I was crossing St James's Park on my way back to the Foreign Office after lunch, I heard the familiar voice of John Henniker behind me: 'I have been looking for you', he said. John Henniker was at that time the head of the Personnel Department. He went on: 'What would you say to going back to the Middle East Centre?' 'To do what?' I asked. 'To be Director,' he replied. I was astounded.

John Henniker-Major had joined the Diplomatic Service in 1938. While serving in the army during the war he had been wounded in the western desert. Later he joined Fitzroy Maclean's mission to Tito's partisans in Yugoslavia. His ambition as head of the Personnel Department – a post he held from 1953 to 1960 – was to modernise the service and make it professional. He recognised that the post-war environment in which the service had to operate was quite different from that to which the old-style diplomats had been accustomed. He had the advantage that senior members of the service regarded him as one of their own and were therefore more likely to go along with the reforms that he had in mind.

So far as British interests in the Middle East were concerned, John took the view that, if these were to be adequately protected and fostered, training in the Arabic language had to be taken more seriously. While there were notable exceptions, many members of the pre-war Levant Service had got by with a superficial knowledge of Arabic. Apart from this, they were regarded by the rest of the Service as a somewhat exotic breed apart. John Henniker had two objectives in this regard: first, to raise the standard of Arabic training and, secondly, to 'normalise' Arabic by persuading members of the Service as a whole that specialisation in Arab affairs was no different from other specialisms and did not close the door to other types of work or to the most senior posts.

From previous conversations John Henniker was aware that I agreed with his approach and that I felt the potential of the Middle East Centre had not been realised. My experience in Amara and Baghdad, where I had to speak and read Arabic for many hours a day, had persuaded me that Arabic tuition at the Centre could be improved in several ways. The teaching texts ought to deal with contemporary subjects and the situations students would encounter in their everyday business. More opportunities had to be created to practise speaking. But there was a more serious problem. The Arab concept of language differed from the European. For religious reasons the Arabic language, had for centuries been the principal medium of artistic expression. Moreover, the Quran was a revealed scripture – the words of God made known to the prophet Muhammad in the Arabic language – and this gave all books a certain sanctity. For Arabs therefore their language was the core of their culture and the richness of its vocabulary one of its esteemed features. This presented the foreigner who had to live and work with Arabs and for whom a knowledge of the language would be uniquely valuable, with a formidable challenge: how best to assimilate a working vocabulary three times as extensive as would be needed in almost every other part of the world. The solution probably lay in a systematic approach over several months.

As we approached Downing Street that summer afternoon, John explained that he had decided that the Middle East Centre had to be re-launched and that he wanted me to do this. It took me only as long as it takes to draw breath to agree. I was excited and honoured.

The Suez Crisis

Jean and I had adequate time to prepare for our move to Lebanon. Through a friend of a friend, we met a charming young woman called Celia Pridham, who agreed to come wih us and help to look after Colin, then nearly four and Alison, nearly two. In agreeing to join our household on this exciting venture Celia can have had little idea of the effect it was to have on her destiny.

The nationalisation of the Suez Canal Company in July 1956 and the crisis this precipitated cast a cloud over our preparations. Although the situation deteriorated over the following months there was no suggestion that our posting would be affected. On 14 October we crossed the Channel with our car by air ferry from Lydd in Kent, drove in stages to Venice and sailed from there on 17 October. The ship called at Alexandria on the way to Beirut, where we arrived on 25 October.

After the enforced camping out at Zerqa in 1947 as guests of the Transjordan Frontier Force, Bertram Thomas had found a new site for the Centre in the village of Shemlan, situated in the hills some twenty miles by road to the east of Beirut. As Alan Trott, the retiring Director, and his wife Hester were not due to leave Shemlan for a few days, we stayed at the local hotel. Alan Trott had retired from his last post as ambassador at Jeddah some years earlier. The Trotts' farewell to the staff of the Centre coincided with Israel's invasion of Sinai. On the following day, 30 October, while we were moving into the Director's house, the British and French governments issued their ultimatum to Egypt and Israel, threatening to intervene militarily if hostilities had not ceased within twenty-four hours. Egyptian airfields were bombed on 31 October and 1 November. On 4 November I was instructed by the Foreign Office to go immediately to Cyprus to take over a radio station. I would be briefed on arrival by John Shattock, the political representative with Middle East forces and Brigadier Bernard Fergusson, who was in charge of the armed forces public relations – the same Bernard Fergusson I had met in Bangalore when he gave an account of the Chindit expedition in Burma in 1944. While I flew to Nicosia on 5 November, British paratroops were consolidating their position in Port Said, in preparation for the seaborne assault.

Diverted to Cyprus

The story I was told in Nicosia was barely credible. Because it was dissatisfied with the way the BBC Arabic Service had been reporting the Suez crisis, the British government had decided to requisition 'Sharq al Adna', the Near East Broadcasting station. This station had been established in Palestine in 1941 and moved to Cyprus in 1948 when the British mandate was coming to an end. Its programmes – news and comment as well as entertainment – were highly regarded in the Arab world. On 30 October 1956, the day the British and French governments issued their ultimatum, the director, Ralph Poston, was informed that the name of the station and its nature would be changed as of 3 p.m. on that day. 'Sharq al Adna' became the 'The Voice of Britain' and on its wavelength messages were broadcast warning the people of Egypt to expect bombing raids. Poston had sought to persuade both the British and the Arab staff to accept the change but, at the request of the Arabs, most of whom were Palestinian Christians, he broadcast the message explaining that they were operating under duress. As soon as news of this broadcast reached allied headquarters Bernard Fergusson ordered Poston and his wife to be placed under house arrest. At this point the entire editorial staff, British and Arab, and the announcers walked out. This meant that the British government had acquired an Arabic radio station, but had no one to operate it. My job was to take it over.

I was joined in Cyprus by three Arabic-speaking members of the Foreign Service from other Middle East posts. On the morning of the following day, 6 November, we were flown to the south of the island where we were met by a squadron leader. He drove us to the broadcasting station situated beside a military camp on a slope overlooking the bay of Limassol.

Our station had an unreal quality. The station had been kept on the air by an engineer, the output consisting of endless gramophone records. My appeal to Beirut to recruit Arabs who could act as announcers produced rapid results. Two brave men, a Lebanese and a Palestinian, joined us within a few days.

On 9 November I received a telephone call from the Political Representative's office in Nicosia. Having identified me correctly, the voice said: 'I am afraid I have bad news for you. We have just heard that there was a bomb attack on the Centre at Shemlan last night. The building has been damaged. Some of your students were injured. Your family are safe.' I was still feeling numb when the telephone rang again. This time it was the British Embassy at Beirut. 'I have bad news for you,' the voice said. The anxiety that swept over me was soon allayed when this turned out to be the same story and not a sequel. Later in the day I managed to telephone Jean in Shemlan. She demonstrated, not for the first nor the last time, her remarkable composure in moments of crisis or distress.

Difficulties in Cyprus

For the first several days we were ostracised by the British staff of the station who had walked out when Ralph Poston was arrested. No doubt they saw us as instruments of a policy with which they disagreed and resented our taking over their functions, however inexpert we were. It seemed not to have occurred to them that we might share their view about the government's handling of the Suez affair, nor did they appreciate that we were in duty bound to carry out the instructions of the government we served to the best of our ability, however disagreeable we might find this. One of them, with more imagination and charity in his heart than his colleagues, did eventually visit us and, when he realised our situation, offered helpful advice on the understanding that this did not compromise his position. Later on others followed his lead.

We were not yet aware that the obnoxious nature of the bombing broadcasts at the time of the Anglo-French intervention had gravely damaged the credibility of the station in the Arab world. But the futility of our endeavours was evident to us all. After two weeks I asked London how long it was intended that I remain in Cyprus; I was anxious to get on with the job I had come out to do. A few days later I was asked to return to London to report. My recommendation that the station and its transmitter be handed over at the earliest opportunity to the BBC was received more stoically than I had expected. I was released and allowed to return to my new job and my family in Shemlan.

A Resignation

On my return to Shemlan on 27 November I faced an immediate problem. One of the Foreign Service students, Peter Mansfield, asked to see me on a personal matter. He said he found it impossible to continue in the service of a government capable of such actions as we had seen over the past several weeks. He therefore wanted me to know that he was submitting his resignation from the Foreign Service. I said that if this was indeed his view, then I had to respect it. He should not assume, however, that he had a monopoly of indignation over the Suez affair. Moreover, there was an alternative to resignation. This was to remain in the Service, contribute to the great effort which would be needed over the coming years to repair the damage done to British interests in the Arab world and use one's influence from within to prevent such folly in the future. This was what I intended to do. He agreed to reflect further, but in the end did not alter his decision. This enhanced my regard for him. Peter left the service and went on to make a successful career commenting authoritatively over many years on Middle East affairs.

Reorganising the Curriculum

I was at last able to focus on the affairs of the Centre. A pleasant surprise was in store. James Craig, a considerable Arabic scholar, had been lecturing in Arabic at Durham University when he was seconded to the Foreign Service in 1955 to become Principal Instructor at Shemlan. He and I discovered that our views on teaching Arabic had much in common: he had already been planning a number of reforms. So there began a creative and enjoyable partnership. We worked late into the evenings compiling a list of some three thousand Arabic words which we arranged in broad order of the frequency of their use in modern literary and spoken Arabic. These three thousand words were then grouped into ten sections, each of three hundred words – the commonest words in the first sections, the less common in the later. The Arab instructors, some of whom were Palestinian Christians who had taught me ten years earlier, were rather bemused but treated our efforts with benign tolerance. We then prepared new teaching texts each of which was related to a particular section of the word list. In this way students would learn from the beginning to use the commonest words which would become instinctive as they progressed steadily through the ten sections. We intended that the vocabulary would be mastered in six to ten months. Subsequent experience justified this expectation. The word list and its companion teaching texts were only the first of our innovations.

Visitors

Visitors to the Centre were a welcome interruption to routine. One morning Freya Stark and St John Philby (whom I had briefly met in Cairo ten years earlier), who happened to be visiting Lebanon at the same time, drove up to Beirut to lunch with us. Rather unfairly perhaps I suggested that they sit in on some of our classes. The advanced students happened to be reading and discussing *Hayati* (My Life), by the notable Egyptian writer, Ahmed Amin. Both of our distinguished guests confessed to me afterwards that they were quite out of their depth. I saw St John Philby's son, Kim, only once but was unable to speak to him; the occasion was a cocktail party in Beirut and he was incapable.

The Search for new Premises

Jean and I toured areas of Lebanon within easy reach of Beirut in search of suitable premises for an expanded Centre. At first the people of Shemlan treated these trips with scorn. They became concerned however when an American Quaker school in the hills north of the Beirut river showed interest in offering us space. At this point, I received an approach from Eddie Hitti, which began a friendship between our families that has endured ever since.

Eddie had graduated in the United States and was effectively running the travel business in Beirut called Hitti Frères. He and his wife, Janet, offered to provide a site for a new Centre on land they owned above the main road that ran through the village. Eddie's motive was clear. The livelihood of many of his relatives depended on our presence in the village. He said half seriously: 'You know my relatives; I'd rather you provided for them.' His original proposal was that he and Janet would provide the site on a long lease and that the British government would build the new Centre. However, after a few encounters with the representatives of the British Ministry of Works, Eddie changed his mind. He offered to build to our specifications and to lease the building and the land to the British government. His only condition was that the building should be adaptable for use either as a hotel or a clinic in the event of the Centre's closing or moving elsewhere. Eddie's price was reasonable and London endorsed the deal.

Work began immediately on clearing the site. This gave welcome employment to the inhabitants not only of Shemlan but of other villages.

Contingency Plans

The Druze leader, Kamal Jumblatt, whose so-called 'forces of popular resistance' were based at Mukhtara, some twelve miles by twisting mountain road to the south east of Shemlan, supported the nationalist cause. This caused some anxiety among the Maronites in our village, but the predominant feeling was that the people of Shemlan should keep their heads down and get on with their work. Some may have calculated that the presence of a British government establishment and some eighty British and other foreign nationals in Shemlan would ensure that they were left undisturbed. They might well have been right. However, one of the four families in the village, the Farajallahs, who had links with the PPS, the Parti Populaire Syrien, a militant right-wing Christian organisation which supported Chamoun, upset this calculation. The Farajallahs brought a number of armed members of the PPS into the village who, on most nights, took to firing at imaginary infiltrators.

Discreetly we drew up contingency plans. The owner of the Hajjar hotel in the neighbouring village of Suq al-Gharb, where Denis and Gillian Mitchell lived, agreed to accommodate our families in the event of our having to leave Shemlan and we prepared provisional allocation of accommodation according to the size of the families. Students with their own cars were advised to keep their petrol tanks filled and everyone was asked to have one suitcase ready containing essentials for a few days.

Early one afternoon one of the PPS gunmen was stricken with panic. He fired at Jeffery Greaves' car, wounding Jeffery in the back. Fortunately, the upholstery reduced the velocity of the bullet and Jeffery was soon able to resume his duties. The culprit was immediately sent away from Shemlan, but my efforts to persuade the Farajallahs to remove the PPS detachment altogether were of no avail. The Embassy in Beirut, whom I kept regularly informed and from whom I occasionally sought guidance, were inclined to suggest that I keep in touch with the local authorities. Since the cause of our difficulties was the complete absence of any authority, this was of little help. But on the occasion of the wounding of Jeffery Greaves my appeal had slightly more impact. On our behalf the embassy asked President Chamoun to have the PPS replaced. This appeal proved equally ineffective but, no doubt as a sop, the gendarmerie detachment in the village was reinforced by the arrival of two elderly reservists charged specifically with protecting the Centre.

Nightly alarms continued. On the afternoon of Sunday, 29 June, Colin Keith, one of the Royal Navy students, was detained by a party of armed Druze while out walking his dog a few miles to the south of Shemlan. While under guard he counted up to thirty trucks full of armed men heading north in the direction of Shemlan. Colin was released after a few hours and immediately reported to me what had happened. Everyone was put on alert. Under an arrangement with All Saints Church in Beirut, the intrepid rector, John Grinstead, who travelled everywhere on a Vespa scooter, visited Shemlan once a month to conduct evensong in the drawing room of our residence. It so happened that he was due that evening. The Third Collect perfectly expressed what was in our hearts and minds: 'Lighten our darkness we beseech thee, O Lord; and by thy great mercy defend us from all perils and dangers of the night'.

Jean and I were wakened in the early hours of Monday morning by the sound of small arms fire. Unlike the night-time shooting over the previous two months, this seemed to have a purpose. From our verandah we saw a number of villagers and some of our Arab instructors making their way down the slope away from the village. At 8 o'clock Denis Michell telephoned from his house in Suq al-Gharb to pass a message from Kamal Jumblatt, which had just been conveyed to him by one of his Druze neighbours. According to this message, the attack about to be mounted was not directed at the British residents of Shemlan but at the paramilitary group belonging to the PPS. Jumblatt advised me to evacuate our people. This message had obviously been seriously delayed. The firing which had awakened us must have been the start of the assault. I asked Denis to get his neighbour to explain the situation to Kamal Jumblatt and to request a brief cease-fire to enable us to move our people out to Suq al-Gharb. We would fly white flags from our vehicles.

Our own suitcases were ready. Jean began tearing up sheets to make white flags. As far as I could see, Jumblatt's men had occupied the old Turkish trenches dating from the first world war on the hill to the east from which they could observe all movement in the village. Except that there was none; the village seemed deserted. At deliberate pace I walked the hundred yards to the Centre. I asked two of the students, Bill Norton and Andrew Johnstone, to call on all our families in the village and tell them to assemble their luggage and cars on the track below our residence. We telephoned the same message to two other families in the village of Ainab, a mile to the south. As the vehicles arrived we formed them into small convoys and gave each a white flag. The two elderly gendarmerie reservists came over to our house from their billet in the Centre. They had in their eyes the same look as family pets when they see luggage by the front door and wonder if they are going too. I told them to take their caps and jackets, put their rifles and packs on the floor of the Land Rover and keep their heads down. They called on the

Almighty to lengthen my life. I recounted this incident several years later when accompanying the Foreign Secretary on a visit to Yugoslavia. One of our hosts said accusingly: 'You interfered in the internal affairs of Lebanon.'

By 11 o'clock the evacuation was complete and we spent the rest of the morning settling into the Hajjar hotel. Colin Keith and his wife, supported by other willing hands, organised activities for the children. News from Shemlan in the late afternoon suggested that Jumblatt's forces had withdrawn to the south. We resumed language instruction the following day in the hotel. When I visited a pharmacist in Suq al-Gharb, who had proved a good source of local information in the past, he said several wounded from both sides in the fighting had been brought in the previous day. He objected strongly to having to treat the wounds of those who received their wounds after they were captured.

A day too late armoured cars and mortar units of the Lebanese army arrived on the scene. To our disappointment they did not replace the PPS irregulars, who were claiming victory. This claim was premature. On the morning of 3 July Druze elements were reported to have returned to the high ground and to be pushing north. Vampire aircraft of the Lebanese air force flew low over the hotel before releasing rockets at positions alleged to be occupied by the Druze. In the absence of decisive and effective action by government forces to stabilise the situation in this area, I felt we had no choice but to suspend our activities. After discussion with senior members of staff I ordered the evacuation of all British personnel to Beirut. The Arab teachers elected to remain with their families. I promised to keep them informed of developments.

The students were dispersed from Lebanon for the time being. Jean and I paid two more visits to Shemlan before she and the children left for home in the middle of July. Soon after the US marines landed in Beirut, I followed.

The Return to Shemlan
Early in September the embassy in Beirut reported that the situation in Lebanon had stabilised. Camille Chamoun had been

succeeded as President by the highly regarded General Fuad Chehab. The Lebanese government were keen for the Centre to return. I flew to Beirut on 9 September and drove up to Shemlan the following day. There were few villagers about, and most of the familiar faces were absent. Our buildings seemed not to have been damaged. Armed PPS were much in evidence, behaving as if they owned the place, which at that moment was probably true.

That evening Ian Scott, the chargé d'affaires at the Embassy, took me to General Chehab's residence on the outskirts of the capital. The President pressed for the early return of the Centre to Shemlan. 'Your presence' he said 'can bring more stability to the area than anything I can do.' I said that I would gladly contribute to a return to stable conditions, but I could not recommend that families be allowed to return so long as the village was effectively under the control of undisciplined irregulars. Within a couple of days a unit of the Lebanese army arrived in Shemlan and instituted what were termed 'joint patrols', consisting of equal numbers of soldiers and irregulars. This device saved the face of the Army's allies in the area. Within a week the PPS irregulars had vanished. Calm returned to our mountainside.

The Background Courses

Before hostilities broke out in the summer of 1958 we had been able to hold the first of a planned programme of background courses. These were designed to give foreigners working in the Middle East a concise introduction to the history of the region, the economic situation in each country, religions, customs and traditions and the main issues of the day. These proved popular. Up to thirty people with different interests and backgrounds from as far afield as Iraq and the Gulf spent five days at the Centre hearing presentations on these subjects from a range of experts, several of them from the American University of Beirut.

David Cowan joined us from the School of Oriental and African Studies in London in September 1959 at the end of Bill Kensdale's term as principal instructor. David, or Daud as he preferred, was a Scottish Muslim married to an Egyptian. He was a scholar not only of the language, written and spoken, but also

111

of Islam. He was also a modest man. He arrived in time for the opening, in some minor discomfort on 1 October 1959 of the first course in Eddy Hitti's magnificent new building. A day or two before Christmas we moved into the new Director's house adjacent to the main building. Once the teething troubles had been dealt with, we all enjoyed and benefited from the splendid amenities.

'To Increase Understanding Among Nations'

When James Craig and I had completed the word list in 1957 and were preparing the final text for printing, we asked our Arab instructors to suggest a motto, which we could inscribe on the title page. The flamboyant Constantine Theodory, one of the Palestinians who had taught me in 1946, suggested a phrase, which while apposite, had the disadvantage that it contained two rather recherché words which we had not included in the list. This needed further work. Our final version was: 'To increase understanding among nations.' Needless to say, this sounds better in Arabic than in English. All of us at the Middle East Centre intended what this motto said, even though we knew that the task would be never-ending and that other forces, either by design or through inadvertence, would promote the opposite.

Sir Donald Maitland GCMG OBE was the Director of MECAS from 1956 to 1960.

MEASURING THE EUPHRATES 1957

Stephen Egerton

I first went to Iraq from Shemlan on my language break in summer 1957. I was attached to the Department of Irrigation's branch at Ramadi on the Euphrates, some 100 miles west of Baghdad. None of my colleagues spoke English, and we had the incredibly boring task of measuring the fall of the river in millimetres three times a day. We walked along the embankment at dawn, midday and dusk and solemnly recorded our findings in a vast book, which was inspected once a fortnight by somebody from Baghdad. This leisurely life gave us lots of time to discuss the situation in Palestine, starting way before the Balfour Declaration and ending more or less at Suez, which had been only the year before. Our diet was mutton, rice and Pepsi Cola. Our daily amusement was to walk down to the bus station at Ramadi as the evening began, and await the arrival of the Nairn bus from Damascus. Talking to the dust-covered passengers as they sipped their sweet tea was a great relief, as one could ask about the price of rice and tomatoes in another country, and listen to the answers in a different dialect. This made a nice change from the Arab-Israel dispute. Of my colleagues the Sub-

Engineers I remember very little, except that they were all mad keen to wangle a posting to Baghdad. Indeed our boss the Resident Engineer was so keen on this that he spent every working day in Baghdad, and of course we never saw him at weekends. Of the countryside I remember the glistening salinity lining every field and watercourse. The sun was so strong for six months of the year that, though there was plenty of water in those days, the dehydration was complete, and little seemed to grow.

Sir Stephen Egerton KCMG attended MECAS in 1956-57. He was appointed Head of Energy Department FCO, 1973-77 and Ambassador to Iraq 1980-82, Saudi Arabia, 1986-89 and Italy 1989-92. His MECAS memoir includes an account of two later periods in Iraq.

LIFE ON AN IRAQI FARM 1957-58

Edric Worsnop

I arrived in Beirut on 2 January 1957, found my way to the Place des Canons in the central part of the city and took a 'service' or shared taxi on an hour's journey of nearly twenty miles, eastwards out of the capital into the foothills of the Lebanon mountain range along the main Beirut-Damascus highway, and then turning south at Aley along a ridge to the small village of Shemlan. At approximately 2,500 feet above sea-level it enjoyed a breathtaking view overlooking Beirut, the Lebanese coastline and the blue waters of the Mediterranean beyond.

A total of 29 students made up the 13th Course: there were eight oil company representatives (Iraq Petroleum Company, Kuwait Oil Company and Shell), nine army officers and three RAF, and nine Foreign Office diplomats (three executive stream officers, and six administrative stream candidates who had recently joined the Foreign Service from university). Some were married and lived outside the Centre, renting houses in the village; the rest of us as bachelors lived on the Centre's premises, an open courtyard separating two large old stone buldings. Both consisted of small rooms around a large central hall, with bed-sitters upstairs and the classrooms downstairs. Life as a student was pretty spartan, with just the basic necessities of wooden furniture, iron bedsteads and coir matting floor covering. Heating in the cold, wet and snowy winters was by means of a tempermental iron stove fuelled by diesel and/or a drip-feed paraffin stove. Many of us bought a large travel rug to wrap ourselves up against the draughts when the storms blew outside. There seemed to be constant problems with the water and electricity supplies. The food in the students' mess was mostly canteen standard. Nevertheless, the paramount impression was excitement at the novelty of it all. There were splendid compensations for any physical hardships: Shemlan lay nestled among olive and orange groves, mulberry, pine and fig trees, date palms and exotic flowers and shrubs, with vineyards below on the terraced slopes, giving unlimited opportunities for contemplative walks. The summer was long, with eternal sunshine and cloudless skies, the heat tempered by altitude. Everywhere one travelled there were spectacular vistas to savour. At weekends, there were visits to the St George's Club on the Beirut waterfront where one could enjoy a hot bath, a good meal and a drink at the bar. There were the friendliness and good humour of the village inhabitants, and the MECAS parties at which we all mixed happily. Above all perhaps, there was the camaraderie among the students.

The beginning of the 13th Course in 1957 coincided with a dramatic change in the method of instruction at MECAS. The Foreign Office had come to realise that fundamental reform was necessary. There was a lack of dynamism and direction. Queries were raised as to the relevance of the teaching to the demands of modern diplomacy. In 1955 the Foreign Office appointed a professional Arabist in James Craig as Principal Instructor (for some years he had been a lecturer in Arabic at Durham University) and in late 1956 Donald Maitland as Director (a young Foreign Office first secretary of high reputation who as an army officer had attended the 3rd Course in Jerusalem in 1946). The Maitland-Craig partnership emarked upon a series of reforms which were to transform the MECAS system. When we arrived in the January, the new atmosphere of drive and energy was almost tangible. A completely fresh Word List was painstakingly constructed, divided ino ten section of 300 words each; the total of 3,000 was regarded as the minimum required to cover the 10-month Long Course. Secondly, the teaching of grammar was improved by the revision of the basic grammar book, again into ten sections to correspond with the sections in the Word List. Thirdly, a new Reader entitled *The Way Prepared* (it sounds better in Arabic) was compiled, in which the vocabulary used in the text progressed hand-in-hand with the Word List and the revised Grammar Book. Additionally, in order to achieve a focus on the spoken word, a series of lessons was devised to make up a Conversation Grammar of Colloquial Arabic; after a few months at MECAS, a Colloquial Fortnight was introduced, designed to immerse us for a couple of weeks in the spoken language before going off on the Language Break. All this represented a huge and sustained effort of labour over several months, carried out by the partnership with enthusiasm and conviction. At the same time the wide-ranging scope of these improvements gave rise to a period of painful adjustment for the Arab staff of eight Palestinian and Lebanese teachers at the Centre, whose wholehearted cooperation in their implementation was crucial to the success of the enterprise.

Meanwhile, for us as students, divided up into small syndicates according to our linguistic abilities, we found ourselves at MECAS at a time of transition and innovation, as month by month the various pieces of the jigsaw were brought into play. There was no disguising the fact that it was tough going, with the constant pressure to master each section of work before moving on to the next; the acquisition of more and more vocabulary was the key to progress. There was also the added competitive stimulus of studying alongside four of my Foreign Office colleagues.

When the prospect of the Language Break began to loom on the horizon at the beginning of June, I was determined to seize this opportunity to escape beyond the narrow confines of Lebanon. There was of course much to explore in that beautiful country, but one also experienced the feeling of being hemmed in, bounded as we were on the east and north by the Anti-Lebanon mountain range, on the south by the state of Israel, and on the west by the sea. When therefore the proposal was made that I accompany

Denys Collier (one of the Iraq Petroleum Company students) to Haditha in Iraq, about 150 miles north-west of Baghdad, I accepted with pleasure. Denys made arrangements for our stay on a farm near Haditha belonging to an old friend of his, Hadji Yasin Da'ud, who as a substantial contractor to the IPC had become wealthy and powerful.

Each morning I was up early since it became too uncomfortable to stay in bed much after six o'clock when the sun came up. Usually after breakfast I went for a long stroll with Khalil round the farm. It covered an extensive area along the banks of the Euphrates with well laid out fruit, vegetable and wheat fields. The whole acreage was irrigated by means of an intricate system of canals, each with its own control point. The water was drawn directly from the river which drove a magnificent six-fold water-wheel. This was a picturesque antique reputed to be 700 years old, and the massive wooden wheels groaned eerily through each revolution. At night, as I lay awake under the stars, the stillness of the surrounding desert would be broken only by the sound of that water-wheel, haunting, lilting, mournful. Also on the farm were about a thousand head of cattle, sheep and goats, all healthy and well-fed. They and the agricultural products of the farm provided food for the surrounding district and the K3 station, where Hadji had a large general stores, a flourishing business administered by his son, Tahir. In order to augment the water supply, especially in the dry season, a single cylinder oil pump engine had been installed near the bungalow; it had been imported from England and was the pride and joy of Ibrahim, the self-styled farm engineer. The main buildings, all mud-constructed, were clustered together and as it must have been in biblical times, the sheep and cattle were herded into the compound as evening approached, the main gates were closed and barred, food was doled out in long low troughs and, with the daily toil completed, man and beast settled down together for the night.

Most of the time Khalil, Muhammad and Ibrahim were my constant companions. None of them knew English, so I had ample opportunity to speak their tongue, and the range of topics touched upon the worlds of nature and agriculture and, inevitably, politics, religion and families. Khalil was very interested in all aspects of life in Britain and curious to know how much any particular article cost so that he could compare with prices in Iraq. Strangely, money seemed to weigh heavily on their minds and they all complained bitterly about the parsimony of Hadji Da'ud. At any time of day, my hosts would suggest a drink of tea or perfumed Arab coffee. This was safer than the water which was drawn straight from the river and crudely filtered. Ice and soft drinks were also brought in every day from Haditha. The heat at midday was very trying and I felt obliged to take a siesta every afternoon. As the evenings drew in, I used to enjoy strolling out to the edge of the farm to sit with the *fellahin* and contemplate the desert sunset. Like a gigantic fireball, the sun sank swiftly below the horizon, lighting up in its ruddy glow the low line of hills to the south. The quiet was only disturbed by the tinkling of the bells round the necks of the leader sheep and the whistles of the shepherd calling his flock back to their pens for the night. Their trampling feet raised a gentle dust cloud that drifted slowly away across the rolling plain.

Throughout my wanderings in Iraq I had encountered nothing but courtesy and friendliness, and had been left with the sense that the average Iraqi harboured a genuine liking for Britain and the British. Sadly, within a year of my visit, political unheaval leading to bloody revolution and the violent overthrow of the monarchical regime had fundamentally changed the face of Iraq. The British Ambassador was shot at and his Embassy burned and looted.

Edric Worsnop OBE attended MECAS in 1957-58. After consular and diplomatic appointments in the Gulf, Cairo, Nicosia, Tehran and Melbourne, he was appointed Consul-General Casablanca in April 1987.

THE MECAS HOME
GUARD 1958

Brian Pridham

In Shemlan: The History of MECAS, James Craig tells how Shemlan was attacked in early July 1958 by Kemal Jumblatt's Druze forces and MECAS was obliged to evacuate, at first to Souq el Gharb and then to Beirut, The attack forced MECAS to close for a few months and to disperse its students to various parts of the Arab world and beyond, The attack also led to one of the more bizarre episodes in the history of MECAS – one which was never accurately reported.

The press covered the attack itself reasonably well, with the palm for creative writing going to Geoffrey Thursby of the *Daily Express*. His account may provoke some wan smiles among those who were there. He misses no opportunity to press the tabloid reporting buttons: the cuddly pet; the small baby; the fierce but chivalric tribesmen; the oxymoronic tight slacks; the absence of useful explanation. Nevertheless, the salient facts were there, and there was nothing to match Scott Gibbons' explanation in the *Daily Mail* that it was all really an attempt to cut the Beirut-Damascus road. The *Daily Mirror* reporter who thought Shemlan was a suburb of Beirut may have borrowed Gibbons' atlas. But press reporting two weeks later was to be far more culpable.

The Worsening Situation

The Middle East in July 1958 was sliding headlong into deep crisis. The *Daily Express* reported on 3 July that 'seventeen wives and children of Britons at the British School of Arabic Studies at Shamlane, 15 miles south-east of Beirut, are to leave Lebanon for England at the expense of the British Government because of fighting in the area.' That decision turned out to be well justified, for the advice of the British and US Embassies on 14 July to families in the Lebanon to leave unless their presence was 'essential' came after the airport was closed. It was the date, of course, of the Iraqi revolution, in which the British Embassy in Baghdad was stormed, looted and set on fire. One member of the Ambassador's staff was killed and he himself was fortunate to escape with his life. It was also the date on which some of the students were planning to leave on temporary postings to other parts of the Arab world. The result was to increase the number of bachelor or unaccompanied students stuck in Beirut.

The Landing of American Troops in Beirut

The revolution in Iraq galvanised the United States and Britain into military action, designed to protect the status quo in the region. British troops landed in Jordan on 17 July but American marines had already landed on Khaldeh beach, near Beirut airport, two days earlier. Crowds of bathers and reporters greeted them and helped them pull some of their vehicles out of the sand when they got stuck. This friendly reception did not, however, entirely remove the fear that there could be a hostile reaction.

The Defence of the Embassy

At around mid-day on 15 July the bachelor and unaccompanied MECAS Foreign Office students were asked to attend the Embassy immediately. There they were shown into a large room, which seemed to be full of firearms and ammunition. The Military Attaché, Colonel Brodie, explained the situation to them: the American marines were due to land at any moment and it had been decided to defend the Embassy against any retaliatory attack from the Lebanese. For that reason it was necessary to load the weapons before them, and to man the Embassy's defences until the danger had passed. Apart from the firearms on display, some boxes of large rocks had been pre-positioned on the stair landings.

Colonel Brodie, of the Black Watch, was what was sometimes nervously described as a 'character'. A few days earlier, he had been attacked in his flat by armed men who abducted his servant after accusing him of signalling to the Government forces. Geoffrey Thursby's account of the event records that Alex Brodie had been wounded nine times in the war and quotes him as saying, 'I fought them but they took him away after tearing out the phone wires. But I know how to mend phone wires and soon had the phone working again.' He was the epitome of the brave and resourceful soldier, and very direct in his methods. He told how he went to see an engagement between Government forces and the rebels, and button-holed the Lebanese Commander-in Chief (General Shihab, later to be the President of Lebanon). 'Tell me where the enemy are' he said, 'and I'll tell you what to do.'

The Protest Movement

During this period the three longest-serving students found themselves agreeing that the whole enterprise was improper. It was against Foreign Office practice and common-sense, they thought, to arm staff and try to fight off a mob intent on storming a diplomatic mission. The suggestion in the press reports that their thoughts turned mainly on the responsibility of the host nation to protect a mission distorts the case. No-one had any confidence in the Lebanese Government's ability at that moment to do much. After all, the first some families knew of the impending attack on Shemlan was the disappearance of the gendarmes assigned to their protection.

The three students formed up to the Military Attaché to put their case and he took them to see the Chargé d'Affaires. The Chargé refused to see them, but sent out a message to say that anyone who wanted to leave was free to do so. Having had their say, the three simply got on with loading weapons and standing guard. The latter part of *The Times* report on this was wrong to regard this as a change of mind. Everything remained quiet, and at about tea-time the

Military Attaché re-appeared to say that he needed to liaise with the American Ambassador on the current situation. For that purpose he called for two volunteers, armed with pistols, as bodyguards. One of the three, and Andrew Johnstone, volunteered. On the way to the American Embassy (through streets that were completely empty), Colonel Brodie remarked that he saw the point of view of the three chaps who had protested, apparently unaware than one of the vipers was sitting beind him. That remark was the last word ever heard by any of the three about the protest. The night remained calm but a tense moment arrived with the dawn. In the half-light, men could be seen manoeuvring near the Embassy and carrying what appeared to be rifles. Fortunately, before a tragedy occurred, calmer minds and sharper eyes saw that they were carrying the morning's baguettes.

The Beirut Three

The tabloid press took up the news of the protest. An edition of the *Daily Express* which has not been preserved made much of the contrast between the brave old soldier (the Queen's Messenger who was stuck in Beirut) and the three young shirkers. The completely fabricated story in the *Daily Mail* about the return home in disgrace and the rejected volunteers is surprising, even to a devout cynic in this field. A possible explanation lies in the fact that all of the students were posted out as quickly as possible after the re-opening of the airport, and three of them, a complete 'syndicate', were sent to work in the Foreign Office in London. The syndicate included one of the Three.

Epilogue

The impulse to protect a mission with armed force died hard. In the aftermath of the Beirut affair the Security Department of the Foreign Office confirmed that the three students had been correct in their appraisal – the approved action in the face of an imminent threat was to destroy sensitive documents and equipment, and then to leave the building. Indeed, one of the Three found himself helping in exactly that process in the Beirut Embassy in 1975/76, during the second civil war. Nevertheless, as late as the early 1970s there were still cases of locally-written security instructions requiring staff to fight their way back through the barriers to the secure zone from which, by definition, there was no escape. The Security Department was alarmed to find out how many weapons, some of them ancient, were still held in some missions and ordered such weapons to be disposed of immediately. 'We were' said the Security Department desk officer, 'caught with our Mausers down.'

Brian Pridham attended MECAS in 1957-9. He served in Bahrain, Muscat, Algiers, La Paz and Abu Dhabi and was appointed Director of MECAS in 1975-76. He was later Director of the Centre for Arab Gulf Studies at Exeter University.

Part Three
1958-65

AN ADVENTURE IN THE BADLANDS
1958

Bill Norton

'Every Englishman has the right to get his throat cut, when and where he wants.' *Lord Salisbury*

The tall, shaikhly Arab came in out of the dark, into the poorly lit interior of the hut in the forest clearing. Like everyone else in the room, he was armed. All eyes were upon him as he strode up to where I was standing. Roughly squeezing my wrists, he clasped them together in one hand. Then leering horribly around the room, he made a gesture with the other hand whose meaning was unmistakable. He was chopping off both my hands at the wrist.

It was a prelude to the most uncomfortably exciting day of my life: a day whose every detail still remains vivid in my mind as I write this thirty-six years later, without the benefit of any notes made at the time beyond a route plotted on a map, and a few bird records.

This mountain fastness, remote from any road, was said to be inhabited by fierce Moslem tribesmen known for their lawless deeds, and headed by the notorious Ja'afar clan. These tribesmen were also known to be in close touch with their counterparts across the Syrian frontier. The frontier itself was wide open; across it, gun-running from Syria into Lebanon was known to take place on a large scale, with the aim of destabilising the pro-Western Christian-dominated government of Camille Cham'oun. So wild and woolly was this whole area that it was totally beyond the reach of the law. The Lebanese police did not dare set foot in it, and even the army generally kept its distance. A grazing plateau was evidently the last outpost of the town before one entered the Badlands.

I had taken this early opportunity of consulting 'The Tourist's Map of Lebanon', the only cartographic authority available. Yes, there it was! For fifty kilometres north from Col des Cedres to the Syrian frontier no road crossed the long spine of Mount Lebanon or even approached it from either east or west. The map showed a largely empty region of mountainous terrain, inscribed with the ominous name of the Ja'afar tribe and including only a handful of very isolated settlements. One feature had especially caught my attention. Most unusually for the manicured, terraced landscape of the Lebanon, an extensive zone of apparently primeval forest, part continuous and part broken, clothed the northern slopes of the great massif as it fell away towards the Syrian frontier. The Badlands, it seemed, could claim the only sizeable tract of forest in the entire country.

As I studied the map, a crazy idea had taken root in my mind: I would go to the Badlands and see it all for myself. Where the Lebanese forces of law and order feared to tread, there I would go, alone and unarmed. The occasion would be provided by the MECAS spring break, and I would tell absolutely nobody of my plans: if the MECAS authorities came to hear of my plans, they would intervene to stop me going. And so the die was cast for the most irresponsible venture I have ever embarked on. Normally the most cautious of mortals, the last one to do anything rash, I had for once got the bit fairly between my teeth.

The political context of my journey needs to be understood. In the early months of 1958 Arab nationalism was running on a high tide. Formally, President Cham'oun's Lebanon stood outside; but it was no secret that his government's interests and sympathies lay wholly with the West and the Hashemites. This had merely served to emphasise the chronic instability of a country whose Moslem majority had to live with a Christian-dominated constitution. Thus, in the spring of 1958, an explosive cocktail of political tensions, internal and external, was being vigorously stirred. Violent incidents were becoming commonplace. Lebanese Moslems were united in their hatred of Cham'oun's regime, and of western influence in general. Hence the gun-running from Syria, a country, incidentally, which had severed diplomatic relations with the UK over Suez.

Although a serving member of Her Majesty's Foreign Service, I was at the time a language student with no diplomatic status. My journey was an entirely private venture. But to the suspicious Arab mind anyone from MECAS – dubbed throughout the Middle East the 'British Spy School' – was automatically branded a spy.

My plan was to walk by a somewhat circuitous route from the coast just north of Tripoli to Hemel, a northern frontier town of the Bakaa plain in the interior. I would carry in my rucksack the essential gear, including a sleeping bag, some reserves of food, and binoculars for occasional bird-watching diversions. I took no tent, reckoning to sleep under the stars, and no cooking equipment, reckoning somehow to find one square meal a day (but prepared to manage without one if need be). I set aside a week for the whole trip. If all went well, the traverse of the Badlands would be completed in the final day and a half, but I had built into my plan one extra day for contingencies. It was just as well that I had.

The first two and a half days took me through friendly Christian territory: across the plain of Zghorta, just inland from Tripoli, where I spent my first night; then for a long haul up the valley of Sir El Dennie. At the head of the Sir Valley, I crossed a high shoulder of Mount Lebanon where I trod the melting snows at over 2,000 metres. Then a northward descent into a lush enchanting alpine valley, where the music of goats' bells vied with a deafening chorus of birdsong which proclaimed that I had now entered Moslem territory. In Lebanon, Christians shoot birds of all kinds; Moslems don't (though both seem equally happy shooting each other).

Those carefree early days of the walk were soon over: a more sinister prospect lay ahead. At Mishmish, my destination for the third night, I repaired to a simple *mat'am* for a communal evening meal with a selection of the Moslem village's male community. Over supper, conversation turned to Nasser and his new union with

Syria. I was asked for my view. In the incredibly naïve belief that Arabs enjoy a good argument, and in my still faltering Arabic, I launched into a somewhat uncomplimentary critique. My words were greeted with a stunned silence.

As we dispersed after the meal, a figure came up to me in the dark and motioned me aside for a word. He spoke in French, and there was a note of urgency in his voice. 'Listen,' he said, ' I am the only Christian in this Moslem village, and I speak to you as Christian to Christian. I am seriously concerned for your safety. These people idolise Nasser. They did not like what you said. I am afraid they will kill you!' Distinctly shaken, I crept off into the night and put some distance between Mishmish and myself before spreading out my sleeping bag on an orchard terrace.

Fnaideq, the neighbouring roadhead village where I made a provisioning stop the following morning, did not live up to the hospitable connotations of its name, 'the small hotel'. The only fare available in the decrepit village store was an egg or two, and some musty Turkish Delight. From Fnaideq, a steep pull took me up to the Grazing Plateau of sombre repute.

The Grazing Plateau or, to give it its Arabic name, Qammou'a, proved to be a singular place. A grassy plain perhaps two kilometres in length and one in width, it was everywhere as flat as a football pitch. A dense fringe of conifers surrounded it on all sides; to the east, they merged into continuous forest that covered the adjoining mountainside as far as the eye could see. It was the beginning of the forest zone that I had seen on the map. Towering over everything, still streaked with spring snow, was the jagged outline of the 2,300 metre Jebel El-'Arouba or Mountain of Arabism. The whole scene had a curiously mid-European, sub-alpine look, which seemed quite out of place in Lebanon.

On the northern edge of the Plateau, a further scenic surprise awaited me. From where I stood, some 1,500 metres above sea-level, everything fell away abruptly to the Homs Gap in Syria far below. Beyond that rose the blue mass of the Jebel Alawi, Syria's northern extension of the Lebanon Range; and there among its foothills was the famous Krak des Chevaliers, *chef d'oeuvre* of the Crusader castles. Perched on a spur beneath me, on the Lebanese side of the frontier, was the ruin of another Crusader castle, Akkar 'Attiqa, clearly positioned for intervisibility with the Krak; between them they dramatically commanded the intervening Homs Gap. The purple-blue Mediterranean filled the western horizon. Exhilarated by this marvellous scenery, I plunged down a long way to the north, spending my fourth night on the edge of a nomadic encampment near the village of Beino. Next day I had a long climb back, by a different route, to the Grazing Plateau which I reached in mid-afternoon.

I had already spotted a footpath leading from the edge of that grassy plain into the heart of the adjoining forest to the east; and on this I now embarked, with a lively sense of apprehension. The Rubicon was crossed: I was in the Badlands, and there would be no turning back! For the next two or three hours, my path contoured with many twists and turns round the northern slopes of the Mountain of Arabism. For most of the time I was in a dense coniferous forest. There were no dwellings to be seen; indeed my surroundings bore no human imprint whatever, bar the path itself. I was in total wilderness.

From time to time I met small parties of Arabs. They rapidly confirmed my impression that I had left civilisation behind. All were male; from now on I was to see very few women at all. All these hill tribesmen wore traditional Arab attire, generally with dark or black *thaubs* – long outer shirts – and baggy trousers. and every single one carried a rifle, swashbuckling *Beau Geste* figures with bandoliers full of cartridges strapped across their chests. Each encounter led to a ritual of enquiry which I dubbed, in my mind, the 'Twenty Questions.' Who was I? From what country? Where had I started my journey? Where was I going, and to what purpose? How long had I lived in Arab lands? Was I married? Not until the full ritual was completed was I allowed to proceed. It was clear that the sight of a westerner in those parts was virtually unprecedented.

Evening was turning to dusk, and my thoughts were on where to spread my sleeping bag, when I unexpectedly found myself in a large forest clearing containing a single mud hut, the first building I had seen since entering the Badlands. Several Arabs were in the offing and, evidently with hospitable intent, insisted on my spending the night in their hut. I should greatly have preferred to spend it under the stars, but had no choice in the matter if I was not to cause offence.

A simple rice-based meal was my eventual reward for a protracted version of the Twenty Questions. With my very limited Arabic, I was finding all this a considerable strain – all the more so after the mildly harrowing episode with which this narrative began, and which occurred in the course of the evening. I was much less amused by the hand-chopping joke than were others in the room. All I knew for sure was that I was at the mercy of these uncouth forest Arabs, with their battery of weapons. In the adjoining shed allotted as my sleeping quarters, I spent an uneasy fifth night.

I was up with the dawn. It was another perfect morning, with a chill nip in the pine-scented air. My anxieties of the previous night were soon dispelled. This was to be my big day: the main traverse of the Badlands lay ahead. The previous evening, I had made known my wish to hire a guide to accompany me through to Hermel. There was a good reason for my uncharacteristic prudence. My very inadequate 1:200,000 map showed that, somewhere ahead, a wedge of Syria stuck, like a sore thumb, a long way into territory which had surely been designed to be Lebanon. There was a problem in how to be sure of avoiding it. I would be safe enough if I kept pretty high up the mountainside to my right, and thereafter kept well to the south. But apart from the effort, delay, and likely physical difficulties involved, such a route would largely by-pass the Badlands, which was hardly the object of the exercise. The only solution I could think of was to hire a guide.

This guide now appeared in the person of 'Abdouh, complete with mule. A brief negotiation fixed the price to Hermel which, he assured me, could be reached within the day. In my elementary Arabic I went out of my way to impress on 'Abdouh my central concern about the route: *'Daiman fi Lubnan! Abadan fi Suria!'* (Always in Lebanon, never in Syria). I repeated it over and over again. 'Abdouh nodded vigorously. That point clearly established, I would simply have to rely on him to see me through. I have a certain knack for picking the right route through difficult mountain country. But this aptitude does not extend to divining the precise course of political boundaries in

Bertram Thomas, the distinguished explorer of the Arabian Peninsula, was appointed the first Director of MECAS in 1944. He is pictured here in Arab dress in the Rub al Khali.

Above: Winston Churchill with King Abdul Aziz (Ibn Saud) of Saudi Arabia. On a visit to Cairo in early 1943, Churchill gave his full support, as Prime Minister, to the MECAS proposals with the proviso that no fit men must be taken away from the front to attend the Centre.

Below left: Aubrey 'Abba' Eban served as the first Chief Instructor at MECAS in 1944-46. He later became Foreign Minister of Israel.

Below right: Gamal Abdel Nasser, President of Egypt and the United Arab Republic. In the 1956 and 1967 Middle East wars, he launched spirited attacks on the interference of the British government.

Above: The First Course of 1944-45.

Right: The Austrian Hospice in Jerusalem, home of MECAS 1944-47 run by German-speaking nuns.

Above: The Course of 1946.

Below: The Course of 1956.

Above: The Advanced Course and the Long Course of 1966-67.

Below: The local potter in the neighbouring village of Jisr al-Qadi.

Shemlan in the 1950s *(above)* and after the civil war *(below)*.

Above: The Long Course visits Byblos, October 1966. Clockwise from left: Tony Arnold, Janet Arnold, Alastair Macaskill, Philip Sadgrove, David MacLennan, Leslie McLoughlin, Patrick Nixon, Charles Wrangham, Ian Lewty.

Below: The MECAS Association returns to Shemlan in November 1997 for lunch in Cliff House.

Above: Archie Lamb, Political Agent in Abu Dhabi, 1965-68, accompanying the Emir, Shaikh Zayid bin Sultan al-Nahayan.

poorly-mapped terrain.

I bade farewell to my hosts of the previous night, and 'Abdouh, the mule and I hit the trail. At first our path wound on through thick forest as before. But soon the forest began to break up. The map, it was clear by now, could not be trusted. The forest I had traversed the previous day was shown on the map as broken but had been continuous; what lay ahead was shown as continuous but was in fact broken. There were still plentiful scattered trees. Increasingly, though, the thinning forest was interspersed with open stretches which had the character of scrub-covered grassy downland. Our easterly course, now with a southerly bias, was taking us across the grain of the country: one by one the myriad wrinkles of the expiring Lebanon range had to be crossed, so that our path endlessly rose and fell, disclosing a series of miniature glens. There was scarcely a trace of human habitation, only rare patches of cultivation.

Suddenly we had run into a party of about a dozen Arabs, carrying rifles like everyone else we met, and they were interrogating 'Abdouh closely. I could not follow what they were saying. I noticed that, unlike the dark-clad forest Arabs we had seen so far, they were all wearing white, or pale, *thaubs*: some tribal distinction, no doubt. The interrogation completed, 'Abdouh told me that we would have to accompany these Arabs to their village not far away, where they wished to question us further. We set off down the hill. I began to get worried. This Lebanese village we were heading for must be very near the Syrian frontier. *'Hon Lubnan, mush heyk?'* (This is Lebanon, isn't it?), I enquired anxiously of the Arab nearest me. *'La, hon Suria!'* came the devastating reply.

I was thunderstruck. The unthinkable had happened: the miserable 'Abdouh, whether through perfidy or incompetence, had led me straight across the border into Syria! We had been following the same path the whole way; evidently it was intended to be a cross-frontier route. As we walked on in silence, the possible implications of this development began to sink into my mind.

In due course we reached the Syrian village – the first proper settlement I had seen in the Badlands. A collection of simply-constructed, single storey houses peered through scattered trees. The male component of the village turned out in force to greet us, and there was a buzz of excitement as the news spread. I observed that, like our escort, they were largely clad in white or pale-coloured *thaubs*. We reached a sort of village green, where I was motioned to sit down on the grass. I was speedily surrounded by inquisitive, staring faces keen to get a close view of the intruder. The atmosphere was not particularly friendly.

A grey-haired village elder, with a lugubrious expression, then took charge of proceedings. Seizing my rucksack, he held up its contents one by one for general inspection. Each item provoked a new outburst of chattering comment. Of special interest were my camera and binoculars, strong evidence, to the suspicious mind, of the nefarious nature of my activities. The binoculars were pounced on by the mob, and everybody in turn had a squint through them.

After Customs, Passport Control. The village elder had discovered my passport lurking in a pocket of my rucksack, and this was now eagerly devoured by all who could get near it. Somebody much have understood a bit of English, and the incriminating evidence steadily accumulated. That I had come from the leading imperialist power was bad enough. But what about 'Profession – government official'? To a suspicious mind, that could only mean one thing! The real excitement, however, was reserved for the final visa stamp in my passport, which showed that I had, only a month previously, visited Jordan. The occasion had been my mother's recent visit to Lebanon, in the course of which I had taken her to see Jerusalem, whose Old City was then part of Jordan. Our trip had happened in the wake of the announcement of the new Jordan-Iraq union. It was the final, damning piece of evidence in the case that was now building up against me.

The pieces of the jigsaw all fitted together. The villagers got more and more excited. The elder summed up their collective opinion: 'You are an imperialist spy – an agent of the infidel Camille Cham'oun, the Western lackey King Hussein of Jordan, and the traitor Nuri Sa'id' (the notoriously pro-Western Prime Minister of Iraq). It might have been scripted for him by Cairo Radio. I vainly expostulated that he had got it all wrong, that I was a simple tourist on his way to Hermel, and that my guide had accidentally led me astray. He brushed it all contemptuously aside. 'You are a spy,' he concluded. 'We shall now consider what we are going to do with you.' He moved off to confer with his villagers, leaving the wretched 'Abdouh, the grazing mule and me a disconsolate trio on the village green.

I took a look at my surroundings. It was plain that the Badlands did not stop at the frontier. I was still in a wild tribal area with no roads, no vehicles. The main form of local transport was camels. The general look of the countryside was similar to that on the Lebanese side – scattered forest interspersed with open stretches, with some cultivation near the village. The scene was still dominated by the snow-capped mass of the Qornet El-Sa'ouda. On its far southern slopes, I reflected, late spring skiing would now be in progress at the Cedars of Bcharré – a world of brightly colour anoraks, of chairlift queues, of spills, shrieks and giggles in the snow. It all seemed light years away.

After what seemed an eternity, the village elder and some of his friends returned and entered into earnest conference with 'Abdouh. I wondered what was coming next. 'Abdouh then collected his mule and brought it across to where I was sitting. 'We are going back to Lebanon,' he said briefly. I was incredulous. But I repacked my rucksack, and soon we were off, watched silently by the villagers. My sense of relief knew no bounds.

We followed a different route back. At first the gradient was easy, but after a while we confronted a 150-metre-high escarpment, up which the path wound steeply and stonily. Upwards we laboured, 'Abdouh riding the mule and carrying both his and my gear, myself walking in front. We were getting fairly near the top when I heard shouts from below. I looked down on an astonishing sight.

Several camels, urged on by their riders, were approaching the foot of the escarpment at full gallop. Strung out in a long line behind them, the rest of the male population was following on foot. I did not at first connect the reappearance of the villagers with myself. A hunting party, perhaps? 'Abdouh was under no such illusion. 'Yallah! Ruh!' he cried, his face contorted with fear, as he spurred on his reluctant mule. The three of us pressed on as fast as we could up the steep, rocky path.

Bang! Bang! Bang! A bullet whistled overhead, then another. It was hard to judge whether this was loose marksmanship – a galloping camel cannot be the easiest base to fire from – or whether they were deliberately shooting high. What was clear was that the Syrians had had second thoughts about letting us return to Lebanon. Another volley rent the air. With an urgency born of desperation, 'Abdouh, the snorting mule and I, strained every gut to get over the crest of the escarpment and into dead ground. So far as I could, I kept the other two in a direct line between me and the source of enemy fire. This was hardly the time to display those heroic officer qualities instilled into me during my National Service.

It was becoming clear to me that the moment when we broke the skyline would be one of especial danger, although there was no way of avoiding it. But it passed without a further volley: the camels, now rapidly gaining on us, had already embarked on the climb up the escarpment. It could only be a matter of time before they caught us up. As we panted up to the crest of the escarpment, we could see that the lie of the land fell away ahead of us before rising again beyond, now with good tree cover. I had not the faintest idea which country we were now in. I ran like the wind down the slope, with the mule, still carrying 'Abdouh and our gear, cantering along at my side. At all costs we must make it to the forest before the camels reached the crest of the escarpment. But it was not to be. As the dead ground opened up ahead, I saw that it contained another village nestling against the forest edge. On the near side of the village an expectant party of perhaps fifteen Arabs, clearly alerted by the sound of firing, had already assembled. We were running straight towards them, and it was too late to avoid them.

These Arabs were wearing dark-coloured *thaubs*. *'Hon Lubnan?'* (Is this Lebanon?) I gasped anxiously as we sped up to them. *'Aiwa – hon Lubnan!'* Allah be praised – we were safely back on Lebanese soil. 'Abdouh blurted out a brief account of our adventures. The villagers seemed reassuringly friendly and sympathetic, a welcome change from the hostility we had encountered across the border. Although breathless from the chase, I began to relax slightly. We would be all right with this lot.

A mounted camel broke the skyline, then another, and another. The Syrians rode up and dismounted. At once a heated argument broke out between the Syrian and Lebanese villagers, which intensified as more and more Syrians arrived. Within a short space of time, the entire Syrian contingent had foregathered. All present formed themselves into a large ring, as if at the start of a Scottish reel, and the acrimonious debate continued. There must have been about fifty Arabs there altogether, the Syrians outnumbering the Lebanese by more than two to one. It was plain to see that the Syrians had the greater fire-power.

At length the argument subsided. The Syrian party broke up into small groups, and started to move off in the direction of their mother country. I wondered what had been agreed. Would I now be left in peace to resume my journey to Hermel, with or without the wretched 'Abdouh? But the Lebanese were motioning me to accompany them, and they appeared to be going off with the Syrians. Puzzled, I asked where we were going. The answer was a bombshell: we were all going back to Syria!

Appalled, I sought an explanation from my would-be protectors, but could establish nothing beyond our destination. Their manner was distinctly less friendly than before. Did they feel that, by being on the losing side of an argument, they had lost face; or had they bought the Syrian tale that I was a wicked imperialist sent to spy on their gun-running activities? It was impossible to tell. The camels had now vanished. I looked round for 'Abdouh and the mule, but they too had disappeared; I never saw or heard of them again. From now on I would have to fend for myself.

I was now part of a long, straggling cortege heading back down the hill towards Syria. We were following a new and different route. After a while, we dropped into the head of a miniature, partly wooded glen. We were descending a straight, rather muddy path which bore a passing resemblance to an English country lane. On the left-hand side of this lane, about two-thirds of the way down, was a solitary mud hut.

As we reached the bottom of the hill, the entire party peeled off to the left of the lane, on to the open grassy sward which I had seen from above. At a point about a hundred yards from the lane, I was told to sit down on the grass. Here the entire fifty-strong company once again formed themselves into a ring – but this time I was in the middle of it! They resumed with fury the raging argument that had begun outside the Lebanese village.

Once again I had no idea which country we were in. The isolated mud hut already mentioned was the only habitation in sight. In my mind I labelled this place 'no-man's-land'. If I was right, the most likely explanation of these antics was that the Syrians, exploiting their force majeure, had insisted on transferring the debate on to neutral territory where they did not stand at a moral disadvantage. The path we had followed was already the third I had used that morning which appeared to lead directly across the frontier: in such a thinly populated area, that had a lot to say about the amount of *va et vient* that took place.

The angry noise all round me soon reached deafening proportions. Everyone present seemed to be yelling at the top of his voice. While it was clear enough that I was the focus of all this, I could not understand why so many had got so worked up over my fate. Were the Lebanese contingent really taking up my cause, and if so why? I was beginning to wonder whether some underlying feud between the two villages had not been unearthed. Bang! Bang! Arabs all round the circle now started to fire their rifles into the air. Apprehensively I wondered where all those bullets were coming down. I felt uncomfortably exposed as I squatted in the centre of that trigger-happy mob: any moment one of those rifles might be turned on me. The whole experience was becoming more alarming by the minute.

I shifted my position a little, away from the dead centre of the circle. Nobody seemed to notice; one and all were totally involved in the quarrel. Mildly encouraged, I edged a little further towards the periphery, dragging my rucksack after me. Still no sign of attention. Bang, bang, bang! Another fusillade was loosed off into the air. There was a small gap in the circle of Arabs at one point. A few more wriggles and I was almost there. Bang, bang, bang! It was incredible, but not one of those fifty Arabs was paying the slightest attention to what I was doing. Almost brushing the legs of the two standing on either side of the gap, I wormed my way out of the circle. More surreptitious wriggles. Now I was several metres outside the circle. Taking my courage (and my rucksack) in both hands, I got to my feet as unobtrusively as possible. Still no reaction.

I stood motionless for quite a while, hardly daring to breathe. Then I started, very slowly and carefully, to move a little further away from the circle. One or two tentative, shuffling steps; a pause; then repeat. With extreme caution, I turned my head and looked back. Viewed from outside, the circle of violently quarrelling Arabs, intermittently discharging their rifles into the sky, was one of the most extraordinary scenes I have ever witnessed. Still a total lack of interest in what I was up to. Another shuffle, another pause. Don't look round this time – it will attract their attention. Already I had covered a quarter of the distance to the point where the lane debouched on to the grassy sward. Shuffle, pause; shuffle, pause. After what seemed an eternity, I was halfway there: fifty metres to go. It was quite incredible that nobody had noticed me. I would remain in full view of them all the way to the lane; if I ever got there, one step would put me behind the tall hedge that would then screen me from their sight all the way to the top of the hill. Don't think about it; just keep moving imperceptibly.

Bang, bang, bang! More fusillades into the air. Just keep shuffling, a step or two at a time. Twenty-five metres to go. The hedge was getting really close now. Gently does it, don't look round. Bang, bang, bang! The tension was almost unbearable. Shuffle, pause; shuffle, pause. And then, amazingly, I was there! One last fearful glance back at the circle of frenetic Arabs, still totally immersed in their quarrel. One tiptoed step to the right, and suddenly I was out of their sight. A moment later, for the second time that morning, I was running uphill, absolutely flat out – for freedom and for dear life.

Euphoria gripped me. My escape was utterly unbelievable. Ahead of me, the empty lane with its continuous screen of vegetation would take me to the crest of the hill in a couple of minutes of frantic exertion. If I got that far, I should be relatively safe, and well on the way back to Lebanon. The bedlam was beginning to fall away, behind and below me to my right. I was running as I had never run before. Only one potential obstacle lay in my path: the small mud hut on the right-hand side of the lane. I was approaching it now. No sign of life from that quarter. Just keep running. As I pounded past the hut, I glanced anxiously to my right. And there, framed in the doorway, was the figure of a woman looking out. As she saw me, she let out a scream which echoed to and fro among the surrounding hills.

It was quickly apparent that her scream had been heard. The hubbub below ceased for a moment, then started again, with individual shouts now audible. Full of foreboding, I looked back over my shoulder. Still nobody in sight. Desperately, I kept running. I looked back again. Oh my God – there they were! At the foot of the hill, the Arabs were surging into the lane. There were more shouts as they saw me. The game was up. It would have been madness to continue: they had a clear line of fire up the dead straight lane: I would have been mown down in an instant. I stopped running. A minute later I was their prisoner again. I could scarcely believe my bad luck. At the very last possible hurdle, my escape had been thwarted by a woman's scream.

For the third time that morning, I found myself being escorted down the hill towards Syria by an unfriendly armed guard. With my escape and recapture, the villagers' quarrel (whatever, precisely, it had been about) appeared to be rapidly forgotten. The large assembly of Arabs began to disperse: the Lebanese back to their village, some of the Syrians, apparently, towards the Syrian village I had first been taken to. I was now with a smaller Syrian party, and we were continuing on the more easterly line we had been following before the drama in 'no-man's land'. After we had gone a certain distance, the houses of another Syrian village began to appear through the trees. Most of the party disappeared into the village; just two remained as my guard.

These two sentries motioned me to accompany them into a partly enclosed area just outside the village. As we entered it, I was startled to find that it was the village cemetery. What, I wondered, could this portend? I was led to a spot in the middle of the cemetery, and told to stand still. My two guards then walked away from me, side by side, and stopped after about twenty paces. Slowly turning round to face me, they now stood shoulder to shoulder, wearing expressions of the deepest gloom. Next, together and with extreme deliberation, both of them loaded their rifles. There was an ominous clicking sound as they released their safety-catches.

I was terrified. My guards were now identified as a firing-squad, and this was to be my execution. There was, one could see, a macabre convenience about the choice of venue. Clearly the Syrians had decided to take no further chances with their escape-prone prisoner, the vile imperialist spy and agent of the Hashemites. I waited for my guards to raise their rifles and fire. In a few seconds I should be dead.

That final act never took place! After an interminable pause, my guards shouldered their rifles and beckoned me to follow them out of the cemetery. The mock execution, it seemed, had been designed to put the fear of God into me.

We were now joined by a boy of about thirteen to whom I took an instant dislike. His role soon became clear: unimpressed by my faltering Arabic, they had enrolled the village's French speaker as an interpreter – although, as soon emerged, his French was no better than my Arabic. At a point on a hillside just outside the village, I was told to sit down. The obnoxious youth then conferred with my guards, and at length sat down beside me. The two guards moved off along the hillside for about fifty metres, where they sat down with rifles at the ready, watching us.

In execrable but just comprehensible French, the boy then explained, not without a certain relish, the fate that lay in store for me. The village elders, he said, were sending for the Syrian army, who would be here in a few hours. I would be taken to Damascus, imprisoned, and tried as a spy. Meanwhile I would be held captive in the village. Gesturing towards the two guards, he sneered down at me as he delivered his parting shot: 'Vous restez ici ou vous êtes mort.' Then he, too, disappeared into the village.

Apart from my guards, a short distance away, I was now left to myself for the first time that day. My first reaction was of enormous, if temporary, relief – relief, of course, to be still alive, but also to be spared the constant, and extremely wearing, attention of hostile Arabs. I began to relax slightly, and contemplae my surroundings.

I turned to look once more at my guards stretched out on their backs, apparently dozing. It was past midday now, and the sun rode high in the sky. It was Ramadhan, when Moslems must endure the long hours of daylight fast; the resulting inaction may make them

141

sleep-prone. It was impossible to tell if my guards were really asleep, but they were certainly in a much less alert state than when I had last looked at them.

I turned back to the landscape in front of me, which I now began to study in earnest. To give myself the best possible chance, I would have to leave my rucksack behind, with all my personal gear including camera and binoculars. The terrain immediately in front of me was ideal for a flying start. I would be halfway down that slope before the guards would tumble to what was happening. They would open fire as I approached the stony bottom. For as long as I was running downhill, I could jink to left and right; but the crossing of the exposed, stony hollow and the short, sharp ascent to the dense thicket beyond would be a period of intense danger. I should have to rely on the occasional intervening tree, poor marksmanship, and my increasing distance from the firing point. Once I reached the thicket, I should be in with a real chance. Desperate thinking, but I was in a desperate situation.

Now I faced the most difficult decision of my life so far. If I stayed put, the future was one I hardly dared to contemplate: as a prisoner of the Syrians, demonstrably guilty of frontier violations in what they could only construe as highly suspicious circumstances. It was not only I myself, but the government I worked for, that would then be in for a lot of trouble on my account. I owed it to them, and to myself, to leave no stone unturned while there was still some chance of escape. The excitement and exhilaration of my recent near-escape were fresh in my mind. An insistent voice within me was urging me to action, to the renewed thrill of the chase, to death or glory, to anything rather than this demoralising wait for the gloom and doom that lay ahead. After all, this voice kept reminding me, I had shown my aptitude in these matters by virtually escaping from fifty armed and very wide-awake Arabs who were surrounding me; the threat now was from two Arabs, some distance away, who gave every appearance of being asleep. There was nobody else in sight. This was positively my last chance of freedom; if I did not seize it with both hands, I might never forgive myself for the rest of my life. Go on ... Go on ... I began to rehearse in my mind the precise movements I should have to carry out: the sudden leap into action, the headlong dash, the jink to right and left at the point where I expected them to open fire, as I approached the sunlit bottom. It was going to be third time lucky. It would have to be.

I can say with perfect truth that I very nearly did it. But I also have to confess that, in the end, my courage simply failed me. The danger was too starkly obvious. '*Vous restez ici ou vous êtes mort.* I had no reason to doubt that, this time, they really meant it. Another voice within me, the voice of caution and sweet reason that generally gets the upper hand, was telling me that, grim as my situation in this Syrian village undoubtedly was, it would scarcely be improved were I to be in the same place, but with a bullet through me.

In any case, the decision was soon taken out of my hands. About an hour after I had first sat down on that hillside, I was conducted into the nearest house of the village, and into an inner room of that house. Here about twenty Arabs, all male, were already sitting around on the floor. I was invited to join them – and at the far end of the room, so that all of them were sitting between me and the only door.

I was to spend several hours in this room. The hostility these villagers felt towards me was sharpened by the tensions that go with the Ramadhan fast. In that respect, however, I did experience an altogether unexpected act of kindness when a meal was brought in for me. I devoured it hungrily under the envious watching eyes of twenty fasting Arabs. I was at first the object of some attention. Questions about my personal circumstances and background were varied by reminders that the Syrian army was on its way to take me to Damascus. After a while, the Arabs simply lost interest in me and reverted to chattering among themselves.

I had little to think about now except my predicament. And the more I thought about that, the more awful it seemed. My government had no diplomatic representation in Damascus at the time and nobody, bar a few wild tribesmen on both sides of the frontier, had the foggiest notion of where I was. The secrecy in which I had planned this whole mad enterprise was now hitting me with a vengeance.

In some ways, I was beginning to reflect, it might be preferable to be taken off to Damascus. At least that would hold out the possibility, which clearly did not exist in this village at all, of finding somebody who was prepared to give serious consideration to my version of what had happened; perhaps an army or police officer, a government official, or a lawyer. It also offered the only chance that I could see of somehow getting word of my whereabouts back to MECAS, our Beirut Embassy and the Foreign Office.

In that case there would, of course, be an international incident. It would not be a low-level affair: these things tend to escalate. In due course there would be appeals for my release from Prime Minister Harold Macmillan to President Quwatly of Syria; perhaps even, with much humble pie eaten on the way, to President Nasser, the Head of the UAR, himself. In the absence of diplomatic relations with either constituent country, those appeals would have to be forwarded through the protecting power. The question of my release would become a bargaining counter among other matters of bilateral concern; I should find myself a pawn on the chequerboard of Middle Eastern politics. My name would be all over the press, to the acute embarrassment of my family, not to mention my employers.

Perhaps, if I was extremely lucky, the appeals might succeed, so that I would eventually be sent home. I should by then have caused a great deal of hard work, trouble, and the diversion of scarce resources from matters of more pressing national concern, to a number of Foreign Office officials and, probably, certain of Her Majesty's Ministers. My own career with the Foreign Office would of course be terminated in disgrace. I should have to find other employment. But I should at least be free.

That, however, was the optimistic version of the Damascus scenario. The realistic one was very different. The circumstances of my frontier violations would speedily convince the Syrian authorities that I was up to no good there. The final nail in my coffin would be their inevitable discovery, sooner or later, that I came from the so-called 'British Spy School'. Ignoring my Government's pleas – the fact that I had no diplomatic status at the time would make it easier for them to do so – the Syrians would stage a trial, find me guilty of espionage and serious frontier violations, and send me to prison for a great many years. I knew little of conditions in Syrian prisons, but did not expect to find them a bed of roses. A variant of that outcome, more likely perhaps in the event that news of my whereabouts never got back home, was that I would simply be locked away somewhere without the formality of legal proceedings. Under either variant, could torture be ruled out?

Another Arab came in. Nothing unusual about that: the *va et vient* was almost continuous. This one, I vaguely noticed, was short of stature and wore a black *thaub*. I was not much interested even when he looked enquiringly round the room and, spotting me in my corner, flashed a brief but kindly smile in my direction – the first I had seen all day.

The newcomer sat down on the ground near me, and at once engaged the rest of the company in lively conversation. As usual I could not follow what was being said, but he seemed to be well known, and to be an immediate focus of interest on the part of all others present. It was also apparent that what he was saying did not meet with their approval. Voices were raised, and a heated argument rapidly developed. Everybody in the room seemed to be lined up against the newcomer, who appeared to me to be fighting his corner with some dialectical skill. Those sitting nearest to him were tugging fiercely at his garments. It looked as if he was in some danger of being physically assaulted.

I began to take an interest. Here at least was a new diversion, although I hadn't the faintest idea what it was all about. Then I began to pick up a few phrases. The quarrel, it seemed, concerned myself. The newcomer, who evidently came from across the border, was trying to tell them that I was just a tourist who had lost his way; the Syrians were furiously responding that I was a spy and an agent of the imperialist powers. Then I lost the thread again. But I had understood enough to feel a faint flicker of hope. Somebody, it seemed, was actually on my side.

The argument raged on and on; the Syrians were getting angrier and angrier. Half an hour passed in this way; then an hour; and they were still arguing. Outside, the light was fast fading. I wondered how it was all going to end. Then suddenly and unexpectedly, the argument simmered down. It was as if everybody had run out of steam. Perhaps the approaching end of the day's fast was beginning to claim their attention. The Lebanese intruder got to his feet and, turning to me, beckoned to me to follow him out of the room. There were objections, but nobody actually barred our way. I did not know what to believe or hope.

In the twilight outside, more villagers were gathered. They watched us speechlessly as we emerged. The stranger led me to a tree nearby where two horses were tethered. 'We are going back to Lebanon', he said simply, just as 'Abdouh had said that morning. I was stupefied. I could not believe my ears.

We mounted our two steeds, and rode off. My father had taught me to ride from an early age. Soon the gathering darkness had swallowed up the Syrian village and all its works; the village noises faded behind us, the only sound now the clattering of our horses' hooves. I was utterly bewildered by the turn of events. I had not the faintest clue who my rescuer was, why he had come to rescue me, or how he had persuaded the Syrians to let me go. All that mattered at that moment was that Providence had somehow intervened.

In the last remnants of daylight, I could see that our route was once again, for me, breaking new ground. Our route climbed gradually up an extended rocky gorge through which our horses picked their slow and stumbling way, guided by the hunched, silent figure of my rescuer. As night finally closed in, the landscape around us was illuminated by the most brilliant full moon that I can ever remember. Every outcropping spur and buttress, each isolated tree, each jungly patch of scrub clinging to the steep slopes above us, stood out with startling clarity. The only sound to be heard was the soft, mysterious call of a scops owl.

Somewhere on that long ride, we crossed back into Lebanon. My rescuer's house, when we at last reached it, proved to be part of another small settlement nestling at the forest edge. He and his pretty young wife were kindness and consideration itself; I was plied with food and comfort, my every need catered for. Overriding my embarrassed expostulations, the couple moved out of their bedroom, the only one in the house, and insisted on my sleeping in their bed. I would not, in any event, have had much trouble sleeping on that sixth night of my journey.

Next morning was the occasion for a photographic orgy. My rescuer was joined by a splendid group of grinning, bandoliered Arabs from the village, rifles slung round shoulders. Posed against the snowy backdrop of the Qornet, under the cloudless blue of another perfect spring morning, my snapshots of these new friends would provide an evocative memento of the Badlands, which I could return to for the rest of my life. Names and addresses were handed over, print copies promised. It was only later that I found I had inserted the film incorrectly into my new camera; the whole thing was a washout.

My rescuer insisted on accompanying me all the way to Hermel, still several hours' ride distant. After I had warmly thanked my hospitable hostess, we were off once again on horseback. Our journey through increasingly arid terrain was an opportunity to ponder the previous day's extraordinary events. The news of my capture could only have come from the Lebanese village where I had last seen 'Abdouh. But that was several mountainous kilometres away from where my rescuer lived. How had the news reached him? From what source had he received a convincing account of my *bona fides*? What possible interest or motive had he for intervening to rescue me, at the expense of a day and a half of considerable effort, and in the face of fierce Syrian recalcitrance? It all remained a complete mystery.

When we at length reached Hermel, the dusty frontier town of the northern Bekaa, I was taken straight to the local police station. I had to answer some questions and hand over my passport for examination. In the end I was released on the strength of an assurance that I would keep well away from the Syrian frontier in future. I bade an emotional farewell to my rescuer, to whom I owed my freedom, perhaps my life. I then returned by bus and service taxi to Shemlan, which I reached that evening. The Monday morning following that weekend, I was back to the dull routine of Arabic lessons: *jasus*, a spy; plural *jawasis*.

There was, of course, an aftermath. I learnt that, in the course of that Saturday, the British Embassy in Beirut had been rung up by the Lebanese Ministry of the Interior. A British subject called William

John, the Ministry spokesman said, had been involved in a strange series of incidents along the Syrian frontier near Hermel. Who was this William John, and what on earth was he doing there? Two members of the Embassy staff had then been kept fully employed right over the weekend, trying to identify the miscreant. It was quite a while before I dared show my face inside the Embassy again.

It all came out in the end, and I had to own up to the MECAS authorities. An interesting piece of feedback then reached me. My rescuer, it transpired, was a corporal in the Lebanese army in disguise, planted there to keep an eye on the gun-running and other lawless activities of the region. It was the nearest the forces of law and order dared go towards having a presence in the Badlands.

Disciplinary action by the MECAS authorities proved to be a double-barrelled affair. First I had to appear before Denis Michell, the Deputy Director. The kindliest, most genial, most avuncular of men, Denis was not ideally suited to this task; it was the least convincing rocket I ever had. On one point, though, he was very firm: I must have no further contact whatsoever with the folk of the Badlands, even those I had come to regard as my friends. In particular, I was deeply disappointed to learn that I would not be allowed to make any recompense to my rescuer.

Next day came the real crunch, when I was summoned before the Director. Fairly quaking in my boots, I duly presented myself. Donald Maitland's features were impassive, but his eyes flashed fire. 'Denis Michell has left you in no doubt of the enormity of the offence you have committed', he began severely. 'Yes', I gasped faintly, wondering what was coming next. Would this be the end of my Foreign Office career? Expulsion from MECAS perhaps? Or a spell of solitary confinement in a Crusader castle, under strict orders to memorise ten thousand Arabic word-cards before I would be allowed out again? There was a long pause. When Donald spoke again, his words astonished me. 'I just wanted you to know', he said, 'That I thought it was a damn good show. We need people who do that sort of thing.' Always provided, he seemed to imply, the entire Foreign Service doesn't go around behaving like that...

William (Bill) J E Norton attended MECAS in 1957-59 as a member of the Diplomatic Service. In the late 1960s he transferred to H M Treasury.

'HONOUR THE CAT'
1958

John Lansley

In December 1959, I was coming to the end of the first term of the Advanced Course at MECAS and this naturally coincided with the end of the first term of the new Long Course which I completed the previous year.

We were standing round the bar of Thatcher's Club the voluntary as-it-were 'Students' Union' of those studying at MECAS and named after the Reverend G. W. Thatcher who had written the Arabic grammar that we then used. As well as myself, there were Mark Marshall, with whom I had been in the same syndicate as we both came to MECAS in October 1958, and one of the 'new people', Stanley Black.

Stanley was a married man in his forties and was having problems – seeing to his house, schooling for his children and so forth (having the same name as the conductor of a BBC orchestra, very well-known at the time, did not help). He was also finding Arabic very difficult.

He turned to Mark somewhat threateningly. 'I understand you finished Thatcher in your first term!' he barked.

'Well, actually three weeks before the end of term.' Mark replied sweetly. This did not please Stanley Black at all. 'How did you do that?' he asked.

'Well,' replied Mark, 'You must remember that I have been a professional student for the past twenty years.'

'Professional student for the past *twenty years?*' expostulated Stanley, 'Whatever do you mean?'

'You see,' went on Mark, 'I learnt my alphabet at the age of three, was reading at four, at which age I started school. I was at school until I was 18 and did not do National Service because of my poor eyesight. Instead I went straight to Cambridge where I took a double first in Classics. I was then accepted for the Foreign Service and immediately posted here last October and have been learning Arabic ever since. I am now aged 23 so that, as you see, I have been a professional student for the past twenty years so that it is not surprising that I finished Thatcher's *Arabic Grammar* three weeks before the end of the first term.'

Honour the Cat

When I was in Morocco serving in the British Embassy in Rabat 1956-58 (before I went to MECAS), I became friendly with a Moroccan grocer from whom I regularly bought fruit. He had a big black tom cat who was always very friendly with the customers and who always liked me.

One day I mentioned to M. Ben Labcen the fact that Muslims everywhere always seemed very fond of cats. He told me that according to Muslim tradition, once when the Prophet Mohammed was kneeling down saying his prayers, a snake crept along intending to bite him. However, a cat saw the snake in time and jumped out and killed it, and that is why Muslims revere cats.

In the middle of the Long Course in 1958-60, the Principal Instructor at the time, David Cowan, himself a Muslim, set us to write an essay in Arabic once a week. He would give us the subject for the essay just as we came in and sat down in the classroom. One week the subject was 'All the nice girls love a sailor' but on the occasion to which I refer now, he wrote on the blackboard (in Arabic) 'HONOUR THE CAT' (*Akrimu Al-Hirr*). He told us that this was a saying of the Prophet enshrined in the Hadith, or tradition of what the Prophet had said apart from what was in the Quran.

Dick Holmes, a lawyer from Aden, was sitting next to me.

'What on earth can we say about *that*?' he asked in despair.

I told him what the Moroccan grocer had told me and suggested this was why the Prophet Mohammed had said, 'Honour the Cat'.

Dick told me afterward that he had written:

> 'I have no idea what to write on this subject but Mr Lansley tells me that when he was in Morocco, a local grocer had told him that once when the Prophet Mohammed was kneeling down saying his prayers, a snake crept along intending to sting him. However, a cat saw the snake in time and jumped out and killed the snake and that is why the Prophet said, 'Honour the cat.'

> 'Now these are the words of Mr Lansley but, *Wallahi*! God knows if he is right!'

What Professor Cowan's reaction was to either of our essays is not known.

John Lansley attended MECAS as a member of the Foreign Service from 1958 to 1960. His memoir includes a further eight anecdotes about MECAS.

IN THE HANDS OF THE MUKHABARAT 1959

Michael Ashmore

One thing that happened to me illustrated the Arab ability generally to operate an internal inteligence (*Mukhabarat*) system extremely well, as compared to their abysmal record outside their own borders.

It being only some three years since Suez, the *Mudir* (Director) told us not to flaunt the fact that we were studying at MECAS and generaly to move around low key. One Sunday afternoon when coming back to Shemlan from a visit to Jerusalem, the service taxi stopped at the Syrian frontier post at Dera'a. As usual I gave the driver my passport and he took it along with the other passengers' papers into the immigration office. After some minutes he came back and asked me to go in with him. the Captain in charge asked me where I was going and I said Beirut. When he asked me why, I said that I was with the Ottoman Bank there. He said that there was no Ottoman Bank there, but an associated bank, Banque de Syrie et du Liban. I agreed with him and when he again asked me where I was going, I told him Shemlan. He smiled and said that I could go, but that he would keep my passport. It would be returned to me at the immigration office on the Lebanese border. I asked him how I would get through the numerous military roadblocks *en route* and he assured me that I would have no problem. Sure enough, there were no problems, and my passport, duly stamped, was indeed returned to me at the Syrian border with Lebanon. I was never stopped again in similar fashion, but the point had been made.

Michael Ashmore, a banker, attended MECAS from 1959 to 1961.

HOW I LOST MY WORD CARDS 1959

David Gillespie

MECAS was intense. My pockets bulged with word cards wherever I went. At night, I poured over word lists and papers on grammar by the light of an oil lamp most of the time. I felt guilty reading or even thinking anything that was not in Arabic. The fortnightly ordeal of searching for one's name on the test results pinned up on the notice board in the early morning was nerve-wracking.

I felt that all the hard work of the week-days earned me some relaxation at the weekends, and it was my custom to drive down to Beirut on a Friday evening to spend two nights at the Excelsior or the Palm Beach, and other places.

On one particular occasion my fellow-student, Jeff Windle, was with me. We shared a large American 6-cylinder Ford. (I had started out with some kind of a Morris, which frequently gave up on the climb towards Aley.)

We set off back to Shemlan on the Sunday evening: I did notice that our Ford seemed to be the only car on the road, but thought nothing more of it. Shemlan was a ghost-town. Not a light visible, not a soul about. The school building was open, but when I got to my room it was empty. All my precious word cards gone, and all my other possessions too. (It was the word cards I was worried about!)

Everything had been as usual in Beirut, so civil war did not spring to mind at once. There did not seem to be much point in hanging around, so we started back towards Aley, hoping to find someone there or on the road who could tell us what had happened. A mass kidnapping? Alien abduction? A *Sawt Al-Arab* attack?

When we reached Aley we spotted a MECAS vehicle and quickly got the story, and our quarters for the night.

It turned out that we had left Shemlan not far ahead of the Jumblatistes, who wanted the village for its position overlooking the airport.

I enjoyed every minute of my time at MECAS, including this little adventure.

David Gillespie of the Ottoman Bank attended MECAS from 1957 to 1959.

THE NETWORK –
A SENSE OF
BELONGING
1959-60

Louis Wesseling

To enter the celebrated halls of MECAS in late 1959 for the first time as a student was scary enough, the more so for a Dutch national and an oilman to boot. I was thirty. My wife and two children accompanied me on our 'sabbatical' in Shemlan and were looking forward to enjoying their holiday to the full. But reality quickly took over.

The main body of students with whom I had to compete (for that is how I saw it) were bachelors in their early twenties. The tone was set by a few cocky but brilliant students, straight out of university with firsts from Oxford or Cambridge, who fully expected to perform outstandingly in whatever assignment they undertook. Amongst them was the grandson of a famous British Prime Minister. A happy crowd they were, too, hiding their hard work learning Arabic behind a façade of riotous partying, quoting Shakespeare when drunk at picnics in the mountains. Together we investigated some of the most enchanting Arab and crusader castles and ruins of dream houses near streams in blossoming orchards. At

155

weekends we stayed for primitive skiing at the Cedars Lodge in the high Lebanon mountains and purely for the record went swimming in the Med at the end of the same day. My brand new coffee-and-cream-coloured Citroen with pneumatic suspension performed sterling transport services. (Even second hand, two years later, it looked still good enough to be bought by the 'Black Prince', a cousin of King Idris of Libya). The students themselves were much in demand for English- and French-speaking evening parties in the city of Beirut, which proudly upheld its reputation as the 'Paris of the Orient'. We actually saw a Saudi Rolls Royce with gold fenders in the streets. Although everyone was fully aware of the well-established armed feuds between Druze, Maronite Christians and Sunnis, nobody had the least inkling that these could lead to the total collapse of the city and of the Lebanon as we then knew and rather admired it. Whenever, infrequently, a car with Druze youngsters raced through our own Christian mountain village, firing their guns into the air, we would merely say: 'Oh well, they will never learn how to fight a proper war' and return to our irregular verbs.

A Spy Among Us

Among the students there was, however, a small but influential contingent of men my age or older, diplomats destined to be posted in the Middle East, military men, business executives like myself and Neville Green of the British Bank of the Middle East, and some who perhaps partly justified the Arab nickname for MECAS 'the spy school'. A future British ambassador to Saudi Arabia and his glamorous wife became good friends of ours and our children were taught by her sister in the same English kindergarten. He exerted a natural moderating influence on the students and was acknowledged as their unofficial spokesman. But one other man really stood out. By far the most proficient in Arabic studies, perhaps because of his Egyptian ancestry, and universally liked by all who met him: George Blake. Great was our consternation when he was arrested and unmasked as a spy for the hated Soviets. His young wife, living near us with two children, was clearly devastated. His young student friends even concocted, and naively signed, a petition to the Foreign Office to protest his innocence, so unimaginable was his double life to most of us. Yet he had never hidden his distaste for the crass commercialism of firms like mine, for the pomp and circumstance and injustice of public life and the Royal Family. But I thought that it was just this freedom and ability to discuss any contrary opinions, which were shared by many of the younger set, that was one of the outstanding features of MECAS.

Thirty years later, after the fall of the Berlin wall, with Gorbachov still in power, on a visit to the Dutch embassy in Moscow, shock and horror were still the only reaction to the mere mention of his name. I met him for lunch at the most decadently expensive restaurant in Moscow, opposite the infamous Lubianka prison. George, now a charming semi-retired general of the KGB, glanced wistfully out of the window and remarked that in the good old days Soviet citizens did not even dare to walk on the pavement next to it, for fear of being dragged inside never to be seen again. Now, inevitably, things had changed, with Dzerzhinsky's statue having been torn down, together with all the other Stalin cult icons. He firmly believed, however, that Communism, in spite of having been let down by Russian human error, still had a great future. He looked back on his Shemlan days as a very happy interval and his current private life, together with that of old friends like Philby (sadly alcoholic) seemed flat in comparison. They had been severely restricted; for instance he had only been allowed to holiday in East Germany, while what he really yearned for was to be allowed to visit his aged mother in Holland. I left with the advice that he should not even apply for a visa.

The very first day at the first introductory lesson, the Director of the school, Donald Maitland, led us through the scribbles of the whole Arabic alphabet, with a senior Palestinian teacher at his side to pronounce correctly all the impossibly sounding vowels and guttural consonants. (Tape recorders were not yet in use for this purpose.) The following day we would have to be ready to work with these in writing and pronunciation, he proclaimed. A famous dictum of his was: 'There is no such thing as a smattering of Arabic. You either learn it properly or you don't'. Now, with hindsight, I would like to comment on that. After finishing the nine months course 'with distinction' I confess that I was distressed at not being able to speak fluent Arabic at all. Yes, I could more or less understand the radio news and read the papers, but truly colloquial conversation with our Lebanese neighbours continued to frustrate me.

To my simple mind there are three kinds of Arabic existing side by side: first, the classical language of the Quran, used by the prophet Mohammed. I later employed several bright Europeans who had studied it at famous universities for five long years, but who could not make themselves understood at all by the ordinary Gulf Arab. Secondly, at the other end of the scale are the many local Arabic dialects spoken by the semi-literate population (and by my wife in the market), which differ very widely from Morocco to Egypt and Saudi Arabia. Local intellectuals use it somewhat condescendingly, with apologies to the foreigner. And finally, there is Donald Maitland's Arabic, the semi-classical universal language of the educated and half-educated, of press and TV, throughout the Arab world. I fully agree with the decision of MECAS (the most practical Arab language institute in the world of the day) to concentrate solely on that last category and on the spoken Palestinian as a useful by-product. But why did I, who speak four European languages with some ease (not including my own), not achieve immediate fluency in that kind of Arabic? Learning a language after infancy is mostly hard work, committing thousands of words and verbs to the brain by repetition. Apart from the intrinsic difficulty of the totally foreign structure of Arabic, the answer to our lack of fluency must be found in our lack of daily contact with real people who had to use it continuously, journalists, politicians, or women. Learning grammar and boring vocabulary can only bring you so far; to a take-off point. Any further progress is up to the individual's imagination, needs and experiences, from pillow talk to business deals. Ask the people who improved their Arabic afterwards. As for the Palestinian and English teaching staff, they were exemplary, performance-oriented in school and sociable outside the office and in the village of Shemlan. They created a sense of belonging to an informal association and that was a major benefit. In East Africa I had already experienced how effective the network of British Colonial administrators could be, but the Foreign Office network of Arabists, based on common study in Shemlan, was to be of far wider importance.

Louis Wesseling, a Dutchman, attended MECAS in 1959-60 on behalf of Shell International. His last overseas position in the Shell Group was General Manager of Shell Vietnam, which he described in his book Fuelling the War (I B Tauris, 2000). His memoir also records his impressions of the first Arab Petroleum Congress in Cairo in 1960 (including time spent with the Saudi Minister of Oil, Sheikh Zaki Yamani), postings to Cyreniaca, Libya and Qatar and numerous visits to the Trucial States and Oman.

THE REMOVAL OF A SPY, GEORGE BLAKE 1960-62

John Coles

Most memories of MECAS are good. But not all. I went there on the then long course in late 1960. I had been in the Foreign Office only a few weeks and it embarrasses me to recall how deeply green I was about almost everything.

These were of course the halcyon days of a calm Lebanon and all the skiing, swimming and picnicking mixture that Mecas graduates of that generation have dined out on for years. But despite the distractions we soon settled into the routine of morning lessons and afternoon preparation for the next day. And then there were the evenings, which were not designed to promote physical wellbeing.

One day, when memory says the skies were blue and all was calm, we were told that two men had come from London and removed one of our classmates: George Blake. For those too young to remember, he was a double agent, supposed to be working for MI6 but in fact, it had been discovered, working for the Soviet Union. He was sentenced to a prison term of some forty years by a judge who made it plain that this man had caused great harm to British interests. He then escaped from Wormwood Scrubs and made his way to Moscow where he spent, so far as I know, the rest of his life.

Now I found this sudden departure of Blake hard to take in. I barely knew what MI6 was, though I had been briefed to talk about 'Our Friends.' I had not given a moment's thought to Soviet intelligence. So it was disturbing. But the disturbance went deeper than that. You see, I thought I knew George Blake. MECAS was a small place. We all knew each other, didn't we? I had come to regard Blake as in some ways a dull swot. He was always walking about with those word cards, checking the English on the front with the Arabic on the back. He answered questions with a broad smile but did not seem to have anything very interesting to say. And we had got to know his family. I remember, these 40 years later, his charming wife, Gillian, and two (or was it three?) blond, blue-eyed children. They would occasionally invite some of us bachelors down to their house for a meal and very pleasant it was too.

But now! I realised that I had been completely deceived and wholly taken in. Also, that the world was a good deal nastier than it had seemed before. Others were pretty shocked too. We used to discuss how we had managed to be so completely fooled. Then we remembered one or two things that we might have paid more attention to at the time. We had formed a dining club, as bachelors will, called, I think, The Mountain. It met from time to time in a good Beirut restaurant, had dinner and spent the rest of the evening variously.

We recalled how the normally punctilious Blake had turned up very late for one of those dinners, probably because he was seeing some agent somewhere in the city. We further remembered going on to the Casino Du Liban and playing roulette. Blake had bet on single numbers. More, he had won a pile on one number and immediately put all the proceeds on another single number. It takes a real gambler to do that. And that of course is the point. We were watching someone who was engaged in a lifetime gamble and got his excitement from living on the edge. But it had not struck us so at the time.

There was another consequence. As all Mecas graduates know, the Arab press almost invariably described our institution as a 'school for spies'. I have now forgotten the 'Line to Take' but we certainly denied it Rightly so. Neither before nor after the Blake affair was it a school for spies. But with his arrest, and all the publicity, it became pretty hard to convince our Arab friends that they were wrong.

About the only thing that gave me any pleasure in this affair was the fact that Gillian and the family, who, I have always thought, knew nothing of Blake's Soviet connexion, were swiftly moved out of the country. I never once saw any report of a press interview with her. I am glad she was spared the ever-ghastly media and hope she had a good life thereafter.

But I can still not quite overcome the fact that I had come to regard Blake as a dull person with nothing interesting to talk about, that he had wholly fooled me. I know he had deceived lots of people for years too but that does not make it much better. And it certainly left me wondering for a long time afterwards who exactly you could trust.

All my other memories of Mecas are exclusively happy.*

Sir John Coles GCMG attended MECAS in 1960-62. He was Private Secretary to the Prime Minister 1981-84, Ambassador to Jordan, 1984-88, High Commissioner to Australia, 1988-91 and Permanent Under-Secretary of State, Foreign and Commonwealth Office and Head of the Diplomatic Service 1994-97.

---

*Not all the students had such happy memories. The top student one year had, in his previous posting, attracted his Ambassador's and FCO attention for his excellent German, He was summoned, as was the custom, to be congratulated on his high marks in Arabic and was asked to express his preference for the next posting.

'Anywhere', he replied, 'provided it was not in the Middle East.' He and his wife disliked hot and humid climates; they had difficulties with the local food and drink; they preferred German home comforts to damp, cold and draughty accommodation. They were frustrated by the poor quality of the drinking water and the unpredictability of the electricity supply and felt isolated from the concerts and cultural life they had come to love. They particularly objected to the exclusion of wives in formal Arab lunches, dinners and receptions.

'Excellent!' replied the Chairman of the meeting, without a moment's hesitation. 'Just what we need in the Diplomatic Service - a clear-headed sense of objectivity' and selected a posting to the most western of the options available.

There is, alas, no happy diplomatic denouement to this particular story. After serving out his three years in North Africa, the top man of his year, with a fast-track career and double linguistic distinction behind him, left the Service.

RANDOM
MEMORIES
1961-62

David Morphet

The always superb view from one's window, except when the mists were down in winter. The best of it was when sheets of rain were sweeping across Beirut airport down below, and you could see the planes taking off. The heavy scent of pines on the road from Souk el Gharb in the summer. The curious little Anglican chapel in the village. Arak and *narghileh* with the *mukhtar* in his cafe up the road.

Catering at the school, provided by Abu Musa and his sons. I always had a ring of *labneh* curd cheese with a touch of olive oil for breakfast, attracting derision from the majority who tucked into bacon and egg.

Skiing at the Cedars. Sometimes, my battered 1954 Volkswagen was the only car which could make it up to the hut – with two people standing on the back bumper, and the weight of the rear engine, it just had enough purchase on the ice.

Christmas 1961. To Jerusalem in the Volkswagen with Kunio Katakura and Jiro Matsumura. A puncture as we entered the city in the dark. Pulling into the side of the road, we found ourselves outside the Garden of Gethsemane. Leaving the car, we climbed up the lane to the Benedictine Convent on the Mount of Olives which was offering accommodation to pilgrims. We were just in time for supper on Christmas Eve – a dish of brains, which my Japanese friends had never had before. The look on their faces when I told them... Visiting a Palestinian Refugee Camp north of Jerusalem.

Dinner one evening with the *Mudir* – John Wilton – to meet the British Ambassador, who entered the room carrying his mother's handbag. Very amusing to a 22-year old.

Once, after all-night clubbing in Beirut, an early morning swim at the Hotel Phoenicia pool, followed by whisky and fried eggs, and straight up the hill into morning Arabic classes. Many other days at the Phoenicia pool.

Organising the Thatchers Club Summer Dance, 1962. We got a spit and roasted a sheep – or attempted to – Alan Rothnie was chief spit-turner. After 12 hours in the Shemlan baker's oven, and four hours on the spit, the sheep only provided a single decent slice off the outside. The rest was almost raw. The carcase had to be buried in the grounds the following day.

At one point we had a brigadier who had great difficulty learning the Word List. One night we called at his room, and found him drilling all three hundred cards of the current list on his carpet, with a pointer. It was the only way he could do it.

A trip to south Turkey with Nick Moy and Andrew Nicholson in my Volkswagen, via Iskanderun. Manhandling the car round a fallen boulder on a remote mountain road near Konya. The crusader castles at Anamur etc – nobody there but us and the occasional snake. No metalled road as far as Antalya. On the way back, the Syrian border closed for the latest coup attempt, and a week's wait in Antioch till it opened. Driving in a long convoy through the night from the border to Hama, escorted by the Syrian army.

'Language break' in Egypt. A fortnight at the Embassy translating. A felucca party. Going up the Nile in the old Sudan Railways steamer – still serving ginger beer, with meat and two veg. Hiring a 1931 Agatha Christie-vintage Chrysler De Soto limousine, with blue curtains in the back, to take me round the

Valley of the Kings. Playing chess one night at Aswan with a Russian engineer involved in the High Dam – he was warned off; we only had one game. Visiting Abu Simbel in its original setting.

A party at the house of a Dutch oilman down the hill from the school, where our one and only Cuban student drank too much and went berserk, hurling gramophone records out of the window etc. When we got him back to the school, I had to sit on him for two hours until he recovered his senses. At one point he managed to bite me in the shoulder. Come to think of it, I am probably the only Britisher to have bitten by a Cuban diplomat.

Helping out for three weeks at the Damascus Trade Fair 1962. Absurdly, the main exhibit on the British stand was a yacht, which many of the country folk had never seen before – historically and socially, Damascus looked to the desert rather than the sea. We did have a television relay on which visitors to the stand could see themselves – they loved that. But the most admired item was a set of large Sheffield knives. We could have sold any number.

Other British diplomats at Shemlan who were there at the same as me, or overlapped, included Roger Tomkys, John Coles, Michael Burton, Rob Hendrie. The Chief Instructor was Dr (now Professor Emeritus) Malcolm Lyons from Pembroke, Cambridge, with whom I am still in touch.

Leaving Beirut on the same day as Philby* – 29 January 1963 – though in the opposite direction. I went south to the Yemen.

David Morphet attended MECAS in 1961-62. He transferred from the Diplomatic Service to the UK Department of Energy in 1974. His publications include Seventy-Seven Poems *(2002);* The Angel and the Fox *(poems 2003) and* Approaching Animals from A to Z *(poems 2004).*

LOSING ONE'S
FALSE TEETH
1962-63

George Rolleston

On Fridays, after lectures, a few of us (usually the same lot) would gather at the MECAS bar for a drink (or twain!) before going in to lunch (screened off from the bar) or going home. On one particular occasion, one of our fellow students, an amiable and extremely humorous Lt Cdr Lou Stone RN (or passed over two-and-a-half as he referred to himself!) asked the barman, Naseeb, if he knew how to make a Negroni. Naseeb admitted that he had no idea; Lou said that it was easy and that legend had it that it was the invention of a notorious Contessa di Negroni (of Naples) who mixed the cocktail for young sailors suitable for seduction!

The drink consisted of: 2 parts gin , 1 part Dry Martini , 1 part Sweet Martini, topped up with soda as Campari soda.

Naseeb duly produced a few Negronis for the assembled group who found them sweet and curiously unalcoholic (we should have known!). By the time our little party had drunk three or four of these sweet cocktails, the alcoholic effect was evident in the volume of our conversation. Such a row did we make that the then Director (John Wilton) came out from behind the screens to tell us that people were trying to have lunch and would we please stop the session immediately. We did as told. The alcoholic effect, however, of the Negronis had the following consequences:

1. Rolleston and Jim Roscoe (RAEC) were expelled by the priest at Suq el Gharb church for playing 'boogie' on the organ using hymn books as percussion. Lou Stone weaved his way unsteadily to the Melkon Hotel where he was lodged. He was promptly sick and lost his false teeth down the hotel loo.

2. Despite his state, and nothing daunted, Lou traced the Melkon's drainage to an airtight inspection cover in the road outside. Having managed to remove the top cover of the drain, Lou peered down the hole, felt dizzy and fell back heavily on the lid of the inspection cover, only to discover that it had been freshly painted and had now imprinted on Lou's trousered bottom the proud logo of Suq el Gharb Municipality. Utterly defeated and exhausted Lou returned to the Melkon and arranged for the Embassy dentist to fit him with a new set of false teeth.

George Rolleston MBE attended MECAS in 1962-3 as a member of the Foreign Service. He died in 2005.

THIRTY NEW
WORDS A DAY 1962

Frank Jungers

I had, over my career, studied Arabic on my own. The company had some basic Arabic language programmes for Americans which were indeed pretty basic. I had taken all of those and had studied on my own. I had a reasonable colloquial knowledge of Arabic, at least at a low level of usage. At one point somebody had decided that they were going to send some people who had demonstrated management capabilities and who had an interest in Arabic to a more formalised Arabic programme and give them a chance to learn. It was not that I really had a choice at that point.

It was a terrifying course, because it was done by a system that only the British use, where all grades and rankings are posted daily. There weren't that many students there. I don't remember how many – 30 or 40 – mostly British, mostly young diplomatic types, fresh out of Oxbridge, academically ready to carry on their studies.

The habit of studying I had long forgotten. In that system, everybody was divided into 'syndicates', as they called them. The syndicate consisted of three people who studied together, shared an instructor and were graded together. If one of the three began to look a little stronger, they'd just move him up a syndicate and then he became the weakest guy in the next syndicate. The best syndicates got the better instructors.

All the grades were posted publicly. So if you went to downtown Beirut one night and got drunk, your test showed it the next morning. Grades were posted on the bulletin board. Arabic is a very difficult language; the vocabulary is very large. An educated English spoken vocabulary is probably in the order of about 3,500 common words, though the reading vocabulary is much larger. An educated Arabic spoken vocabulary is more like 10,000 words, and the written vocabulary is correspondingly larger.

How do you learn 30 words a day?* Well, you put the English on one side of a card and the Arabic on the other, and flip them until you've got them. But now you have to go over the 30 you learned yesterday and remember them, and the 30 before that, and the 30 before that! So you have stacks of cards and must continually go through them just to memorise them.

Frank Jungers was sent by ARAMCO of Saudi Arabia to MECAS in 1962. On return to Saudi Arabia, he was promoted rapidly to the position of CEO. As such, he played a key role with Sheikh Zaki Yamani (Saudi Oil Minister 1962-86) in the OPEC pricing confrontation and Arab export embargo of October 1973. We are grateful to Peter Iseman (1974) for obtaining these comments.

---

*The process of concentration needed to remember 3,000 words was not dissimilar, as many MECAS students have observed, from the process whereby all over the Islamic world for the last 13 centuries, classes of young boys seek to commit the entire text of the Koran to memory, some by the age of nine.

In the 1960s some students had been pre-selected by completing the approved Language Aptitude Test. This took the form of a one-hour examination in a completely artificial language whose vocabulary bore no relationship to any other language on earth. Students were given a booklet and told to fill in the question at the foot of each page. Each page had a new list of words – nouns, verbs, pronous, adjectives, adverbs and their meaning The question at the foot of the page required you to translate a sentence from English using the words on that and all previous pages. If you had forgotten anything, you could turn back to check, but this wasted time. A bell was rung to mark the start and finish. Shortly before the end, the invigilator walked round, noting down the page reached by each candidate and thus knew instantly more or less who had passed and who had failed.

'ONE WHO LEADS
ASTRAY' 1963–64

Rosalind Ward Gwynne

I was a student at Portland State College (now Portland State University, Portland, Oregon, USA) when I began to study Arabic in 1962. My interest was not in the Middle East but in language in general; so intriguing was Arabic, however, that once involved with it, I never abandoned it. After the equivalent of nearly two years of Arabic, I was interviewed for the NUPOSA program at MECAS by Prof. Gustave von Grunebaum. I read a bit of Arabic aloud for him from the Ziadeh and Winder textbook. But once he discovered that I had been studying French for five years, he asked, *'Bien, on peut continuer en francais?'*, to which I replied, *'Mais oui, bien sur'*, and on we went for the rest of the interview. Perhaps it was my French that got me into MECAS.

The seven NUPOSA students did a summer intensive course at Georgetown University before going on to Lebanon. Thus within three months this West-coast jazz-and-coffee beatnik experienced a quadruple culture shock: East Coast ivy-league, Lebanese mountain, Mediterranean francophone, and British Empire. For example, when I finally got up the courage to switch from French to Arabic and order *'tneen 'ahweh'* in the restaurant of the hotel where we two women students first stayed, the waiter literally sniffed in disdain and corrected my Arabic back to French: 'Deux cafes!' And I had to adjust to the fact that some Foreign Office students flatly denied that the US had had anything at all to do with winning the second World War.

At first, Alyce Page and I, both from PSC, were the only women students at MECAS, though we were later joined by another American and a Dane, both Christian missionaries. Women could not live in the MECAS dormitories at the time, so Alyce and I were at the hotel until we moved into rooms in the house of the butcher, Salim Hitti. Each of us had our own room, comfortable for us but much less so (though more profitable) for the Hittis and their six children – Said, Amin, Therese, Nada, Nabil, and little Bassam. Neither the parents nor the two youngest children spoke English, so we had a far more pressing need and greater opportunity to learn colloquial Arabic than did most of the male students. The NUPOSA course lasted from late August until mid-June, a month longer than the normal US academic calendar. Two of our students left early, one for financial reasons and the other to be with his wife, who had become pregnant just before we left the US. Sooner or later, I believe, we had classes with most of the instructors at MECAS. I don't remember particulars of our four hours a day of the usual grammar and vocabulary; different – and very difficult – were the classes we had in simultaneous translation. Having used a number of textbooks before coming to MECAS, we were less in awe of the MECAS grammar and word list than were many of our fellow students, and at some point we finished *The Way Prepared (al-Tariq al-Mumahhad)* and went on to the next volume. Its English title was *The Way Paved*, but its unfortunate Arabic title, *al-Tariq al-Muzaffat,* literally meant 'the tar-covered road'; the students called it zift for short, a word which meant 'tar' but in colloquial Lebanese was also a euphemism for another dark, smelly substance.

As this was before we knew about the Wehr dictionary, and the Hava dictionary was largely useless for newspaper Arabic, instructor Constantine Theodory strongly encouraged (to put it politely) his students to buy his own even more useless work, *A Dictionary of Modern Technical Terms*: Arabic English, remembered as the source of the eternally mysterious term 'electric egg' (p. 375 – yes, I still

171

have my copy). Quirky, fussy, and exacting, Mr. Theodory may have been the acid test for new students. A test of another kind was Mr. Ibrahim Dallal, seemingly a red-faced, opinionated tyrant but in fact one who liked nothing better than to have his students stand up to him. 'Missss Ward!', he would fume over some shortcoming on my part; 'Mister Dallal!' I would fume back, looking him in the eye, at which point he would explode with laughter.

Behind his back, naturally, students changed the first letter of his name from an ordinary d to a palatised d, thus turning him from 'one who guides' into 'one who leads astray'.

Life with the Hitti Family

As long as I was living with the Hittis, my social life was closer to the village than to MECAS. Ms. Hitti was the best cook in the village, and within a month I had gained six pounds and learned a good deal about Lebanese cooking. The view was beautiful, but once I looked down and right below my window was a newly slaughtered animal waiting to be cut up. On fine evenings everyone would take a sunset stroll in the village and greet everyone else: *leileh sa'eedeh sa'eedeh, sa'eedeh m'baarkeh!* The Hittis had one of only two televisions in Shemlan, so many of the neighbors used to come over for an evening of TV. This was especially true on the Thursdays when *zajal* was broadcast. *Zajal* is poetry improvised on the spot, making it very attractive to a fan of another improvisational art – jazz. There were two Christians and two Muslims sitting at the table, plus the (Christian) leader Zaghloul of Damour. Zaghloul would recite a piece composed for the occasion, then throw the lead to one of the other poets, who would improvise lines on some aspect of the same topic. A male chorus accompanied by *derbakke*-players (drummers) and other musicians would then repeat the last line or two as a refrain, during which time the next poet would be composing his own offering. The process was aided (if I am not mistaken) by glasses of *araq* for the Christians and cups of coffee for the Muslims. The audience in the Hittis' living room would repeat the lines along with the chorus, and sometimes one of them would anticipate the next line, to great applause from all of us present. But when the poet produced something wholly unexpected, using the set vocabulary and theme, we all exploded in delighted laughter.

When winter came, I moved to my own apartment. The Hittis heated only one room of their house, and I could not do my homework or relax in a room with six children, two parents, two tenants, numerous visitors, and a television. Now the focus of my social life shifted to MECAS itself. I had three meals a day there instead of one, drank far too much Scotch (I, a bourbon-drinker!), and listened to great stories about oil, the Foreign Office and the Trucial Oman Scouts, learning more about the world and politics but far less colloquial Arabic than before. Still, there were always trips to Beirut – Khayat's book store, Rue Bliss and Faysal's Restaurant, Hamra Street, the Suq al-Tawila, the Bourj, and the Automatique for ice cream – and conversations up and down the mountain with the *service* drivers and passengers.

Vacations and day trips took me to the Cedars, Zahleh, Damascus, Baalbek, East Jerusalem, and Jericho, the last two still under Jordanian rule. For the language break, I took a boat to Alexandria, then the train to Cairo, Luxor, and Aswan, one week before Khruschev presided over the diversion of the Nile to enable construction of the Aswan Dam. From there I took the Nile steamer to Wadi Haifa, then the train to Khartoum, where I stayed with the friends of a MECAS graduate for two-and-a-half weeks. Most people I met wanted to practise their English, of course, but Arabic was necessary from time to time in real life. For example, the only hotel in Luxor that I could afford was the rock-bottom Hotel des Familles, with its quarter-mile, lizard-infested hallway between my room and the bathroom, and the bedbugs that for days turned my legs purple. I often passed for Lebanese, with my blue eyes, blondish hair, and Lebanese mountain accent thick enough to cut with a knife. My return to Lebanon thus was almost a homecoming.

After returning to Portland State, I finished my degree while working as an undergraduate teaching assistant in Arabic. Then I worked full-time in the library cataloguing Arabic books and newspapers, eight hours a day for three years, an exposure that gave me the ability to skim Arabic. When the University of Washington was suddenly given some NDFL graduate fellowships in Arabic, I pounced on the opportunity and moved with my husband to Seattle. After completing the MA and PhD, sometimes also working as an Arabic teaching assistant, I accepted a job teaching Arabic at the University of Tennessee but gradually made the transition from teaching language to teaching Islamic studies, a field much closer to my graduate work. My book, *Logic, Rhetoric, and Legal Reasoning in the Qur'an: God's Arguments* was published by RoutedgeCurzon in the summer of 2004.

Rosalind Ward Gwynne attended MECAS in 1963-64 as a member of the NUPOSA programme, which sent American university students for a course at MECAS.

A LANGUAGE BREAK
VISIT TO SHAKHBUT
AND ZAYED 1965

David Gore-Booth

I joined the Foreign Office on 3 September 1964 and was sent to MECAS two weeks later. At the time I knew nothing about Arabic – or even the Arabs (an omission which the next 34 years certainly rectified). In the summer of 1965, as all the students prepared themselves for the five week Language Break, I received an unexpected instruction to spend it not with a family in 'Amman, Damascus or Jerusalem, as was the norm, but 'in the Gulf'. No embellishment, no forecast of a forthcoming assignment to the Political Residency in Bahrain or one of its quasi-colonial sub-posts down the shore of the Arabian Peninsula, no nothing.

Peter Williams was then Third Secretary at the Embassy in Beirut, having graduated from MECAS a year or two earlier (and to the amazement of us students the employer of a daily maid called Um'Atif who produced mountains of chips for hungry MECASians). He kindly offered to drive me and Adrian Fortescue to Kuwait – in a Sunbeam Talbot as I recall. There Christopher Battiscombe was the newly installed Third Secretary, fighting off the amorous attentions of a predatory nurse (successfully). Thence

I took a plane to Bahrain, where I was scooped up by Sir William Luce, the Political Resident. He announced that he was about to pay a pastoral visit to his Agents down the Gulf and would take me with him. So off we went to Abu Dhabi where the airline 'terminal' consisted of a tumble-dowm shack. He opened a Hawker Siddeley power plant, the first of its kind (and perhaps one of the last for Hawker Siddeley) – and went on to have lunch with Sheikh Shakhbut in his sandstone fort. But he was careful to reinsure (significantly in the light of subsequent events) by having breakfast the following morning with Sheikh Zayed in the desert.

One lasting memory is of running out of Duncan Slater's house straight onto the beach and into the sea for an early morning swim and another is having dinner with the legendary Hugh Boustead in his funny upside down premises with the residence downstairs and the office up. Then on, via RAF Sharjah and a four-wheel drive across the sand, to Dubai. There my first ever Queen's Birthday Party took place on the tennis court of the Agency (which then fronted directly onto the Creek) and for which I borrowed Michael Tait's 'Gulf rig', Michael having fallen down a *jebel* days earlier to the fury of his boss, the otherwise gentle Glen Balfour-Paul, Then up to Qatar where Ranald Boyle looked after us in what was the sleepiest of city states and back to Bahrain – and Shemlan where my Arabic was found not to have improved as much as that of my more family-based colleagues. But what an introduction to Arabia.

No assignment to the Gulf followed. I was sent instead to Baghdad, whence I was evacuated – to the safety of the Shah's Tehran – after the breach of relations following the June War of 1967. With the brief exception of a visit to Abu Dhabi in 1988 as Head FO Planner, accompanying the Minister of State. David Mellor, I was not to set foot in the Gulf again until 1989 when I was appointed Assistant Under Secretary (Director in the contemporary parlance) for the Middle East. Early on in my time I accompanied the Foreign Secretary Geoffrey Howe on visits to Saudi Arabia, the UAE, Qatar and Bahrain. What an amazing contrast! The UAE had been transformed. Skyscrapers and supermarkets (not just Spinneys) everywhere. No longer direct access to the beach in Abu Dhabi or the Creek in Dubai. No sea frontage in Bahrain. No Trucial Oman Scouts. And certainly no raising and lowering of the Union Jack at dawn and dusk to the sound of a bugle. But what astonishing progress, The Gulf Rulers have succeeded triumphantly in disproving the thesis, promulgated by Gamal Abdul Nasser and expressed by the likes of (then) 'Red' Fred Halliday, that the Arabian peninsula would shortly be cleansed of Sultans. Dubai is not as picturesque as it was, with the wind towers outshadowed by tower blocks of a much taller kind, but it is clearly more prosperous. Ditto Abu Dhabi – where the British Embassy now resembles a monastery surrounded by high rise cloisters – Doha, and even Bahrain; which had a head start because of the British air force and naval presence and the earlier discovery of oil. Politically they are on the march too as Bahrain and Qatar blaze trails that surely the Saudis and Emiratis will eventually have to follow, though Dubai seems likely to remain a special case.

The Hon. Sir David Gore-Booth KCMG, KCVO, attended MECAS in 1964-66. He was appointed Assistant Under-Secretary of State (ME) in the FCO in 1989, Ambassador, Saudi Arabia in 1993-96 and High Commissioner, New Delhi in 1996-98. On retirement, he was Special Adviser to HSBC and Chairman of the Windsor Energy Group until his death in October 2004.

ARABIC IN A COLD CLIMATE 1965-67

Shirley Kay

We walked down the steps opposite our old school, feeling as shattered as the battered village around us. Everything was wrong. Plants grew in the paths and lanes, brambles in the gardens. The little church, just below the road in front of the school, was roofless and lacking door and windows. Opposite it, the open terrace which was the garden of 'our' house, had been walled off and the wall topped with barbed wire, but this had not kept the looters out. Outside no door, no windows; inside no fireplaces, stoves, cupboards. All that could be moved had gone.

The houses round about were peppered with holes, lacking part of their roofs. Only two buildings in sight were in fine fettle. One was a huge and hideous new concrete villa, built on the terrace just below 'ours', and completely blocking the breathtaking view down over Beirut, with planes coming in to land directly below us. The other was the school. This had now been renovated, modernised, made more visually appealing. It was pristine, and was just about to reopen now in 1998, as a school for the mentally handicapped. A comment on our time there, perhaps?

For learning Arabic in this mountain village had never been an easy ride. Challenging, exciting, unforgettable maybe, and certainly providing some of the best times of our lives, but also frustrating, boring and oddly unreal. Slowly, oh so slowly, we had managed, some 33 years earlier, to exchange a few words with the ever ready villagers, who had watched the school bring welcome prosperity to Shemlan.

Our young children were less hesitant. The two-year-old toddled off to Eliyya Tabib's shop one day and exclaimed confidently 'biddi bowza'; he kindly got someone to bring her home, clutching the ice cream she had demanded. But in our next posting, Algeria, such mountain talk got them nowhere, and they gave up in disgust. Only on a later holiday in Aitat did they find it paid; by then relying on me for such comunication as we could muster, they asked me to get them sweets. I told them firmly to ask for themselves, which they did, and were amazed when the shopkeeper almost threw her arms round their necks – 'Such beautiful Arabic!' – and showered them with sweets. We, meanwhile, sat down each night to learn our word lists. Heated only by a stove, we moved nearer and nearer as the evening wore on. With the stove doors closed we gradually froze; with them open we were eventually smoked out. At that time Jolyon, I and Patrick Seale of the Observer were all studying together and living in the house. Finally one or other could bear the stinging eyes no more and closed the stove doors. Until the charade began all over again. Paraffin stoves proved little better. A back room of the house was a splendid library belonging to our landlord, the Palestinian academic Prof. Walid Khalidi. While we were out one day the paraffin stove there flared up and blackened everything in sight. We were lucky no further damaqe was done.

Bathing was just as demanding. Well, showering actually, since there were no baths. The water was heated by *nerite* stoves, *nerite* being bags of resinous wood shavings to be lit just the right time before the shower, in order to heat the water but not let it cool down again. On one trip to Jordan we stayed with the family of the ambassador, Philip Adams, who had briefly been our much loved neighbours in Shemlan. Their nanny was appalled when our two-year-old screamed and refused at first to set foot in the bath. After all, she had never seen one within her memory scan. After the first year the Khalidis returned to Lebanon and we moved to a flat in one of the original huge buildings which had housed the school. The rest of the building was empty, and we had no open stoves. The rooms were high and elegant, the lay-out typical of a mountain house with a huge hall in the centre upstairs, and rooms off all round. But as winter crept on we realized why the building was empty. When it rained water ran down the insides of the great stone walls; heating was just a mirage. But the word lists were by now mostly mastered. The secret was not to sit still. One night when we were out, a visitor came to the door. Our nanny ran to open it. She apologised sadly in the morning. She had gone, of course, in her pyjamas and anorak, in which we all slept. She was most upset that she had publicised the fact that the Kays slept in their anoraks!

By that time, however, spring and the real world of work and embassies, was just round the corner. We could get along now in Arabic and it was beginning to pay. Once, on a trip to Jordan, I paid a surprise visit to Palestinian friends in Bethlehem. '*Ahlan* – welcome! – We have been expecting you for a couple of days' they said. 'How could you, when I did not know myself that I was coming here'. 'Oh well, one of our neighbours saw a fair haired woman speaking Arabic at a petrol station in the Jordan valley a couple of days ago, so we knew you would come.'

We had also learnt to field the inevitable response of 'so you are at the spy school.' Even today, in Lebanon and Jordan, I still sometimes hear it. But our only known experience of it was one morning when all the teachers were in high spirits and mistakes were viewed benignly. Blake, a former student and convicted spy, had just escaped from prison in the UK. He was completely charming they assured us – who cared that he was spying for the wrong side? Once Patrick Seale asked me to warn Jolyon that people thought he was a spy, because he had previously worked at Harwell (the nuclear energy research establishment). Then Jolyon told me that people thought Patrick was a spy, because he worked as a journalist. I had worked at GCHQ but no one ever suggested I might be a spy. How could they, a fair-haired woman who spoke mountain Arabic.

A better memory than ours was keeping tabs on us too. Some ten years after we had left Shemlan, our original toddler went into the shop and was greeted by Eliyya Tabib with. 'Oh Delia how lovely to see you again'. 'I'm not Delia Rothnie, I'm Katty Kay' she replied somewhat indignantly. Only recently Anne Rothnie had kindly given Katty a dress that had been Delia's, the dress she was wearing that day.

Shirley Kay attended MECAS in 1965-67. She is the author of 15 books on the Middle East, numerous other travel guides and articles. Between 1986-89 she wrote and presented 18 documentary films for Dubai TV.

RIDING WITH
GLUBB'S GIRLS
1965-66

Michael Baddeley

I joined MECAS in August 1965, having completed my Arabic studies in Durham. The course was, unfortunately, unaccompanied (the Army only allowed wives to accompany husbands if the course exceeded a year) which was sad, as I had only recently got married to Barbara. But as luck would have it, this problem was resolved, for the Craigs (James and Margaret) who were in Beirut with the Embassy took Barbara on as a help in looking after their young family and I would bus down from MECAS to stay at weekends which was a real bonus and a welcome contrast to the arduous Arabic studies which occupied weekdays. They were very good to us both during those happy months we spent in Lebanon. With regard to MECAS, our Arabic teachers were practically all Lebanese who spoke English well. Just occasionally we were rewarded with the odd unforgettable howler which put us all in a good mood. I remember on one occasion the teacher concluded the lesson by saying: 'Now be sure to put your text books back into your pigeon's hole.' There was a teacher, I remember, called Fauzi Khouri who would be called upon to give us Arabic lessons. He had recently come to MECAS having previously been teaching at CALSAP in Aden. He was probably in his late twenties and had a hacking cough, which could be heard from some distance away, giving us due warning of his whereabouts. But this became somewhat confusing when we discovered he had acquired an African Grey parrot who would imitate his coughing bouts so realistically that we were unable to differentiate between the two. We mingled with the Foreign Office and civilian groups but the Service or Army group was taught separately from the others. David Gore-Booth and Adrian Fortescue were with us then and were looked upon as being among the elite of the Foreign Office intake. As the date for the final examination approached we were allowed to go on a mini-sabbatical to polish up our spoken Arabic. I chose to go to the Wadi Rumm in Jordan and George Wadia kindly drove Bill Fullerton and myself in his Land Rover. I remember we stayed on Christmas Eve at the Aqaba Hotel whence we moved on to the Wadi Rumm where I got out and left Bill and George to continue their journey elsewhere. There I lived in the *Beau Geste* fort surrounded by high mountains and breathtaking scenery. There were many interesting birds to study including the lammergeier, a somewhat rare winter visitor. My Arabic might have prospered more had I chosen to stay in a less remote, more suburban area. The topic of conversation was rather limited but the Bedu there taught me quite a lot about the local flora and fauna one might encounter.

The Bedu Guard – Glubb's Girls as they were called because of their specially-designed long cloaks which they wore when riding camels, their usual method of conveyance – told me why, for instance, foxes made messes on flat stones in the desert instead of on the sand. Such information, fascinated though I was to hear it, was hardly conducive to acquiring a high mark in the Civil Service Exam which I was due to take in a few weeks time on my return to Beirut. The last few days of my sabbatical were spent with the Ibn Al Aas Regiment at Zerqa where I was welcomed by the officers and invited to play chess with the Commanding Officer on most evenings. He won every time and was quite obviously much better than I. Curiously enough the Jordanian officers were under the impression that I contrived to lose and was just being diplomatic – 'It never pays to beat the Colonel' – and I did not attempt to disabuse them of this idea! My trip, which was organised by the British Defence Attaché in Jordan, also entailed my attempting to discover what state of readiness the Jordanian Army was in against foreign attack. My report, I remember, stated that it seemed to be fully capable and competent. When I finally returned to Beirut to be met by the Craigs and my beloved Barbara, James said to me 'You never got in touch to tell us how you were getting on. Poor Barbara was getting worried'. This was some forty years ago when the pristine solitude of the deserts of Jordan would have courted the approval of even that desert die-hard Wilfred Thesiger; But I dare say that the Wadi Rumm may well have a red post box and a telephone kiosk installed by that magnificent grey-stoned fort today.

Michael Baddeley, an army officer, attended MECAS in 1965-66.

THE NUPOSA
PROGRAMME FOR
US UNDERGRADUATES
1965-66

Benjamin Foster

The National Undergraduate Program for the Overseas Study of Arabic, funded, I believe, by the Carnegie Foundation, was intended for US undergraduates, with career interest in Arabic or the Middle East, who wanted to master Modern Standard Arabic in advance of beginning graduate work. It was administered by Princeton University; the Advisory Council included faculty from Michigan, Columbia, Portland State, Harvard, UCLA, and Princeton. The effective director was R. Bayly Winder, professor at Princeton and the mover and shaker of its Middle East Studies program. He had married the daughter of Philip K. Hitti and inherited from his father-in-law one of the most active and productive departments of Middle Eastern studies in America. Hitti had pioneered in America the teaching of Arabic as a modern, living language, in preference to the read-and-translate classical Arabic approach of most American departments. Winder had a spectacular office in the tower of Firestone Library and it was there he first recruited me, a timid sophomore, for the NUPOSA program.

Students could not apply, but were considered by nomination only. My nominator was Hanna Mikhail, as generous and talented an Arabic teacher as anyone could hope for, a native of Ramalla. Winder was an imposing presence, with a tendency towards pomposity, but was also encouraging and supportive. I was not by nature adventurous, in fact was retiring, rather self-absorbed, and happy under my comfortable paternal roof, so it took a good sell to make me think seriously about going to Lebanon, of which I knew nothing. I had, of course, never heard of Shemlan, and imagined a dusty, desolate place with an ancient church, rocky roads, and no trees, rather like a Roberts print of the Holy Land.

These were the balmy days of the National Defense Education Act (1958). This infused liberal and easy cash into the teaching and learning of 'critical' or 'less-taught' languages, including Arabic, Persian and Turkish. The United States goes through periodic crises of conscience when it finds that many Americans are not proficient in foreign languages deemed of political import at the time. NDFL (National Defense Language Program) was supposed to address that by making it attractive for young people to study languages the American government wanted its subjects to know. Participation in the NUPOSA program required an intensive summer course in Arabic before departure, in my case at the University of Michigan under the direction of Ernest McCarus and Raji Rammuny (summer of 1965). The former was an accomplished linguist and Arabist; the latter a former employee of the Jordanian Broadcasting company and a hard-working, first-rate teacher. McCarus was low-key whereas Rammuny put passion into the class. Ann Arbor, Michigan was hot and tiring in the summer. A good morale-builder was that Rammuny put Arabic music at intervals on the tapes in the language lab. The lab technology was limited, to the extent that the entire tape was played through from a central station, so you just had to tune in on it and listen to the whole, like airline earphone entertainment (in the Princeton lab we each had individual tapes; of course everything was better there). The people in the other courses soon tumbled to our special treat, so we developed a general signal when the music began, and everyone else would tune in, including the hirsute hippie types studying Pushtu in preparation for the Elysian fields of Afghanistan, then a destination for the laid-back in pursuit of poppies. I was fortunate that I had friends with me there, notably Jim Holman, whose grandparents had a house in Holland, Michigan, a resort town on the western shore of the state, and Fred Donner, later to become professor of Arabic at the University of Chicago. The Michigan program was top-flight and left us well prepared for MECAS. I was thus coming to MECAS with the equivalent of three years of Arabic study behind me.

Shemlan

The school, in good British fashion, stood aloof from the village. The village population was mostly Maronite Christians, whose church occupied a small square in the centre of the village. The priest was a jovial fellow with a bushy black beard and a very dubious servant. Shemlan was the home village of the Hitti family, and one night Winder took us to call on Philip Hitti's brother, who had been a minister in some Lebanese government. This old gentleman reminisced about his service in the Ottoman army in Palestine, quite fascinating for an American college student.

Like most other people, I had bouts of depression and discouragement and was sometimes laid low by the food and climate with the most acute pains in my stomach as though someone were boiling water in there, and minor convulsions. Did anyone escape this at MECAS? This plus rounds of keen homesickness made the first days of study a little grey. I was praised for my ability to read aloud but my colloquial accent was obviously painful even to experienced interlocutors. I decided to try my feet at mountain climbing.

Went down the road a piece and started in. Since the mountains have little shoulders and ridges I didn't realize where the top was until I got there. There was of course a magnificent view of the coast and Beirut and some spectacular though not really huge mountains to the southeast. Then I headed east and found myself face to face with an excellent view of several valleys and then a great range of purple mountains that I suspect must mark the frontier of the Syrian desert. I sat on a stone for a while contemplating that magnificent sight, with lots of hills and ridges between us with little villages caught in them like snow in the crotch of a tree. On the way back I ran into a gang of about six Lebanese urchins, the oldest about eleven, and the youngest two or so. After some initial this and that, I found them very friendly though I had problems understanding all of them but one, who was very articulate, and toward the end of the afternoon would address questions to me in classical. I had a long dissertation on religion, about Allah making men from clay and breathing life into them and the blessed savior. I watched a long re-enactment of a wrestling match and answered many questions about the USA as best I could – some were rather embarrassing. Wasn't the white man's pushing out the Indians like the Jews in Palestine? Why did they fight with the Indians? Have I ever seen a cowboy? What direction does the sun rise in America? Are the people rich? Are there mountains in the USA? Which is more beautiful, Lebanon or the USA? Which is harder, English or Arabic? They laughed at my periodic stammering, told me all about their father and his American car, wrestled violently, socking and kicking, but all in fun, etc. etc. I spent about three hours with them. It was very interesting and my first real human Lebanese contact...'

The Word List
The bane of everyone's existence was, of course, the famed MECAS wordlist of the 3,000 most commonly occurring words in Modern Standard Arabic. This was a departure from traditional English instruction, enshrined in Thatcher's grammar, where the vocabulary was a mixed bag, including such lexemes as *zuhd* 'abstinence', *kasir* 'ramping,' and *jalada* 'flog.' One translated lines like 'An astrologer was crucified and it was said to him: Did you see this in your star?' There was no short cut to mastering the MECAS list – where else in those more peaceful times would I learn Arabic for 'mine sweeper' and 'land mine'? There was a weekly word quiz and we soon learned that the English grading system was much more severe than its American counterpart. I memorized the list by folding a paper over each half of each column and writing in turn the English and Arabic words until I could do the whole column

twice without a mistake. It was a dreary routine and the book seemed awfully thick. By mid-September we were up to list IV. We had little pre-printed flash cards as well. But already in October I was fussing to myself, 'How can I possibly fill my bloated brain with so many words, words, words?'

The English Community

We were surprised by the English community. Some seemed to go out of their way to bait us. We were, however, so serenely convinced of our innate superiority that none of that really bothered us. There was an entity called the 'Thatcher Club' which collected trifling dues in order to maintain some magazine and newspaper subscriptions for the school lounge. As a great concession, Time Magazine was added to the roster, and I recall an English student named, I think, Tony Harris, he who later fell in love with the blonde American, holding it out to me disdainfully, as if I had some kind of responsibility for it by the unhappy accident of my birth, and saying something like 'Do you really consider this to be English?' The Brits, as we called them, ragged each other mercilessly as well, according to some social distinctions that were invisible to us. They were also fond of being rude to the food-serving staff, peering at a proffered dish with an elaborately sarcastic 'shu hadha?' (what's that?). I made no real friends among them. The older men mostly looked on us as a lower form of life, and were worried that somehow a round of mutually obligatory invitations would get us involved with them. A bright exception to this pattern was the Adams family. He was relaxed and friendly and his children were cute and delightful, with the exquisite manners and beautiful diction of their class. The younger Englishmen were pretty much impossible, condescending, or non-communicative. For example, I spent a delightful evening in a bar in Beirut with a Scottish banker in training for a branch in Abu Dhabi, and I don't think more than three syllables passed his lips in fifteen minutes, despite the free flow of alcohol. I doubt he enjoyed It either. I have forgotten nearly all their names. We soon learned that when you went to an English party, it was not polite to introduce yourself to strangers, the hostess was supposed to do it (even if she was not sure who you were), and that the diplomats left in order of rank. The highest-ranking was always pukka enough to leave early to make way for the others.

Professor Benjamin Foster attended MECAS in 1965-66. He pursued an academic career, most recently in the Department of Near Eastern Languages and Civilisation of Yale University.

Part Four
1966-78

NO COHABITATION IN THE OFFICERS' MESS 1966–68

Tony Reeve

In my era (1966-68) the school's car park was plentifully stocked with white Cortinas. Pam and I lived initially at *Bait Maalouf*, a charmless flat along the main road where the early morning Beirut-bound traffic, horns a-blazing, appeared to pass directly through the only bedroom. After a few months we retreated to the house of George Tabib, halfway up the hill behind Elia's shop. Life at *Bait Tabib* was quieter but the plumbing more uncertain. Our lives were ruled by those twin combustibles, *mazout* and *nerit*. Attempts to run the *mazout* stove on a more economical basis, by slowing down the drip, led to loud explosions, which filled the room with diesel fumes, threatening the well-being of our unborn child. When it rained, water dripped through the kitchen ceiling. We kept an umbrella alongside the stove in case of inclement weather.

From a perspective of nearly 40 years, my memories of school life that first autumn are of a seemingly endless succession of mellow, blue mornings. Once the early traffic had disappeared down the road to Aley, a profound silence descended, disturbed only slightly by the sweeping of a brush outside the open classroom windows. There were of course some flies in the ointment. Leslie McLoughlin's morning grammar lessons, where we wrestled with the mysteries of the diptote and tried, unsuccessfully, to piece together our broken plurals, provided a testing start to the day. Leslie's method was to lob questions at those spotted gazing out of the window. If, while gazing, you knew that *kaana* was a hollow verb or, even better, that the first person singular of *kaana* was *kuntu* – well and good, though Leslie would often slip you another poser later in the lesson, just to make his point. Pretty soon it became obvious that the Word Lists were forming a sand-bar which would require an exceptionally high tide. There were countless words impossible to remember without a mnemonic. The trouble was that, to take a couple of examples, 'D'ya read – newspaper, or 'Well, I see yer, Ma' for 'especially' (*jarida* and *wala siyamma*) were rather too approximate, when regurgitated in Arabic, to produce the pin-point accuracy required by Leslie; so re-takes of the word-lists were a not infrequent occurrence.

After the coffee break our tutors would loiter outside their respective rooms down the long corridor, awaiting their next customers with enticing smiles that would have done credit to the Reeperbahn.

Afternoons (when not re-taking the word lists) were spent largely on the Melkon tennis court or down in Beirut, stocking up with food and extraordinarily cheap liquor at the Lebanese Supply Company. In the evenings, often by the light of flickering oil lamps when the power had failed, we were treated to the thoughts of Joe Malone and other AUB luminaries on (and how right they were) The Crisis Still to Come. Or we descended on the nightclubs, or simply sat around drinking the cut-price gin while listening to Lennon & McCartney on our reel-to-reel tape recorders. Only gradually, as the need to master grammar and word lists grew more pressing, did it become apparent that some sustained academic effort was going to be required.

That first year, which culminated in June 67, seems now to belong to a different, and more benign era. My language break with Olga Wahbe, just a few yards from the de facto cease-fire line at Bait Jala near Bethlehem, was a civilised affair: excursions to the refugee camps where, in return for some Arabic conversation, young men (many of them doubtless long since dead) gratefully taught themselves to drive the Cortina; suppers with Olga's sisters and friends; visits to the neighbourhood Orthodox church to hear vespers. We left Jerusalem only a week before the Israelis swept in for good.

Evacuated from Shemlan while the war was gathering pace, we found ourselves in a makeshift MECAS at the officers' mess at Beaconsfield. Women had never set foot in the place before, let alone slept there; so it was, I suppose, to cushion the shock to male susceptibilities that Pam* and I were assigned separate rooms. The fresh-faced adjutant was embarrassed when he broke the news but firm on the unacceptability of cohabitation**. We were therefore mightily relieved to get back to *Bait Tabib* in the autumn and a few months later, after a midnight dash down the hill to the Khalidi clinic, to introduce our first-born to Shemlan society. For the rest of the advanced course I rather enjoyed being Abu James.

Twenty years later, when eventually appointed to Amman, I had an agreeable reminder of the old days. Constantine Theodory appeared from nowhere 'to pay my respects'. The great lexographer looked much older, his booming voice cracking a little under the strain of his uncertain English syntax, but he was still in excellent fettle, still radiating the affection he felt for all his students. When we parted, he kissed me wetly on both cheeks. And that was the last I saw of him. *Fi amaan allah, ya ustaaz!*

Sir Anthony Reeve KCMG, KCVO attended MECAS from 1966 to 1968. He was Ambassador to Jordan 1988-91 and High Commissioner (at first, Ambassador) to South Africa 1991-96.

---

* Several weeks later, after the port had circulated several times at dinner, the Adjutant explained to me that the problem with the Reeves concerned the batman bringing in the early morning tea. He would be embarrassed to find a lady in bed, whereas a batwoman delivering the tea to a lady would be equally put out to find a man there. I suggested that the batman and batwoman might deliver the tea together. The Adjutant, a Hussar in full dress uniform, stiffened visibly, shrugged his chain-mail epaulettes and turned a steely eye to what I imagined was a distant horizon, a small movement of a tiger, a signal flash or a puff of smoke? ... Answer came there none.

** At this time, wives of full-time Diplomatic Service students were offered the choice of a part-time course in Ladies' Colloquial Arabic or the opportunity to compete against their husbands on the Long (10-month) and Advanced (4-5 month) Courses. Pam Reeve was one of several wives who opted for the full-time training.

DEFENDING THE
SCHOOL 1967

Robert Walmsley

When the danger of an Arab/Israeli conflict increased towards the end of the week 22-27 May 1967, I considered whether precautions should be taken in the form of extra patrols, or asking for police protection, but decided against. A fairly powerful explosion then occurred at the US Embassy, while the international situation began to deteriorate. I decided on 27 May that precautions should be taken against the only kind of threat which seemed significant at that time, namely the deposit of bombs by a few fanatics or violent Arab Nationalists coming from outside Shemlan, as had happened on one occasion in 1956.

The security situation was seriously affected by the Egyptian allegation early on 6 June that British and American aircraft were assisting Israel. Demonstrators smashed windows in the Embassy during the morning and were not driven off until reinforcements arrived from 'Squad 16'. I saw the instructors at 8.30 am and said that we could not go against the Lebanese order for the closing of schools: they need not re-appear till Friday at the earliest.

Planning the Evacuation
I telephoned the Embassy in the morning and raised the question of extra police protection for the Centre. Meanwhile, I advised the married students that although the risk of attack in the village was small, it could not be ignored, and it would be worth keeping a bag

196

of essentials handy and knowing the best line of retreat. Any attack, of course, would come from outsiders; the Shemlanis were very well-disposed. The same evening the Embassy telephoned their view that I might consider moving the entire British staff and families down to a hotel or hotels where they would be concentrated and better protected. Nine of the eleven American students took off from the airport that evening or at dawn next day.

The next morning (Wednesday, 7 June), a reliable informant reported that two persons in the next village whom he knew to be reliable, but who did not want their names to be mentioned, said that they had overheard adherents of Kemal Jumblatt talking in a taxi the previous day about a plan to 'shoot at' and 'blow up' the Centre. (Such a conversation in a public place was not surprising in the atmosphere at the time.) In view of this and the still further deteriorating situation, I telephoned Mr Craig in the Embassy who agreed that the time had come to move students and families to Beirut. He said that families should come prepared to evacuate direct from Beirut if necessary. I informed the students at 11.00 am and they then had to pack one suitcase (about 44lb), leaving the rest to to be stored in their room or house. Goods in the houses would eventually be removed to the Centre for storage and forwarding. Lists of contents were made.

Most people left by mid-afternoon, but the last only just in time to arrive before dark. The route was by the side-road, via Shweifat, Khalde and the coastal motorway. Accommodation was in two hotels, the Mayflower and The Orient Prince. I stayed the night myself with the owner of the Melkon Hotel, a few hundred yards from the Centre: my wife went to Beirut under protest. On this day the Lebanese Government announced the stoppage of oil supplies to the USA and Britain, and that it was 'considering' breaking relations. Egyptian allegations of US/British complicity continued to be very widely publicised. The denial received very little notice.

Big Demonstrations Expected
At noon on Thursday, 8 June, after the defeat of Egypt and Jordan was clear, the Embassy considered that although the situation was better, it was only slightly better And there was still a risk to British

lives and property: this was the unanimous view of all concerned. The Embassy thought it premature to decide on a return to Shemlan. On this day the Lebanese Government decided to expel the British and American Ambassadors, though not to break relations.

The Lebanese guard at the Centre on the evening of Friday, 9 June, was reduced to two, both of whom were discovered asleep by Mr Green on a round at dawn the next day.

President Nasser announced his resignation on Friday evening. Next morning, and long before he withdrew it, the Embassy said it was out of the question for students to return to Shemlan: big demonstrations were expected, all British subjects should keep off the streets, and the Embassy was being put in a state of siege. Two of Spinney's shops had been attacked in the night, and the British Bank in Tripoli ransacked.

We then considered the erection of some defence along the wholly unprotected side of the Centre, facing down a slope to the main road. A high wire fence could not have been erected in time. Mr Green suggested, and supervised with admirable efficiency, the making of a low-wire entanglement, strands of barbed wire criss-crossed between posts about 20' above ground, with old cans strung on them to give the alarm. Mr Green, Mr Shepherd and Mr Nixon, with the gardener, hacked down bushes over a wide belt to clear the skyline. The iron stakes and wire and old cans (salvaged by Landrover from a nearby rubbish-dump arrived by about 2.00 pm and by 4.00 pm a belt about 75 yards long by several yards deep had been protected, covering the two normal footpath approaches up the slope. The school houseboys assisted with zest and surprising skill. Much was also owed to George Tabib, the village carpenter, who procured materials at times when all the shops were shut and who handled barbed wire with his bare hands for choice.

Weapons available were two iron bars and unlimited rocks. The gendarmes' rifles were a doubtful asset. Since we ourselves had no firearms, the question of instructions about these did not arise.

Three Bursts of Automatic Fire
On Sunday 11 June, the Lebanese authorities imposed a drastic curfew, lifted only between 9 and 11 am and 5 and 7 pm. All

assemblies of over five people were forbidden. Any cars with slogans or carrying shouting passengers would be confiscated. There were no reports of incidents on that day. The Macaskill family was allowed to move up from Beirut to Suq el-Gharb, and my wife returned also in the morning.

At 2.30 pm on 2 July there were three bursts of automatic fire from the direction of Ahmed Shukairy's house, overlooking Shemlan from about three-quarters of a mile away. All the electricity in the neighbourhood was cut. The least unnatural presumption is that some madman loosed off at an electricity pylon. The Shemlan Municipality was excited into action by this and made strong representations to the gendarmerie in Aley for the removal of Ahmed Shukhairy's followers.

The late Robert Walmsley CMG was Director of MECAS from 1965 to 1969. Under the pseudonym of Nicholas Roland, he published several novels, one of which described the adventures of an ancient colony of Stylite monks, not dissimilar from his own students in Shemlan. These extracts are taken from a detailed 9-page account of the 1967 evacuation forwarded by Mrs Frances Walmsley.

A SUMMER WITH
THE MILITARY 1967

Paul Tempest

On the second day of the June 1967 war, we were instructed to abandon our belongings and cars and to stand by for evacuation from Shemlan – first to be tucked away discreetly in two small hotels in Beirut and then by air to Athens and on to London. There were touching scenes at Beirut Airport, when we discovered that the aircraft carrying us to safety had just brought back a full plane-load of our American friends, who had been told that the danger was over.

We were to continue our studies in the cloistered summer calm of an Oxford or Cambridge college. By the time we reached London, the Foreign Office (or perhaps HM Treasury) had had second thoughts and settled for an army camp at Beaconsfield.

For the few of us who had already enjoyed Army hospitality during two years of National Service, there was the prospect of observing how the rest might react to military discipline and acute discomfort. So it was with mixed feelings that one blazing early July day, almost eight years after joining the Bank of England and thirteen after joining the Royal Corps of Engineers, I reported to the guardroom of the Royal Army Education Corps, Beaconsfield and, with a case in each hand and my word-cards and dictionaries in my haversack, staggered up the half-mile drive.

Prep with a Prince

The RAEC surprised all of us. Shorn of wives, children and babies, with most of our clothing and belongings two thousand miles away, and quite unable to find anything to match the distractions of Beirut nightlife and the Lebanese countryside, one or two of us learned more useful Arabic there than in the previous nine in the Lebanon. We had a team of experienced Arabic teachers from the London University School of Oriental and African Studies, but most important, we were placed under military discipline, parading for daily word-tests, spot vivas and frequent exams. Everything, including Arabic, seemed to be done at the double.

The Royal Army Education Corps had, of course, no assault bridging, tanks, armoured cars, field guns, heavy artillery or other paraphernalia of modern warfare. Schoolmasters in fact need little more than a sharp pencil and a well-directed piece of chalk. But what the RAEC did have at that time, learning Russian, his Aston Martin parked every day and most evenings on the Officers' Mess forecourt, was his Royal Highness, Prince Michael of Kent.

I have no idea how the RAEC behave normally, but I suspect the presence of royalty had not been entirely without effect. The whole place gleamed with whitewash, polish and order. Whole regiments drilled to and fro across the parade-ground. Buglers wakened us at reveille and reminded us to get on with prep at sundown. Campaign and gallantry medals were worn at dinner where there was ample wine and port, some excellent food and a constant variety of regimental ritual. While we were there, a new tower block was opened, appearing to tilt or wilt slightly to one side and providing brand-new sporting and drinking facilities.

The Commanding Officer and Adjutant were not a little perturbed by the arrival of a motley rabble of civilian MECAS refugees. We were lectured, cajoled, implored to smarten ourselves up. Several senior diplomats were instructed to get their hair cut. Bankers and oilmen were told not to slouch along behind the CO's parade, nor to sit watching it on the ornamental cannon.

Just Breaking in, Sir

The nadir of our military adventures came on the third Monday morning. I cannot remember whether the train from St Pancras was on time or not. What was evident as it worked its way slowly out of the north-west suburbs was that, if we got off at Beaconsfield and walked through the town, along the main road and up the drive, we were definitely going to be late. However, we had observed from the previous week that the railway ran quite close to the back of the camp and that the train made a short stop at a halt nearby. We therefore disembarked to a man. Between us and our objective lay several heavily overgrown fields belonging to the army and currently unused.

We scaled the first fence quite easily. But the undergrowth was worse than we had imagined. Here and there the brambles were head-high. It had rained most of the weekend. The foliage was sodden. Soon, so were we. One sector consisted of a series of overgrown flooded slit trenches into which we fell.

Finally, only a few yards from our objective, we were faced with a high barbed wire fence. We were already late. Summoning all our combined energy, wit and courage, we mounted an infantry assault worthy of the Gloucesters. Torn, bleeding, caked in mud and trailing briars, we dropped down into the compound and straggled towards the classroom. There, outside the entrance, walking up and down, impatiently, but still in step, were the Adjutant, the Regimental Sergeant-Major, who had turned brick-red, and the Commanding Officer himself, waiting to inspect the entire garrison drawn up on the parade ground. I cannot record precisely those few and – as I remember – terse and unappreciative words which passed between us.

Paul Tempest attended MECAS from 1966 to 1968 and again for a month's refresher in 1974. He was employed by the Bank of England from 1959 to 1981, including a secondment as General Manager of the Qatar and Dubai Currency Board (1970-71). He went on to two years in the World Bank, Washington, six with Shell International, London and eight as Director-General of the World Petroleum Permanent Council. He is currently Vice-President of the British Institute of Energy Economics and the Director and CEO of the Windsor Energy Group.

I cannot record precisely those few and - as I remember - terse and unappreciative words which passed between us

"...hanging the carcase for butchering from the tree in the front..." see page 207

Drawings by Dennis Denahy

ARAK, LABNEH AND LAMB

The Consequences of a Language Break in the Valley of the Grapes 1967-68

Paul Tempest

Shortly after our return to the Lebanon in September 1967 following our two-month evacuation on bachelor status to Beaconsfield, UK, I found myself again abandoning my wife and infant son (then seven months old). The Advanced Course language break lasted just short of three weeks. Thanks to some dedicated reconnoitring by the Chief Instructor, Leslie McLoughlin, I was assigned to the Wadie al-Arayish, a Christian Maronite village close to Zahle in the Beka'a valley.

The approach to the village is dramatic: up a steep, narrow, twisting gorge skirting many waterfalls and cascades to arrive at a scattering across the mountainside of small white box-like houses, many reached by steps and steep footpaths. Beyond, in the west, at the head of the valley brooded the snow-capped mass of Mount Sannine.

There was a warm, kind welcome from the extended family – Youssef Suliman Hariqa, his wife Therese, their two young children, Youssef's younger brother and two sisters, all of whom slept on the floor and benches in the living room while I was given the double-bed in the only other room in the house. No amount of remonstration would deflect them from this arrangement.

In the first week, a daily routine was established with breakfast of labneh, fruit and hot, fresh, crisp mountain bread at 8.00, followed by attendance at the village school at 9.00 consisting of daily *imla* (dictation) and arithmetic sitting with the 8-9 year-olds and followed by singing and games.

The weather was unsettled and the vendange in full swing, so the first afternoons were spent climbing steeply up narrow tracks to an extensive plateau where the vineyards were located. We all worked hard harvesting the grapes.

The Linguistic Effects of Arak
Before I had embarked on this rash adventure of pressurised language-learning*, I had taken the precaution of asking an elderly Knight of the Realm and former British Ambassador for some sound advice. 'Ideally', he had patiently explained, I should follow the view of our greatest British oriental linguist of all time, Sir Richard Burton**. To achieve fluency to an acceptable standard, he had insisted, it would be

---

*At MECAS, I was told, we would be graded in four categories:
1. *mumtaz* (excellent); 2. *tayyib* (good, but implying we could do much better); 3. *yaani* (OK perhaps but conveying doubt and carrying a warning that we had to do very much better); 4. *wallahi* (May God help us!). No student was ever told he was *mumtaz* in case he or she became complacent or lazy. Those graded *wallahi* knew they were already into the process of being rapidly recycled elsewhere in the Middle East or sent home. The results of the fortnightly word-tests and end-of-term exams were posted on the Centre notice-board at a known hour. However, it was impossible for a student to get anywhere near, given the press of the wives, all busily comparing the results. Repeated failure meant being sent home in disgrace with a career in tatters. On the upside, but barely perceived at the time, was the probability that survival would be accompanied by a life-long love and respect for the Islamic world, with the additional bonus that, if eventually admitted to Paradise, one would have at least a smattering of the local language.

**Sir Richard Burton (1821-1890) spent much of his time travelling on Government service in India, Africa, the Middle East and North and South America. One translation story of his was the occasion in India, when he had been selected to interpret for General Napier at a *durbar* for the local Princes. The General spoke for about half-an-hour non-stop in English on the reasons why the British presence in India was necessary to protect the Indians from the Russians. Burton fell asleep and was wakened by a sharp prod as the General sat down beside him. 'Burton, translate!' he ordered. Burton got up, went to the rostrum, spoke for 45 seconds and returned to his seat.
'Damned concise language! ' remarked the General. 'Yes, sir' Burton replied.
'But what did you say?' asked the General. Burton paused.
'I said, Sir: "The Big Man has spoken and you must obey!"'

necessary to fall deeply in love with an attractive, intelligent and gentle local maiden, absorbing sub-consciously through each night her cadences and rhythms, her grunts and her moans, her chatter and her cries. Alternatively, but less effective, was the need to sink each evening into alcoholic oblivion in an environment where no English was spoken. As, clearly, the former was, for me, a newly and happily married man, completely out of the question, the latter became an urgent imperative.

This was no problem at all in the village. Each evening, we gathered in the village houses or the school hall to consume the ultimate product of our labours, the local, home-made arak, about 80% proof diluted with water to form an apparently harmless, milky-coloured liquid, which, after one tumbler, greatly enhanced fluency; after two, it fully removed most inhibitions and after three, consciousness itself. Before ten, we had been taken gently home and put to bed.

A Memorable Party

At the end of the break I invited the entire village back to a party in our house in Shemlan. The journey by rented coach takes about two-and-a-half hours and we had no idea how many, if any, would come. About forty arrived in a coach followed by various taxis and cars. They came laden with home-made arak and enough grapes to give each of the 20 or so course students and other guests a one-kilo bunch on departure. We had warned the village restaurant that we might need large quantities of grilled chicken, *mezze* and pitta bread and these were duly delivered. Our large, warm, comfortable and beautifully furnished house in the centre of Shemlan became a seething party spilling out on to the long pillared balcony and the patio and garden terraces of olives and fruit trees. Entertainment included a form of karaoke, *aoud* (Arabian lute) playing, *dabke* dancing and sword dancing using the razor-sharp swords taken from our walls, and course croquet played to the local Tempest rules. A very good time – with mercifully no injuries or damage – was had by all. Jennifer has often remarked that the lethal mixture of our whisky and their arak produced an astonishing effect which she has never experienced before or since.

Off to Australia

Six years later, in 1974 on a month's refresher at MECAS, I took fellow-students Derek Plumbly, Peter Iseman and Kathy Vignos back to the Wadie al Arayish. Again the whole village turned out and the tables were laden with roasted sheep, mountains of rice and the full range of the Lebanese *mezze*. A notable feature of the photographs we took was the line of blue plastic Domestos bleach bottles placed down the centre of each table and used for water to dilute the arak.

There was a big surprise. Youssef and Therese and family had toyed with emigrating to Australia and had asked me to give a reference and help with the paperwork. They had gone. For about four years I corresponded and exchanged photographs with an address in a Melbourne suburb. Then they moved abruptly and we had just moved into our present house. We lost contact.

A Well-Remembered Family

It was another ten years before Shell International despatched me on my first visit to Australia. We landed at Melbourne Airport on a Sunday morning and I hired a car and drove immediately to the old Hariqa address. The street was full of life with children playing, much clipping of hedges and tinkering with motor-cars. The house I was looking for was boarded up; but visits to the neighbours produced inimitable Australian hospitality freshened with ice-cold tinnies and a warm stream of memory.

'Yes', I was told, they and grandma all remembered the Lebanese family. They were the ones who kept sheep in the back-garden and slaughtered one each holiday, hanging the carcase for butchering from the tree in the front and, on the last occasion, ramming the entrails and bones down the main storm-drain of the street, causing blockages, floods and an appalling smell.

Despite a visit to Melbourne City Hall and various enquiries in local Lebanese restaurants, I never managed to find the family. I must try again. Somewhere out there, they will be tending their sheep and goats, perhaps growing their own grapes and vegetables, gazing at the star-spangled sky, and thinking, most probably, of their old home.

VISITING KUWAIT AND BAGHDAD 1971

Peter Clark

I decided to look up friends Ahmad in Kuwait and Ilham in Baghdad, so I drove to Damascus and took a plane to Kuwait. I booked into a cheap hotel, and wandered around the town, spending afternoons on the balcony of the oldest hotel in Kuwait, Funduk al-Jazira al'Arabiyya, built in 1946. I caught up with Ahmad, who was head of the Kuwait Planning Board. He was a bright as ever and asked about Beirut. 'People from the Gulf no longer go to Lebanon to enjoy themselves,' he told me. 'There are too many of our friends, family and neighbours there. We go to Athens instead.'

Kuwait was far more interesting than I had anticipated. I talked to anyone, and met Syrians, Yemenis and Palestinians. I sailed on a dhow to the island of Failaka, the price of the ticket including a communal meal eaten off a reed mat on the deck of the boat. I enjoyed the variety of communities, Arab, Iranian and South Asian, who made up the working population. I was fascinated by the museum illustrating the life and work of the pearl fishers.

Baghdad

I moved on. I found my way to the *service* station early one morning and took a shared taxi to the Iraqi border. Then another car took me on to Baghdad, at great speed, through the Marshes, 'Amara and Kut and reached the capital in the middle of the afternoon. In Baghdad I stayed with Gail and David Wright. David had been Administrative Officer at MECAS and was now doing commercial work in the Embassy. Their house was my base for a few days.

I now set off in search of Ilham. I had a telephone number and an address. The former did not work and locating houses that matched addresses in the Najab Pasha quarter was not straightforward. I eventually found Ilham's mother, who directed me to the Centre for Petroleum Studies, and there I met Ilham.

I showed off my Arabic, which amused her greatly.

'What a cute Lebanese accent you've got. You say *kuwayyis* [good] and *muta'assif* [sorry] and *min fadlak* [please].'

'That's what I've been taught. What am I supposed to say, then?'

'*Zain* and *aasif* and *rajaan*.'

'Well, I'll try while I'm here, but they'll laugh at me back in Lebanon if I use them there.'

'Come to a party on Sunday evening with some of my friends.'

And what a party that was. Just before sunset we boarded a boat and sailed down the Tigris to Jazirat al-Khanazir, the Island of Pigs. There were 20 or 30 of us, friendly sympathetic people. Among them were, I noted, men and women, Muslims, Christians and Jews; people whose first language was Arabic, Turkish and Kurdish. We landed after dark on the island that was unoccupied and uninhabited. By the river some of my new friends got a fire going. They circled the fire with sticks and a few plaice-like fish were skewered on to the sticks: *mazgouf*. Food, conversation, laughter, games, music and dancing: this was not the grim Iraq I had been led to expect.

The following day I had to return westwards. I took the Nairn bus to Damascus. 'A long bus for passengers is attached to an articulated lorry. It is air-conditioned inside, with small windows, tunnel-like and resembles the inside of an aeroplane,' I noted in my diary. Then over the desert – Falluja, cross the Euphrates at Habbaniyya, and on and on to Rutba. Leaving Rutba and Iraq was no trouble, but the entry into Syria at Khan Abu Sham took three pitiless hours, between 1 and 4 in the morning. Damascus by mid-day.

Syria

I collected my car and decided to wander off north of Damascus, without any clear objective. There were always people hitching lifts. I picked people up, imposed my Arabic on them, remembering to drop *zain* and *aasif,* and to revert to *kuwayyis* and *muta'assif.* I took people to Rankus and was invited in for lunch. I went on to Yabrud and was invited by a teacher to stay the night.

Next morning the teacher, Abd al-Rahman, showed me round the village. It was a summer resort, two-thirds Muslim, one-third Christian. The hospital was provided by Yabrudis who had migrated to Brazil. A stream flowed through the courtyard of the mosque. Roman masonry formed part of the fabric of the church. Back at the house, my hosts asked if I would take a startlingly attractive young relation, Bushra, back to Damascus. I agreed, surprised at the trust given to me.

'Bushra is seventeen and Muslim. Her father is dead,' my 1971 diary records. 'She admires the easier relations between the sexes in the West and is impatient about many traditions. Her brother is a soldier and there is a plan to marry her off to a cousin. She would like to travel, and to study French at the university. She is very outspoken, relaxed and friendly. I enjoy talking to her immensely. It is very hard for the likes of me to get to know the likes of her.'

And this was the beginning of a beautiful friendship. I met her mother and her sibs and kept in touch with Bushra who married the following year, but not to her cousin. Nor did she go to the university and study French. Through the 1970s and 1980s I often visited Damascus and would always see her, her husband (who had a clothes store in Bab al-Barid near the Umayyad Mosque) and her growing family. When I went to live and work in Damascus 21 years after first meeting her, I became part of Bushra's extended family. And on the last night of my five years' residence in Syria, I stayed with Bushra and her family. Bushra is now a grandmother.

I stayed on for a day or two in Damascus. Someone at MECAS had told me of an experimental play by an angry young Syrian playwright and I secured a ticket to see it at the Qabbani Theatre. The play was a Brechtian piece called *An Evening's Entertainment for the Sake of 5 June* and the author was Sa'dallah Wannus. The play started with the recorded voice of Nasser after the 1967 war. The play was a challenge to the lies of official propaganda, statements that contradicted people's everyday experience.

That evening sowed the seed, though I knew it not at the time, of another friendship. When I re-opened the British Council in Syria in 1992, I got to know Sa'dallah, read his plays – and translated one of them – and took every opportunity to see any performance of them. During the 1990s he was slowly dying from cancer. The illness turned an otherwise morose personality into a man who valued life and creativity. He was writing right up to the end, challenging the illiberalism, oppression and hypocrisy of the contemporary Arab world with savage humour. He died a few days before I left Syria in 1997 and I wrote his obituary for *The Guardian*.

Dr Peter Clark OBE attended MECAS in 1970-71. He was the Representative of the British Council in Damascus in 1992-97. His 11-page memoir recounts his experiences in the Middle East before his studies in Shemlan and subsequent experiences in Iraq and Syria.

A BOMB AND A
DOUBLE FUNERAL
1970

Ann Hopkins

As we had promised some Durham Course people a picnic, I
drove them away on Sunday, leaving poor John in bed with a
migraine and taking no notice of anything, until forced to do so by
a frightful wailing and screams just below his window. Women
were writhing on the ground and emitting that piercing screech
peculiar to Arabs; huge crowds had gathered and the commotion
was extreme. Munir and Rosetta's mother had died and was to be
buried that day we knew. She was Assad Hitti's sister and he came
down to see the body in the coffin against advice and fell dead in
the road at the sight of it being taken from the hearse, which of
course caused the uproar and distress. He was taken in the hearse
to the doctor at Souk, where he was said to be dead. They therefore
cancelled the first funeral in favour of a double one the next day,
the first in living memory and of immense length and pomp,
attended by professional chanters and a brass band from Aley.

John came home at lunch on Monday with the news that your
old house was evacuated temporarily, while they dismantled the

bomb found at the gate to the mountain by your back-door.

The Bomb Disposal Squad was called. They arrived at lunch-time and pronounced it a dangerous one, containing 10 kg of gelignite plus two bombs and a brand new watch set for 3.00 pm and ticking smartly. It was, by all accounts, a sophisticated and well-constructed affair, capable of causing considerable damage, but had been placed so as to do rather little. It was only just on the mountain side of the fence and would have blown out the *Mudir's* windows, but not much more. It rather looked as if it were meant to be discovered.

The following letter was written in Shemlan on Friday, 13 March 1970 by Ann Hopkins, wife of John Hopkins, Principal Instructor at MECAS 1968-70. It was addressed to Frances and Robert Walmsley (Director 1965-69). Dr John Hopkins before and after his stint at MECAS was a lecturer in Arabic at Cambridge University.

KIDNAPPED IN
BEIRUT 1973

John Doble

In April 1973 the Israelis murdered four Palestinian leaders in their beds in the middle of Beirut, including the elderly head of the Lebanese/Palestinian Friendship Association, who intervened whenever tensions arose between the Lebanese and the large Palestinian refugee population. I believe the Israelis wanted a confrontation which would result in the eviction of Palestinian 'terrorists'. Soon after, a confrontation occurred with the kidnapping of Lebanese senior army NCO's by Palestinians. There was a lot of fighting, even raids by the Lebanese air force on refugee camps.

In early May there was the first of many cease-fires. I drove out to see how it was holding and, as a result, the Ambassador sent a telegram to the FCO. The next day, Saturday, I had to go into the Embassy. On the way home, I wanted to listen to the Cup Final and 2000 Guineas on my car radio (clearer than the one in my house) and thought I would drive round a more extensive area, to see what the situation was. It was a lovely day. My thoughts were half in Newmarket. At a roundabout near the Sabra/Chatila camps, I took the wrong exit.

At once I saw my mistake. There was a road-block with a mass of armed men. I reversed into a side-entrance to turn. They signalled for me to stop. I had to decide whether to race away, possibly knocking people over, getting shot in the process, or to stop. I stopped, was hauled out of the open MG and led beyond the road-block, as the car was driven off. I was led into the ground-floor room of a modern high-rise block, where lots of other people were also waiting for questioning. I was taken into an office and all my belongings (watch, diary etc) were taken off me and I was briefly questioned as to who I was and why I was there. I was then returned to the outer office.

After a long time waiting, I decided I should not allow myself to be detained in this way. When the man in the inner office was free, I walked in, saw my possessions still on his desk and picked up my diplomatic card and said politely:

'You've no right to hold me here. I have explained why I was in this area. I am a diplomat here. The time has come for me to go.'

At this he seized the card, tore it in half (I still have the two halves as a souvenir), saying:

'We don't recognise diplomats here, only human beings.'

And gave me a hard clout on the side of the head, knocking me down and leaving my ear singing and oozing liquid for days. I was returned to the outer office under guard.

Eventually he questioned me at length. As an ex-Army officer it occurred to me that I should refuse to answer anything but name and rank. But I was not a prisoner-of-war and there seemed no harm, possibly some use, in talking to one of the Palestinian terrorist/freedom fighters, whom normally we did not meet. My job was open and innocent; my sympathies already very much with the Palestinians. But clearly he thought I was a spy. He questioned me precisely on which building in London I worked in (they clearly knew where MI6 HQ was) and whether I worked for a man in the Embassy, who was the MI6 station head. I said that he was just a colleague in chancery.

Finally, I was taken down to the basement where lots of people were being held. A poor, scruffy man was turfed out of a little room (10' x 6') and I was chucked in, with one disgusting Chinese blanket. A light was burning all the time. Of course I wondered how long I would be there and if would ever emerge: only six weeks before three diplomats had been shot dead at a party at the Saudi Residence in Khartoum. Through a grating in the ceiling, I heard people working the bolts of firearms, possibly just cleaning them.

There I stayed for two and a half days, expecting, of course, that it would be a lot longer. I was given a bottle of water each day and twice a day some Arabic bread and jam or olives. My big fear was diarrhoea. So I ate and drank sparingly, using much of the bottle to give myself an all-over wash. Twice a day, I was led out to a foul latrine. I worked out how I would pass the time. I decided to do exercises and walk round and round the cell, having worked out how many circuits necessary to do a mile. I imagined going on walks in my favourite areas at home, trying to remember every tiny detail of the landscape and vegetation. My Christian faith helped. I prayed and tried to recite some of my favourite hymns and prayers from the Book of Common Prayer. I did not worry much about myself, although I did about how my disappearance must be upsetting my family. When one is totally helpless and can do nothing whatever about one's fate, it seemed to me a sort of fatalism set in, coupled with faith. There is no point in worrying, so one doesn't.

One remark of my interrogator had been somewhat ominous when he asked why I had driven there. I replied that I had wanted to see what was going on. He commented: 'Curiosity kills the cat.'

No one ill-treated me or spoke to me. I heard no sound of others in the basement being ill-treated, although when being taken out to the latrine, I saw some sticks and clubs leaning against a wall

Eventually (early Monday afternoon) I was led back up to the same man in the same office. I thought – More questioning. He was smiling, while he had been grim before. I thought of nice/nasty questioning techniques. To my amazement, he said I was to be released. He had on his desk all my possessions. He wanted me to go through them carefully and to ensure that nothing was missing. They had been extremely suspicious of some c.1945 vintage detailed British army maps of Syria in the car, which I had had purely for a Christmas trip to Aleppo. They had seemed unconvinced, although I pointed out that if I had been on some intelligence mission, I would hardly have had maps 30 years out-of-date. I noticed later that my watch had had its back forced open with a sharp object: they had obviously examined it for possible communications equipment.

All smiles, the interrogator said my car was at the door ready for me to drive away. I should check it too, to see that all was OK. I then had the extraordinary experience of driving at speed through Beirut with escort vehicles bristling with gun men in front and behind, to some Lebanese army camp, where I was handed over to Tony Cawston, our Defence Attache, who had to sign for me (a note I still have) as if for a piece of equipment.

After a few days in the Residence, I went back to the UK on leave (I had been in Beirut for eleven months). While there, I saw James Craig and others in the FCO. It was decided I should never return to the Middle East. The PLO knew me and would always be liable to pick me up again.

No blame seemed to be attached to me for what had occurred, although the episode resulted in large part from my foolishness. Indeed the Ambassador, Paul Wright, a lovely man, seems to have wanted to use the incident to develop conversations with the Palestinians; this was not allowed by FCO. His obituary says this – but there is more in his autobiography, *A Brittle Glory* (1986).

I was devastated, as I loved the area, the work, the people and also my house – I had got back a glorious old house in an olive grove on a steep slope above Pigeon Rocks, which had been the British Consul's house pre-1914.

As I have found elsewhere, disaster can turn out for the best. Had it not been for that affair, I would have served repeatedly in the area and retired in 2001 with a life largely spent on an issue that was worse than ever. As it was, I spent eleven and a half years in Africa, being involved with the Rhodesian and South African changes: an immensely interesting, enjoyable experience.

How and why was I released so soon? Being a bachelor, no one knew I was missing until Monday. That morning a Palestinian walked into the Embassy. One of our people was being held. He had noticed me, as I was wearing a suit and tie, unlike all the other mass of people there. The Embassy at once contacted the Lebanese

Government who contacted Yasser Arafat, saying he must not hold diplomats.

Then the Palestinians valued their sanctuary in the Lebanon so much that they complied and released me. A few years later, it would probably have been different. Almost as soon as I was released, fighting worse than ever started again. So, possibly, that Palestinian saved my life. He had wanted to go to Berlin and HMG arranged this with the Germans. Being grateful to him, I sent a glossy book on Britain with a thank-you letter to him, having found out his address in Berlin. I received a brief letter of thanks. After retirement, I thought it would be interesting to follow up this fellow and get to know him. But, given the complications, suspicions and dangers of the Middle East situation, I decided not to.

John Doble OBE attended MECAS in 1973, while he was a member of the British Embassy, Beirut. He was a Captain in the 17th/21st Lancers before joining the Diplomatic Service. He was appointed High Commissioner to Swaziland 1996-99.

NOTHING LIKE A
GOOD ARGUMENT
1973

Rex Baker

For me, one of the abiding memories of MECAS was the courteous tolerance shown by the Lebanese whenever they were subjected to our practising Arabic. Only once was I rebuffed; by an assistant in a smart Beirut shop who refused to respond to my overtures in Arabic, which she described haughtily as *'la langue du peuple'.* There were, however, constraints, not least of which was the limited range of topics around which to build polite conversation. Moreover, it was not only the paucity of our vocabulary, at least in the early stages, but often the very politeness of our interlocutors which made it difficult to sustain a dialogue. What was lacking, in my view, was emotion, particularly the sort of emotion induced by argument. After several months at MECAS I had reached a level of competence which enabled me to write short but reasonable essays on international relations and even to translate Bertrand Russell into Arabic. When it came to speaking, however, I found it no easy matter to engage in conversation. And even when I succeeded, I had little to say. Until the Jehovah's Witnesses called at our flat!

At home in Britain, such visits had been irksome and embarrassing. But these two charming young Lebanese gentlemen prevailed upon me to let them have their say. I hold fairly orthodox Christian beliefs. To me, the tenets of the Witnesses, though sincerely held and meticulously defended, are implausible, even outrageous. So we plunged into theological argument ... in Arabic.

They spoke no English. It was a vigorous debate and my tongue was loosened. The emotion aroused by our differences and my eagerness to refute what for me were absurd contentions dissolved the language barrier. Maybe not linguistically, but, more importantly, psychologically. I was using Arabic not as a channel for polite chatter or commercial convenience, but as an instrument for argument, persuasion, intellectual cut and thrust. There was nothing tentative or artificial in my wielding of the language. For the first time it was for real. They did not convert me but I am grateful to those young men for helping me to introduce a strong element of genuine feeling into my discourse. There's nothing like a good argument to get the tongue wagging, in whatever language.

Rex Baker OBE attended MECAS in 1972-74. He was British Council Representative in Baghdad 1974-78, in the Sudan 1978-80 and in Sri Lanka 1984-90.

'A MIXED BUNCH'
1973-75

Brian Stewart

We were a mixed bunch, that 1973 Long Course. The previous generation were all embarked on the Higher Course and seemed infinitely wise. When we moved on to the Higher course we were joined by the serious Arabists who had already done years of university study and knew their way around the region. Edward Chaplin (now Ambassador in Baghdad), tall and slightly aloof. Mark Allen, who turned up with hawks, which he kept on his bedroom balcony. A regular supply of day-old chicks from some poultry farm kept them fed, and Mark would disappear with them at the weekends to go hunting with Bedouin friends in the desert east of the Jebel Druze. Years later, on camping trips from Damascus out towards Qasr al Heir and Deir ez-Zor, we would occasionally encounter Bedouin who – once they knew we were British, and from the Embassy – immediately asked if we knew 'Mark', and enquired after his health.

The pressure on the FCO to economise, and the debate over the cost and viability of MECAS – to which we were oblivious – had stimulated a drive to bring in more private and 'foreign' students. So we found ourselves alongside Canadian and Australian diplomats, British bankers, Japanese businessmen, even Americans (were they really employees of oil or cigarette companies?). Many went on to illustrious and incident-filled professional careers in the region. John Woods, as First Secretary in the Australian Embassy in Cairo, was in the line of fire on the rostrum when assassins sprayed bullets into President Sadat, and narrowly survived thanks to emergency surgery and medevac to Frankfurt. Dave Richards became, I think, Australian Trade Commissioner in Cairo. Terry and Jill Collins Williams proved that the Canadian Ministry of External Affairs follows as perverse a postings policy as the FCO: MECAS training has led them to postings in Tokyo, Ottawa and Geneva. Gunter Mulack is renowned as one of the leading Arab-world experts in the Auswärtiges Amt. Werner Michel completed his career as Swiss Ambassador in Libya.

Once we had got through the initial period of grimacing, throat-clearing noises and other sound effects that necessarily accompanied efforts to memorise a completely new alphabet, the serious voyage of discovery through the MECAS Grammar and Word List began. Ten forms of the verb; the mysteries of the 'construct'; irregular plurals; and much else that was incomprehensible at the time and remains obscure thirty years later.

Our linguistic experiences were not, however, limited to the classroom. All the course members looked forward with enthusiasm to the 'language break'. After months of study, the idea of two weeks immersed in the fleshpots of Phoenicia Street, or exploring the souks of Damascus, or roaming round the far ruins of Palmyra and the desert beyond, all had a certain appeal.

Life and Leisure

Our time at Shemlan was spent variously between study and recreation, work and pleasure. Afternoons were spent shuffling word-cards, or with headphones clamped to our ears in the language lab (oh what hi-tech modernity!) repeating the Dialogues already known word-perfect by every shopkeeper in the village. Evenings slipped away at *beit* Selim Hitti with my good friend, Chris de Glanville of Rothmans who lodged there. With a glass or two of *arak* and dishes of *fustuq halabi* (pistachios) on the table we learned the legerdemain of the Lebanese at the mosaic-inlaid tric-trac board; and when – as was inevitable – we were struck down by the effects of Abu Musa's goatmeat stews, Mama Hitti would counsel the medicinal virtues of *laban* (yoghurt) as a cure for all digestive and gastric problems. Weekends saw us down in Beirut, exploring the Burj, talking our way into the beach clubs of Raouche, even (dare it be said) sometimes finding our pictures in the pages of 'Monday Morning' or Peggy's gossip column in the *Daily Star* after being caught on the margins of the social life of the Beirut of those 'Paris of the East' days.

East, over the Dahr al-Baidar, lay another world. The hashish-growers of the Bekaa; the plumes of smoke from the pottery of Jisr-al-Qadi; and the road to Damascus. And there the Hamidiyeh, and '... *filigrane, and paste of apricots and coffee tables botched with pearl, and little beaten brassware pots*'. Damascus offered – as it has through the millennia – a gateway to history, and a people whose warmth and friendship has been a lasting pleasure of my time in the region. As a MECAS student I had experimented over innumerable cups of sweet tea and bitter coffee with those conversations one has about politics in a country where people look over their shoulders, then lean forward before offering, in a whisper, what they want to say rather than what they think you want to hear. Twenty years later I was posted to the Damascus Embassy. I took a walk down souk Midhat Pasha and found the shop in which I had spent so many hours as a young student. The owner, now an old man with failing eyesight, looked on as the son who I remembered as a five year old urchin welcomed the visitor: then '*Ya Burhaan! Waynak hal ghaibeh... zamaan ma shufnak*'. "Where have you been, stranger? It's ages since we saw you.") As if I'd been gone a week, not a couple of decades.

Getting Around
Revelling in the novelty – for most of us – of having a car of our own to drive, we used to compete for the fastest run down the hill to Beirut, and the fastest drive back up. And somewhere I still have my trophy (a polished cylinder-head ornament designed – of course – for use as an ashtray) to remind me of the Liban-Syrie rally sponsored by Chris de Glanville's employers, Rothmans, in which I

was rash enough to get involved.

Three sleepless days followed on the road and in the desert, through the mountains of the Lebanon and across the desert to Palmyra, then to Homs, Hama and Aleppo. Driving, with headlights blazing, through the dark border post of el Qaa... a pause, red-eyed and dust-caked, in front of the water-wheels of Hama and the old mosque (subsequently flattened, along with half the *medina* by Hafez al Assad when his tanks went in after the Ikhwan ...). And finally the finish, roaring into the forecourt of the same Beirut Holiday Inn that, many years later, became such a nest of snipers

Not all of my colleagues were quite such experienced drivers. It was a standing instruction (perhaps apocryphal) to all students who brought cars to MECAS that if, when driving through the local villages, one had the misfortune to hit someone (a child... or even an errant goat), one should not stop. There was – so we were led to believe – a risk of being beaten up, lynched or held for blood-payment.

Despite this, one FCO member of the course who had not passed his test in UK, bravely decided that he should learn to drive while at MECAS. All local driving instruction took place on the old Beirut airfield, using stripped-down Second World War Jeeps or similar vehicles. These did not have such accessories as indicators or rear view mirrors, and learners were not allowed on to the public road until they had passed their test (on the airfield). This seemed to explain a lot about Lebanese driving habits.

But in one sense the Lebanese driving test was well ahead of the UK equivalent. Part of the test was a formal examination on the Lebanese Highway Code. In this document was found the following gem: 'Vehicles going uphill must give way to vehicles travelling downhill ... because the vehicle going downhill may not have effective brakes'.

The End of the Innocence

We did not know it then, but these were to be the last of the golden days. Darker clouds were looming. The Palestinian state-within-a-state was unbalancing the fragile Lebanese body politic. By late 1974, and as we moved on to the Higher course and a new group of beginners arrived, the mood was changing. One of the new Canadian students, driving back from town late one Saturday night, took a wrong turn by the airport and, heading towards Choueifat through a Palestinian area, failed to see, or to stop at, a PLO roadblock. He and his car caught a burst of automatic gunfire. Had he not been super-fit (he had been a downhill ski-race champion) he might well have died. In February 1975, I moved to Amman

Epilogue

MECAS struggled on for a year or two, as the country slid into violence. In Amman we heard stories of bravery and narrow escapes. Friends from Beirut passed through, refugees moving onwards to the Gulf, Cyprus or further afield. Some of the 1976-77 course actually relocated to Amman with a handful of instructors, and as the junior (and ex-MECAS) Chancery Officer, I found myself looking after a small group who became, in effect, among the last 'graduates' of MECAS. Soon after, the Centre closed for good.

Maybe sometime I'll go back. I'll buy a Coca-Cola and drive up through the villages to the hills of the Chouf and gaze down again towards the sea. But as someone once said, the past is a different country.

Brian Stewart attended MECAS in 1973-75. He was appointed Ambassador to Algeria in 2004. These extracts are taken from his 10-page memoir on his time at MECAS.

'THE COLDEST
AND THE HOTTEST
IN THE LEBANON'
1973-74

Tony Millson

It is now over 30 years now since I left Shemlan at the end of my Arabic course – *en route,* via London, to my first posting in Libya (where the very different type of Arabic was just waiting to make me realise how little I had learned!).

Perhaps, after so many years, odd flashes rather than coherent memories. But vivid all the same.

My first experience of a mosquito net. The sound of bullfrogs in the night. The endless water shortages. Abu Musa's cuisine. Darts before dinner. Naseeb's famous araks (five for the price of a gin and tonic though one was enough to make me brilliant at darts and two sufficient to ensure the board became indistinct...). The humiliation, after a few months, of being beaten at darts by Japanese students who had not seen a dart until they arrived in Shemlan. The desk with the graffiti, 'the moon's a *sukun*'. The look of wonder on the faces of the Australian students when they first saw snow. The lazy hours spent sitting outside the Modca café in Hamra drinking Almaza beer and listening to MEA's 707s scream low overhead.

And then there was the language break (which, when I first saw the timetable, I erroneously assumed meant a total break from Arabic). Two nights at the Funduq al Kabir in Damascus (which was far from Grand). Despite Leslie McLoughlin's assurances, flourishing the MECAS grammar and wordlist in the lounge did not produce lots of guys willing to chat, but rather looks of total mystification. Lying in bed, convinced I was being eaten alive by bugs, and listening all night to car horns (the *AA Book of the Middle East* assured me that it was forbidden in Syria to sound horns after 11pm – clearly no one had thought to tell Damascene drivers). The look on the face of a policeman when, in my Hillman Avenger, and totally lost in the Suq al-Hamidiyyah, I ask for directions, in my best Arabic, to Amman.

I could go on. Picnics at Jisr-al-Qadi. Skiing at Faraya (where a group of us rented for the season the coldest house in Lebanon – the only time in my life when I have put on extra clothes to sleep). And, paradoxically, playing squash in the hottest court imaginable – on the school roof.

Tony Millson attended MECAS 1973-74. He was Ambassador to Macedonia 1993-97 and High Commissioner to the Gambia 1998-2000.

BENEATH THE
IRON BEDSTEAD
1973-74

Mark and Kate Evans

What bliss: no receptions, no entertainment – just parties: no in-tray, no out-tray – just a word-list. A last pleasurable year of university life, lived out in a world of oddities and confronted daily by the fantastic view from our apartment – the sea, the sea, and below us terraces of fruit, the city of Beirut, and the sweep of coastline to Byblos. The word 'apartment' does not do justice to the splendour of our huge terrace where three-year old Anneliese and her German friend Mischa swept round and round in their Kettcars, while adults sipped cool Ksara Rosé or drank Turkish coffee.

Such a blissful existence must be paid for. This was, after all, the first year when the authorities admitted wives to the Arabic course as full students in their own right. So while our daughter sped round the huge terrace, we chanted the Word List to each other or grappled with the idiosyncrasies of our apartment. Why were there holes in the upper wall? – to provide for a stove-pipe, said some, but through these holes came the cold air in the winter and the mosquitoes in summer. We learnt the alternative use of the

MECAS Grammar – thrown flat, it would crush the mosquitoes nesting on the ceiling, fifteen feet above our bed.

Plasticine from the toy-box was pressed into action to cover the mousehole – not very successfully, as a Lebanese mouse gnaws through it and re-appears in the kitchen. Closing the kitchen door firmly, Mark was left armed with his umbrella to battle with the mouse.

The household, fortunately, was run by the redoubtable Fawzia, who plied us with her wickedly fiery *hommous badinjan* from her own kitchen. Having discovered that the oven soared to 250° Centigrade and stayed there, we restricted baking to the 1/4 hour required for Green's Sponge Mix which was made for all possible occasions: what a relief, particularly after we had seen the damp packets and puddles at the bottom of Elia Tabib's deep-freeze.

This was not only the year in which wives and other foreign bodies joined the course, but also the year when MECAS changed from the traditional 'Services' course with its rote learning to the audiolingual approach brought in from Ann Arbor University in Michigan – a change definitely not to the taste of our tutors. Shana'a (he of the short fuse) memorably shouted: 'This is not a course.., this is not grammar.., this is not even Arabic!' Perhaps he had a point when faced for the first time with students from without the gilded circle of British schooling who had never heard of the Ablative Absolute and similar Latin-based short-cuts to language acquisition.

It is amazing how much we did learn given the range of our illnesses. Anneliese managed the full gamut from a rash on the wrist and face, confidently diagnosed by another mother as 'caterpillar trouble', to the dreaded hepatitis, confirmed on the day we sold our car.

Beneath the Iron Bedstead

The only cloud on our horizon was made by the Phantom jets of the Israeli Airforce, who on reprisal raids targeted the Palestinian School just behind the Abi Sa'ab mansion. With our daughter we cowered beneath the iron bedstead as these planes dived towards us: certainly, more frightening to her than the discovery of a scorpion in her shoe! But she went on from laboriously traced Arabic words at school in Souq-al-Gharb to study Arabic at Cambridge.

When we left Beirut airport in August 1974 it was to the now entirely unremarkable sound of mortar fire: we had grown used to the sport of shooting all birds and had, after all, greeted the New Year with fireworks on the MECAS balcony that had been answered by gunfire and church bells. The orange tree in the garden laden with fruit, covered in snow and lit up by spectacular lightning is our enduring, less threatening image of Lebanon's contrasts; sitting on our terrace in the winter darkness of a power-cut, looking over and down to the brilliant lights of Beirut, we had a prophetic insight into the civil wars to come the following year.

Mark and Kate Evans attended MECAS in 1973-74. Mark Evans CVO joined the British Council in 1969. He was Director, Canada 1988-92 and Director, Austria 1996-2000.

HAWKS AND
FALCONS
1974-75

Mark Allen

I first went to MECAS in 1971. The undergraduates' four week course started in late June. Hugh Pilkington and I arrived at Beirut by air, in his two seater, single engined Piper. We had flown down from Oxford, five days of lunching and dining across Europe and the Aegean. Our plane seemed very small in the spiralling stack of large jets, waiting on hold south of Beirut airport. We felt like a gnat with wheeling storks above us and made a very fast landing, tail between the legs, as the airliner following behind us filled the rear mirror.

Up at Shemlan, it did not seem fun to get down to work. This was supposed to be the long vac'. At our first class, to separate the sheep from the goats, Mr Shana'a made us take down dictation. This was very difficult – I had never had experience of this kind of thing at Oxford where Arabic was still taught as a classical language, in other words, a dead one. Alan Jones, my tutor, had told me during one of my moments of despair, that of course Arabic was difficult, but not to worry – 'the first 25 years are the worst'. I was a goat and was put in the bottom set with Edward Chaplin.

Waiting for the Migrants

As soon as I could, I got away to Damascus to look for hawks and spent my twenty first birthday at Rahaibah in the country north-east of the city. There I fell in with a party of hawk trappers who invited me to a big dinner party in a courtyard. The trappers, Syrians from Rahaibah and various bedouin visitors, were looking forward to the beginning of the autumn migration. The first hints of cooler weather, much later of course in Syria than up north, would herald the arrival of the birds. The first migrants would soon be followed by a flood, pulse upon pulse, wave upon wave, of hundreds of different species – half the bird contents of the Palaearctic on the move south. Above, below and amongst them, would be the hawks, together with eagles, buzzards and harriers of every kind. During the summer, the trappers made up their stock of traps and snares. Plaiting and twisting thread stretched on a loop around the big toe, they worked away in the circle of cross-legged men.

The trappers wanted to know about falconry in England and I was cross questioned. I am neither a natural linguist nor an actor and I found it difficult to overcome my self-consciousness about speaking my bad Arabic. These people spoke no English, but we had a great love in common – falconry. So we got on and they kept talking. They were sympathetic and amusing. They told long stories which made everyone shout and laugh at once. It was a noisy, but intense introduction to spoken Arabic. I trace back to that evening a theme running through the years since – my liking for tribal Arabs, the people of the countryside and the desert. They accepted me and because we had such a lot to talk about, I took them for normal. I never saw them through the lens of a viewfinder. I never found them 'romantic', any more than I had the country people at home where I was brought up. The romance of the desert is found in two places: in the imaginations of those who have not spent much time there and, amusingly, in the imaginations of the Bedouin themselves. Like all heroic poetry, the desert song is nostalgic and the Bedouin are addicted to the most fantastic stories about honour and a glorious past.

Ahead of the season, there were few hawks at Rahaibah, but I bought a young sakeret, a male of the large desert falcon, the saker, which Europeans first encountered during the crusades. I took it back to MECAS and thence to Egypt and back to Oxford.

Life at MECAS was different. We were 'the students' and 'language student' seemed painted across our foreheads when we went into the village or down to the Cliff House for a meal. I remember on my first walk being stopped and offered coffee by Philip Hitti who also gave me a gardenia. That shot my concentration on 'forms of greeting' because the gardenia made me think of the girl I had danced with at the Magdalen commem' a week before. Thirty three years later, I still start at the hospitality of the Arab and can only offer the silent tribute of remembering it. I don't suppose I ever really learned how to speak Arabic. Countless generous and hospitable Arabs kindly talked me into it.

There were some Foreign Office students still in Shemlan who seemed imposingly confident and grown up. Henry Hogger was still a bachelor and had a racing car and Paul and Suzanne Bergne brought real style and pace to pre-lunch drinks at that otherwise rather soulless bar. At a party one night at Bait Callan, there was a belly dancer. Bill Carden was the Director and apparently the only grown-up. He seemed to run the place on a long and gentle rein. A number of students wanted to visit Jordan after the course, but there was still an atmosphere of insecurity there following the 'Black September' of the year before. When Bill announced that we were not to go there, everyone accepted this as nothing but kind and friendly advice, despite the disappointment. He was equally good humoured and confidence-giving when I ran into him three years later. I got muddled up in a coup attempt in Khartoum where he was then ambassador. He told the Sudanese to reopen the airport because it was time for his mid-tour leave. They did; BA sent a plane; and I got a lift out on it.

I had my first full strength dose of Lebanese brio and glassy charm when Peter Joy invited me to a cocktail party down in Beirut. I remember Roger Bland was wearing a white dinner jacket and the Lebanese women an awful lot of make up. An introduction to a different aspect of life in the Middle East was an invitation to visit Kamal Abu Deeb, a don at the Oriental Institute at Oxford, who was summering with his family near al-Husn in Syria. We were offered raw liver for breakfast with a yolk-yellow sauce made from garlic and Edward Chaplin ate it.

I remember being struck at MECAS that all the Foreign Office people seemed to know everybody else. They talked easily about people in embassies throughout the Arab world.

Being admitted into that community of friends was a powerful encouragement to me when I later joined the Office. MECAS was a strong factor in creating these bonds which helped us overcome the work and think of the Middle East as a region, a community.

I returned to MECAS nearly four years later, a signed-up beneficiary of all that I had sensed during my first stay. I arrived bored and conventional on a ferry from Venice with a new car-loan, boring and conventional car. Having had a gap year after Oxford, spent in Jordan following up hawking leads among the tribes there, I was remitted the Long Course. Edward Chaplin who had gone on from our undergraduate course to spend a year in Bahrain before his final year at Cambridge, also arrived to start the Advanced Course. The students from the long course were already inculturated into MECAS, not to say institutionalised. They gratefully ate the hospital food served by Musa and his father. They didn't jib at the local tomato ketchup from Spinney's and were on easy terms with the teachers, even the alarming Mr Shana'a. 'My name is Shana'a. It means 'Ugliness'. Remember that the key to the kingdom of Arabic is words…it is always words….always learn the new words.' I felt like a hobbit being given survival instructions for Mirkwood. The Long Course lot had got the top floor rooms with the better view of the sea. Edward and I had rooms above the garage, alongside some very long suffering Japanese students. Nick Witney ran that year's racing car and Brian Stewart ran a rally round Lebanon for a Rothman's representative also on our course. Brian had a white Ford with white hubs and 'added specifications'. I headed for Damascus with a homing instinct.

By the end of the course, my Hillman was all but trashed. I had driven 25,000 kilometres, a good bit of this off the tarmac, and was unable to find a buyer for it. Almost every weekend, I had headed east, into Syria or down to Jordan, to meet up with friends in the Beni Sakhr, the Howeitat and the Ruallah.

The Ruallah Shaikhs

The Ruallah shaikhs were camped on the Hamad near Jordan's borders with Syria and Iraq. The Hamad is a wide swathe of limestone steppe which runs down from Syria, east of the lava country round Jabal Druze and west of the Iraqi Wudian, down to the Nafud sands in Saudi Arabia. This beautiful open country, dotted in those days with bedouin and their tents and camels, was good hawking country – trapping in the autumn and hunting in the winter. Many of the shaikhs were hawking fanatics and had become friends. They had had European friends off and on for over a century. Lascaris, the Napoleonic agent interested in the land route to India; Wilfred and Anne Blunt who were looking for horses and founded the Crabbet Stud on Ruallah stock; Alois Musil, the Austro-Hungarian agent, general and priest who wrote a large ethnographic study of the Ruallah; TE Lawrence for whom they were the gatekeepers to the Syrian desert and Damascus; Carl Raswan who made a film about them called 'The Sheikh'; Glubb Pasha who sometimes tried to arrest them; and William and Fidelity Lancaster, also from MECAS, who wrote a brilliant work of anthropology about them. The shaikhs accepted me as another 'occasional'. I visited when I could, as did they, in Beirut, or later on during my postings until today in London.

On the Hamad there was no Spinney's ketchup. There was no belly dancer, no Japanese, no exercises and no drinks before lunch. We ate little and slept in the afternoon, stayed up late into the night, talking, talking, talking. There was gossip from across Arabia and no television. My Arabic got ahead, spurred on by teasing and mimicry from the Bedouin. The Syrians from Rahaibah visited to buy newly trapped hawks. One of the senior slaves (whose wife told me she was already a teenager when TE Lawrence arrived on the scene) was the chief falconer and very good to me. His technique with wild new hawks was graceful and assured, giving them, within days, confidence and peace of mind. His experience was vast, probably unequalled in Europe since the decline of falconry in the seventeenth century. He taught me a lot and with the desert Arab's reserve about new things took little interest in the bits and pieces I had brought him from London. The Hardy's 12 lb monofilament fishing line did go down well. It was just right for making snares. We spent hours and days scouring the Hamad for hawks, and later, when they were trained, hawking for houbara and hares. They would not let me drive much, saying, 'If there's bump in the desert, Mark will find it.'

Edward Chaplin sometimes came with me. He caused a sensation on the Hamad. The tallest man in the world, as far as the Ruallah were concerned, was Hajji Khalil, a retired white slave who had belonged to the Ibn Muhaid shaikhs of the Fid'an, another branch of the 'Anaizah, north of us in Syria. They were always quite stuck up and had once made it a matter of prestige only to have white slaves. Khalil was proud of his height. When Edward got out of my car and advanced towards the tent, the tribesmen saw the point at once: *'Wailun ya hajji khalil! Ya khabr! Ma ja'k atwal mink!'* (Bad new for you, Hajji Khalil. Here is someone taller than you."

Several times I was late returning to MECAS for Monday morning's classes. John Moberly, the Director, was very forgiving, though he once delicately explained that my ambassador, if I got a posting, would probably expect me to be at my desk at the start of work. The great and merciful absence was the 'Language Break'. On return from it, we had to fill in forms with details about the family with whom we had stayed. A dull ennui settled on me. What should I say? Tell the truth? Say the shaikhly clan numbered about a thousand males, with slaves in scores? Fill the 'main activities' box by saying I had been hawking hares across the border in Iraq? I remembered telling a Palestinian in Amman that I would be away a few days in the desert. He was shocked and said the Bedouin would kill me, possibly eat me. I did not suppose that Mr Theodory's view of my progress in grammar would be lightened by news of such goings on. I recalled the morning we heard that Haile Selassie had been killed and the staff view that he was a 'feudalist' (and had it coming to him). These were early steps in learning about the mistakes of taking sides in the Middle East and being careful with some about who your other friends might be.

The morning in May 1975 when I packed up my car at Shemlan to drive to Abu Dhabi for my first posting, there was trouble down in Beirut. We had had a number of air raids during the autumn and

I was not particularly alarmed, though shocked now at a new level of violence: a school bus had been attacked in Sinn al-Fil and a lot of children killed. It later turned out that this outrage was the detonator for a civil war which would engulf the Lebanon for years. And MECAS would be one of its casualties.

I was lucky to be one of the last generation for whom MECAS and the old Lebanon, its salons, cafes and casino were welcoming and insecurity and violence not so much of a worry, a generation for whom Christmas at the Zenobia at Palmyra or hawking on the Hamad seemed simple and quite natural. Salad days, indeed. And how nostalgic is that? Did something rub off, somewhere? As it happens, for the first time since I left in 1975, I shall go back to Beirut in a fortnight's time. I shall have dinner with one of the shaikhs and doubtless we shall be maudlin by midnight. *Wailna al-ayyam.*

Sir Mark Allen was in the Diplomatic Service from 1973 to retirement in 2005. He attended MECAS in 1974, having graduated in Arabic from Oxford University.

SECURITY
DETERIORATES
1975-76

Nicholas Armour

The 1975 intake arrived in Beirut in September. The FCO was to abolish sea travel entirely early the following year, but we arrived in the traditional style by Adriatica Line from Genoa. Two days in Alexandria/Cairo on the way gave many of us our first taste of the Arab world. We sailed into Beirut harbour with smoke rising over the city and the sound of small-arms fire clear in the morning air. The Embassy had tried without success to get a message to the ship that we remain on board. We landed; it sailed without us; a police escort took us to the Embassy through the deserted streets of Beirut, with just a couple of bodies visible as we sped past. Our luggage and vehicles remained in the port and we wondered when or if we should see them again. Installed in Shemlan three hours later, the sound of gunfire was even louder but no one turned a hair: it was the usual weekend activity of shooting small birds.

We were able to collect our belongings from the port a few days later, on only one of the four visits to Beirut proper which 'the events' permitted over the next few months. Spinneys, the supermarket, remained accessible for a while, as did Sonny Mann's riding stables by the end of the runway. We soon settled into the routine of Shemlan life: lessons in the morning, tennis at the Melkon, squash on the roof, *arak* with Freddie Tabib (in his new house built around a rather sad pine) and weekends in Syria. This routine was interspersed with power cuts, occasional food shortages and, more seriously, the increasingly frequent inability of the teachers to get to us for lessons. Visible drama was provided by the firefights and explosions in Beirut below, much more real than television in some ways but also more remote as we sat on the balcony with a crate of beer beside us.

By the end of October, it was clear that Shemlan was no place for those who did not need to be there. Wives and families were evacuated with a promise that they would return within a month or that we should follow them. Shemlan itself was relatively safe. With the neighbouring villages, a cordon was set up around the whole area at dusk. Young fighters, when not on duty to protect that cordon, would slip down to whichever side of the dividing line in Beirut their religion dictated. The situation never improved markedly enough to allow the wives to return nor did it deteriorate sufficiently to necessitate further evacuation that year. We students felt we were at MECAS on borrowed time and made the most of the opportunities to travel throughout Syria and Jordan before the plug was pulled. We were always advised to check with the Embassy in Damascus whether it was safe to return, but the duty officer there invariably referred us to the taxi drivers: if they were plying trade to Beirut then it was safe, otherwise not. In Shemlan, the problematic shortages were of heating oil and teachers, for many of whom the journey to Shemlan was now positively dangerous. Furthermore, we were reinforcing the regional myth that we were a school for spies: who else would stay on in such circumstances? I have only witnessed one aerial dogfight for real and it was from above, looking down on two ageing Hunters chasing each other over the airport.

On St Andrew's night, the Scottish country dancing suffered for lack of female partners. Singing In Ainab, with Win Gosling to accompany, was wonderful therapy. Win also coaxed the harmonium in the Anglican Church back to wheezy life.

The Melkon hotel and Cliff House café had few customers apart from us. Husbands got mercy flights home at Christmas (and I believe that every British wife bar one produced offspring the following September). Not all the students returned after Christmas. By mid-January, we had lost count of the ceasefires and the airport was usually closed. At the end of January we finally evacuated to Damascus, the Japanese by taxi and the rest of us in two convoys on consecutive days. HMG did not speak to the PLO in those days; so, through intermediaries, it was arranged that a heavily-armed Palestinian convoy would happen to be passing MECAS as we happened to be leaving. There was much camaraderie as they escorted us through over 50 roadblocks, one armed Palestinian much enjoying his ride on the bonnet of a white Pontiac Firebird. Just beyond Sofar, we bade our Palestinian escorts fond farewell and drove round a bend into the thin sliver of mountain territory controlled by elements of the Lebanese Army. From Chtaura to the frontier we seemed to be on our own. Lebanese officials quibbled for form's sake over expired visas or out-of-date carnets but made no serious attempt to send us back to ministries in Beirut.

At that stage, we were fondly expecting to continue with MECAS either in Jordan or, possibly, Syria. The Embassy made it quite clear that there was no room to stay in Damascus and we headed for Aleppo to await Training Department's verdict on our future. Three days later, the six of us FCO Long Course members with cars set out on the long drive home, each equipped with a 500 Deutschmark note which none of us ever managed to cash. Anatolia was covered in deep snow. Three cars, with efficient fuel pump filters that needed cleaning, ended up spending three days in snow-bound Belgrade. We caught the first ferry from Calais late one night and, God bless somebody's system, word reached HM Customs and Excise in Folkestone of our predicament only ten minutes after we had begun to engage in the potentially protracted battle over possible duty payable on our cars.

We had continuing flavours of the Middle East during our seven months with the Royal Army Education Corps at Beaconsfield. 1976 was one of the driest and hottest summers on record; Arabs studying there kept our enthusiasm alive; and four of us lived in a village called Jordans. A handful of staff from Shemlan turned up to help teach us. It was with relief that we returned to the region in October for a stint at the Jordanian University, again accompanied by erstwhile staff from Shemlan. There we had snow, sheep holding up the rush hour traffic on the Third Circle outside the Embassy, and further travel in the region (the Holiday Inn in Aqaba had opened in our absence, a sad improvement on the Red Sea Hotel with its eight beds to a room and banging fly screens). We even had a terrorist attack on the Intercontinental Hotel, just to remind us of the sound of aggressive gunfire

A Posting to Beirut

From MECAS, I was posted to Beirut in February 1977 as part of the rebuilding of the Embassy following the imposition of peace under the Syrian-led Arab Deterrent Forces. Shemlan had been relatively unharmed by the tides of war and the villagers there always welcomed back any of us who came up for the weekend. As security deteriorated again from early 1978, the main building was occupied by a Palestinian rejectionist group and I was sent up to evict them. It was somewhat surreal spending the night in the Director's house and then wandering down in the morning to drink tea while discussing some form of dialectic with the armed intruders. I saw quite a bit of Janet Hitti in those days and, when a Fatah group from Aley were in residence at MECAS, she was adamant about the reason for their presence. Not for her my suggestion that MECAS was the largest building in the Chouf, overlooking the whole of Beirut and its southern approaches, standing on the principal supply route to the Palestinian camps of southern Beirut; Fatah knew that her mortgage on the premises was with the Arab bank whose principal shareholders were the Hashemite family and thus it was Yasser Arafat's way of getting back at King Hussein for Black September. I have had difficulty with conspiracy theories ever since. I engaged the help of the red-haired, befreckled (Crusader throwback?) Syrian captain in charge of the village roadblock on that occasion. We were joined by a young Palestinian from headquarters who arrived in a flurry of dust. He explained to the occupants that the mortars were in slower vehicles, about ten minutes behind. He spoke beautiful English, learnt at Sandhurst, where he had thrown up the chance of a career in the Egyptian Army and joined the revolution.

MECAS did re-open briefly in Shemlan in 1978. I suspect the re-opening was doomed from the start. As I drove to collect from the Syrian frontier some of the new students arriving by car, I stopped on the balcony road in Aley to see why everyone was looking over the edge. The noise of bombardment was always exaggerated in the mountains, so it was some time before I realised I was standing under the arc of fire from a battery of Syrian mortars. I am glad that our cohort at least had a taste of Shemlan. Four of them are currently (February 2004) serving as Ambassadors in the Arab world, more than can be said for my own intake.

I managed a day trip to Shemlan in April 1982 while on a short holiday in Lebanon escaping the pressures of a London desk. Freddie Tabib, as in the late seventies, had persisted in his ideas to rebuild MECAS, initially centred on his own house in Shemlan but later looking at buildings in Broumana. Other Shemlanis seemed more resigned to our absence. I did not get back again until 1991 when, with then Ambassador David Tatham, we picked over the remains of Shemlan. Most of the buildings were still standing but all had been looted and even the wooden window frames taken for firewood. The Maronite Church had obscenities written on the walls. The last page of an English hymnal fluttered on the steps outside the Anglican Church: the harmonium, designed for mule-back transport, accompanying those early Anglican missionaries, existed no more.

Nicholas Armour attended MECAS in 1975-76. He was posted back to Beirut in February 1977 and covers here the period to the closure of MECAS in 1978.

THE END OF THE ROAD 1978

Duncan Campbell-Smith

The Hittis' home sat towards the bottom of the village. Salim shuffled out to greet us, silent but grinning gleefully at my arrival. Behind him stood his wife Nouha. Clapping her hands, she gabbled excitedly and ushered us into their kitchen for coffee and cakes. Nouha Hitti was a saint, and I was swept up by her warmth and generosity from that first moment.

Salim and Nouha could speak no English whatever, so it was a relief when two sons appeared. Bassam was 16 and still at school. His older brother Amin was 25, newly married and worked in Beirut for American Express.

On my first Saturday, Nouha gathered together a huge supper party in my honour. I marvelled all day at the elaborate preparations that filled the kitchen, and watched fascinated as Bassam helped his mother shave all of the hairs off the skin of an entire sheep's skull that then disappeared into one of several huge cooking vats.

I should, of course, have been prepared for the sheep's eye, but wasn't. Didn't everyone in England know that Arabs were fond of eating sheep's eyes, and wouldn't it therefore be disappointing for me to find a first celebratory supper without one? So the meal that

243

evening included, along with dozens of wonderful native Lebanese dishes, a vast mound of mutton atop an ocean of rice – from which Bassam triumphantly extracted a large lump of gristle, with an unmistakeable black cornea attached. This was dropped onto my plate, amidst much raucous comment from all sides. I duly squirmed and wriggled, then downed it with a suitable grimace. Squeals of laughter all around – and that was the last sheep's eye I ever saw in the Lebanon.

The Syrian Peace-keepers

Life quickly settled into a happy routine. I would breakfast with the family, then walk to the school for lessons starting at 8.30am each morning. My route led up the steep hill outside the house for a couple of hundred yards, then off to the right along a path that led through a small meadow and provided a short cut to the main road.

In the meadow sat a green Russian T-62 tank, and beside it a small camp occupied by a dozen or so Syrian soldiers of the Arab Peace-Keeping Force. It was often raining, sometimes heavily, and the men sat huddled in their tents leaving only a sodden sentry or two to nod miserably in my direction as I scuttled past under my umbrella.

There was never anything remotely threatening about their presence – unless you happened to be a small bird, in which case the meadow was definitely best avoided. I would often spot one of the soldiers huddled intently at some distance from the camp, with a .22 airgun trained pathetically on a nearby bush. Certainly it was rare to hear a blackbird or a sparrow in Shemlan – the airgun snipers had done for them all. (The same, it was said, accounted for Lebanon's lack of seagulls, which was probably apocryphal but seemed plausible enough.)

Lunch alone with Salim and Nouha should have been a strain in my early weeks, when we could hardly communicate at all. Yet it never was. Nouha was a patient teacher, always ready to help me work though some new bit of vocabulary – telling the time of the day, say, or identifying some of the foodstuffs in the kitchen. Salim would sit, hunched silent and watchful over his plate.

Then I would retreat to my room, to tackle the latest page of the Selected Word List and the rest of the day's homework, until at 4pm without fail there would come the same daily invitation from Nouha to join her for tea and cakes in the kitchen.

Evenings at Home

This brought the second opportunity of the day to review Nouha's preparations for the evening meal and any bits of ironmongery laid out for the task. The kitchen was often filled with more contraptions than I'd seen on one bench since quitting physics at school: some were for grinding up or mixing or hollowing out, others for stirring and stretching and sieving. There were wheels and pedals and pulleys that Nouha could sit working at for hours in her daily regime. Even in the last, cold rainy weeks before the spring, little ever seemed to come out of a tin or even a packet. She prepared food as one could imagine generations of women in her family had prepared it before her.

And Salim, doubtless also true to countless generations before him, sat and smoked while she did it. His duties as the village butcher were not onerous. Once a week, on a Friday evening, he would take delivery of a sheep that would spend the night tethered in the garage beneath the house, and early every Saturday morning he would lead the sheep across the road to his shop and cut its throat.

For a few hours, there would then be the sound of much hammering and sawing, while the street flowed red with blood. After which, Salim would return contentedly to his main routine – challenging all comers to trik-trak (aka backgammon) on the rickety table outside his shop, and steadfastly puffing his way through several packs a day of Marlboro cigarettes.

I provided him with a fresh opponent to be humiliated at the trik-trak board. My monthly rent was certainly a matter of little consequence to Salim compared with the incalculable pleasure it gave him to fox me with the dice each night. He would scuttle away after supper and sit waiting in the living room for my arrival at the board. If ever I dallied too long at the table, there would be much coughing and a clattering of counters that would grow louder by the minute. Finally, unable to tease him any longer, I would step round the living room door and feign surprise to find, yes, a beaming Marlboro Man poised and ready to roll.

And then there would follow a bout of excruciatingly bad TV – almost always Lebanese (or, worse, Egyptian) soap operas featuring dysfunctional families or star-crossed lovers. Nouha would sew and Salim would smoke, while hysterical in-laws bickered on the small screen for an hour or so. Finally, the Lebanese national anthem would blare out, to announce the arrival of the main evening news.

Weekend Pursuits

By way of grading the importance of this or that disturbance, the foreign press in February 1978 was still inclined to compare them with other events 'since the civil war ended'. True, there were random explosions somewhere in Beirut on most nights, and constant reports of fighting between Palestinians and Christian militiamen in the far south near the Israeli border. These, though, were not seen as the harbingers of renewed civil war. They were rather the dying embers of the war that had supposedly burned itself out in December 1976. For the most part, life in Lebanon was supposed to be edging back to normality.

And so it seemed to us in Shemlan, based on our weekend forays into West Beirut. These were hugely enjoyable. After the single-minded focus all week on Mr McLoughlin's Course in Colloquial Arabic, and the commitment to memory of five times our daily 30 words, it was no small thing to be able to escape down to the city for a day. Few other students had cars, but several would crush into the back of mine or make their own way down each Saturday morning in service taxis via Aaitat, Ain Aanoub and Choueifat.

We would generally congregate in the late morning at one or other of the British-style pubs in the city – more often than not, The Rose and Crown. Fresh newspapers could be read and swapped over cold beers and olives. Then we would move on to one of our favourite restaurants in the city – often, once the summer arrived, a marvellous place in Raouche between the Corniche and the sea. It had a huge open courtyard, where we would sit under canvas umbrellas, looking across at Pigeon Rock in the middle of the bay.

After a long self-indulgent lunch, it would be time to return to Shemlan, or perhaps see a film. And on some Saturdays, there would be invitations to be gleaned from new acquaintances or embassy staff, for a party in the city that night.

Chantal

It was at one of these parties, early in March, that I met Chantal Pule. Petite and ravishingly pretty, her father was a Lebanese of French extraction, her mother Italian. So Chantal spoke English, French, Italian and Arabic almost interchangeably. She seemed almost impossibly exotic, and I rashly invited her to lunch the following Saturday at a restaurant of her choice. Rather to my surprise, she accepted.

She also picked one of the best and most expensive restaurants in Lebanon. I collected her at noon from the offices of Merzario, a container shipping line where she worked as an international booking agent, and under her directions we set off north out of Beirut and up to the small harbour town of Jounieh. Just short of the town itself was a long stretch of pebbled beach, where a row of narrow piers provided access to a string of glamorous looking restaurants. Chantal, confident and *tres chic*, stared down the hard men on the door who were clearly appalled by my shabby student clothes, and in we went.

The waiters were in bow-ties and French was *de rigueur*. There was a pianist playing quietly in the corner, and tables at the centre of the restaurant sported huge statues made of ice. Conspicuously, though, most tables were empty. We were almost the only customers that day. It was easy to imagine such days were now all too frequent.

It made no difference to us. The food was exquisite. The window views along the seashore were surely no less beautiful than they had been before the war. And I made Chantal laugh, which seemed a good start if we were going to see each other again.

Not necessarily, though, in Jounieh. Chantal, thank God, made no pretence of being a regular. Indeed, it was quickly clear from everything she told me about her family that the Jounieh jet-set was as alien to her as to me: she lived with her parents and her younger brother in a small apartment in West Beirut. The civil war had been a difficult time. It had forced them out for a while, and they had taken refuge with her grandmother's family in the mountains. Chantal offered to take me the next day to see the village where they'd stayed.

I cannot remember now the name of that village. But I have never forgotten the shock of finding it utterly deserted, most of its houses blackened by fire. Chantal had given me only the most cryptic of warnings before we arrived. Now she wanted me to see what had happened to dozens of mountain villages in the war. It was especially distressing to see so many personal effects strewn about. Children's clothes, a pair of pyjamas, old photographs and bits of broken furniture lay scattered inside the houses. Many people had died here, though fortunately Chantal's family had left and taken hotel rooms in Cyprus a short while before the village was attacked.

Until this time, I'd really had only a little bookish knowledge of the war. Hearing of Chantal's personal experiences of it was a very different matter. And by the end of March I think I had a rather better appreciation of how lucky we were as MECAS students to be cocooned in Shemlan. Or more to the point, perhaps, cocooned in a beautiful corner of the Chouf where Maronite, Shia, Druze and Greek Orthodox communities seemed to have happily coexisted, despite everything.

Expeditions to Syria

So cocooned, in fact, that even the Israeli invasion of the South in the third week of March seemed at first to be of no concern to us. During the mid-morning break between classes, we could stand with our coffees on the balcony of the school and just about hear the sound of distant Israeli artillery, shelling the villages south of the Litani river. But the South seemed another country: the invasion made no difference to plans that several of us had, to visit Syria over the short Easter break just ahead.

Three of us had cars – enough for a sizeable party to travel together to Damascus and back. We drove north to Aley, then east via Bhamdoun and Zahle into the Beka'a valley. I suppose we must have stopped to look at the ancient Baalbek temples, though I have only the dimmest recollection of the place. What sticks far more in the memory is the crossing into Syria.

I was the last to reach the border checkpoint, with Chantal and two fellow students in my Beetle. The other two cars were through the border in minutes. The customs man took one look at my carnet document for the VW, however, and disappeared with it into one of the tents beside the road. Only then, to my intense embarrassment, did I recall the large red letters across the back of the document: INVALID FOR SYRIA. How could I possibly have overlooked them?

The rest of the party, sensing trouble, sat glumly in their cars looking back. I made a show of coping heroically with the usual bureaucratic ineptitude and tried not to think about the humiliating drive back to Shemlan. Perhaps a brave face would see us though after all. Moments later, our customs man reappeared with my carnet – and an invoice to be signed. Entry would cost me fifty Lebanese pounds and that was that. On we went to Damascus.

It was the first of three such expeditions. A group of us went again in May between the spring and summer terms, and a third time in the mid-term break in June. Always we encountered the same unwavering friendliness and warmth: wherever we stopped, nothing was too much trouble to the Syrians. Of course this was in part a simple taste of traditional Arab hospitality, and no doubt our gallant attempts to converse in Arabic endeared us to the café owner in many a remote country village. But it also dawned on us quite quickly that we were not exactly the first intrepid travellers from Shemlan to Syria.

On one long drive through the desert, we came upon a bedu walking with his camel a few hundred yards from the road. He was the only human being we had seen for an hour or two, and he waved at us frantically. We pulled up, and he came running across to us, hitching his heavy woollen *jellabeh* up to his thighs with one hand and clutching his scruffy head-dress with the other. It was baking hot. He glugged gratefully on a bottle of water and two small cans of orange juice that we handed over. Then he flashed us a big smile, offered thanks to Allah and said: 'Wa intu al-jawasees min Shemlan?' ('So you're the spies from Shemlan?')

Every trip brought surprises to be savoured for years afterwards: the sight of spring flowers after rain in the Syrian desert; the grandeur of the Roman ruins (and the glorious old Queen Zenobia hotel) at Palmyra; the scale of the cobbled roadway leading from the drawbridge up into the interior of the crusaders' castle at Krak des Chevaliers; the sublime quiet and stillness within the great Umayyad mosque in Damascus, where we watched white-bearded elders reading stories to groups of illiterate working men clustered at their feet.

Bathing in Aleppo
Best of all, perhaps, was the surprise we got in Aleppo.

We stayed at the Baron Hotel. The rooms were full of mosquitoes and the plumbing groaned and chuntered all through the night. But the famous bar was still there, as visited by Lawrence and Churchill and de Gaulle. As of 1978, the old place still seemed to enjoy more than its fair share of Western tourists in the city.

Inevitably, this attracted a good many citizens of Aleppo to hang around the doors of the hotel offering their services as a guide. We were a dozen or so in our party on the night we stayed there – a prize haul for any successful salesman. Leaving the hotel to find a restaurant for dinner on the first evening, we turned down a good many offers. Some way down the street, though, we were skilfully corralled by a clearly very practised operator. He told us he was a masseur in Aleppo's famous Turkish baths. He would await our return to the Baron and promised an interesting end to the evening.

It was almost midnight when we returned and our prospective masseur was all but forgotten. There he was, though, on the steps of the hotel. His name, memorably, was Ardon. The women in the party sloped off to bed, but most of the men followed him to the baths in a troop of taxis.

It was a famous night. Ardon was as good as his word. The taxis took us deep into the souk quarter of Aleppo where the baths were housed in an old Ottoman redoubt. Once inside, we undressed in cellars deep below street level and were shown through to the steam rooms. These filled an area as large as a cathedral crypt, which it resembled with its stone pillars and ceiling of ribbed arches. We sat in a line along one wall, towels wrapped modestly round our waists, wondering what had happened to Ardon.

We did not have long to wait. He reappeared, wearing virtually nothing at all, and carrying a large bucket of loofah sponges and soaps the size of bricks. Most of Ardon was dark and swarthy, but not the palms of his hands and undersides of his fingers, which we now saw were almost translucently pale. He held them up to impress his professional status upon us, then asked for a volunteer. There was a long pause. Smiling happily, he reached for the nearest arm and yanked its owner after him and off to the hammam.

The rest of us waited rather sheepishly for their return, exchanging nervously ribald remarks and wondering if all was quite as innocent as we were supposing. The question hung in the air as Ardon returned alone for his next client. One by one, he led us off. There was no going back.

We need not have worried, of course. Ardon soaped, scrubbed and pummelled each of us with a rare expertise. And when the massage was over, we were collected and escorted to a sublime Turkish lounge. Here we were all reunited among mountains of thick white towels and plates of sweet pastries. We sat on a ring of white woollen sofas, smoking enormous hookah pipes while attendants ran back and forth with dates and freshly sliced oranges and melons. If this was how the Foreign Office trained its future ambassadors, I had to reflect, then it was a diplomat's life for me.

We stayed there most of the night. Then Ardon organized everything perfectly, and a fleet of taxis swept us back to the Baron. I stared sleepily out of the back windows of my taxi, only for a moment jolted awake by the magnificent sight, in the half-light of dawn, of the citadel of Aleppo rising like a mountain above the streets.

For most of my time at Shemlan, Syria was rather more accessible than East Beirut. In fact, I can only recall a single visit to Ashrafiyya, one of the main residential districts of the Christian half of the city. And the significance of that visit had nothing whatever to do with Lebanese politics.

I went with Nouha and Amin in his car to visit an old family friend in hospital there. I cannot now remember her name: let us call her Maryam. She had been widowed or divorced some years earlier (I never did discover which), and lived in Ashrafiyya with her daughter, a painfully shy 17 year-old called (I think) Hanna.

It must have been the early summer. Maryam had been diagnosed with a brain tumour late in 1977. At great expense, she had just been to New York for major surgery. Now she was back and recuperating in a private clinic quite close to their apartment. She spoke excellent English: she had done a little interpreting for me back in my first month. Now perhaps three months had gone by – and what followed was a tiny epiphany of sorts. Mr McLoughlin's Colloquial Arabic and all those innumerable dialogue sessions with our infinitely patient MECAS teachers had wrought a magic that I only now began to appreciate.

As Nouha, Amin and I squeezed into Maryam's private room, I was able to greet all of the other well-wishers with the appropriate courtesies in Arabic. When Hanna perked up the courage to ask about my progress at school, I talked for a good few minutes of this and that, in Arabic. Hanna could hardly disguise her astonishment. And her mother, who had seemed to be lying asleep in her bed, opened her eyes wide and stared at me as though it were my brain not hers that had been seriously tampered with. A marvellous moment – though no doubt Nouha, beaming proudly beside me, had seen it all before.

Maryam made a good recovery. It was Ashrafiyya that took a serious turn for the worse. Fighting in the South was one thing, battles in Beirut quite another. A five-day battle between Christian militias and the Syrian army in the Roumanieh district in April had caused widespread alarm. In May the battle resumed and spread to Ashrafiyya.

A Serious Deterioration

It was reported that Syrian checkpoints on the roads had come under sniper fire. The response from the Syrians was savage, with tanks firing shells point blank into apartment blocks suspected of harbouring the snipers. When tank fire destroyed apartments in their own street, Maryam and Hanna left for Paris and I never saw them again.

As things turned out, they timed their departure perfectly. The May battles marked a serious deterioration in Lebanon's condition. This much was apparent to everyone at the school. Through the afternoons, we started rushing on the hour to catch the latest BBC World Service news bulletin (and I have never since heard the World Service's signature tune without scenting the smells of Shemlan). At the regular roadblocks between the villages in the Chouf, soldiers of the Arab Peacekeeping Force were now checking our British Embassy identity cards with a new seriousness. When we drove down into West Beirut, it was plain to see that an influx of Shiite refugees from the South had been a disaster for the private beach clubs lining the coast road. Several clubs, poised for the onset of their summer season, seemed to have become refugee camps overnight.

One might suppose that all of this must have made one thing very clear: we students of the '77-78 class were in Lebanon on borrowed time. Yet it did not seem so at the time. However much things on the periphery of our little world were changing, we were not to know that the civil war was simply in remission. We went on working hard and revelling in our weekends, as no doubt our predecessors at MECAS had done for 30 years.

With the arrival of summer, the Hitti household took on a new importance in Shemlan. The door from the kitchen opened onto a large veranda, where we now had our family meals – and where any number of neighbours might gather at any hour of the evening to sit, work their worry beads and exchange the village gossip.

There was one draw, of course, that it is safe to say counted for more than Salim's conversation: Nouha's hospitality. Each day she cooked enough for a small army, and many evenings each week a not-so-small army gathered from all directions to eat it. Or to be more precise, gathered for a neighbourly chat, happily in time to be offered a little supper before leaving.

Sunday evenings were the most important of the week, when Salim and Nouha would return from church just across the road, invariably accompanied by two or three of the congregation's middle-aged bachelors. Some of the shopkeepers who sat all week in the street with Salim would then appear and pull up a chair (usually hailing their friend Salim as though they were Stanley greeting the long-lost Livingstone). Finally, we would be joined by the priest and his two assistants.

And Nouha never seemed less than genuinely delighted to have them all there. She would sit through supper watching the men with the loveliest grin on her face. It often seemed as though the only thing that could give her more pleasure than cooking for them was the thought of clearing it all up afterwards – which was just as well, since she usually did that single-handed, too.

Even on the hot afternoons, as she sat on the veranda preparing vegetables or making dough, Nouha would often have one of the village's elderly gentlemen to keep her company. Men like the gloomy Nabeel, a huge and stooping figure who used to totter in slow motion around the roads of Shemlan in between long spells of sitting on village walls, clasping his walking stick in front of him and staring morosely at the ground. Years later, I heard that Nabeel had been shot dead by Israeli troops during their 1982 invasion: it was poignant to think of the old man no doubt being taken wholly unawares by the speed of the soldiers rushing around him.

Aside from Nouha's suppers, the other notable social event of early summer was the start of Shemlan's village dances. For the most part, the young women of the village kept their distance from the school, no doubt very sensibly. But they were always friendly enough – and many of them were gorgeous-looking girls. So whenever there was a dance in the village hall, there was likely to be a table or two of students in attendance, enjoying a beer and admiring the sights on the dance floor.

It must have been at about this time that Chantal introduced me to the Commodore Hotel, where the staff adored her and she enjoyed a kind of honorary-guest status. The reliability of its telexes had ensured the Commodore a full complement of Western journalists during the 1975-76 fighting, and now many of them were back again. The hotel was centrally located, a couple of blocks from the Hamra in West Beirut, and its bar was the best in the city for catching up on political gossip and rumours of the situation on the streets.

It was a strange time, with the threat of so much violence in the air and the hotel full of so many people drawn to it with conflicting motives, all of them naturally pretending not to notice that anything out of the ordinary was happening. The foreign correspondents of the London and Paris papers brought their own brand of cynicism. The staff from the British Embassy affected an air of professional detachment. And most of the local political figures who milled about the place (including a pinball-obsessed Walid Jumblatt, leader of the Druzes) seemed happy to treat the hotel as a welcome strip of no-man's land, where sectarian squabbles were to be avoided at all costs. Not quite Rick's Bar out of Casablanca, perhaps, but cast in the same mould.

Mounting Tension

The second half of the MECAS summer term ran from early June to the end of July. Every aspect of life in Shemlan grew more intense. There was no escaping the mounting tension. In the Lebanon at large, things were falling apart.

For our (mostly Palestinian) MECAS teachers, as for the villagers, it must have been a time of acute anxiety. One of the them, poor man, had to move temporarily into the school when his city apartment was destroyed. Most of the time, though, the teachers were remarkably stoical and went about each morning's classes as painstakingly as ever. And our Arabic, each morning, inched a little further forward.

By now I had accumulated half a dozen or so of the small orange HMSO exercise books in which we kept our Grammar Notes, our Colloquial Phrases and our Homework Assignments. We were also two thirds of the way through *The Way Prepared*, a collection of short Arabic texts used in MECAS since time immemorial for translation practice.

It was striking how many of the texts adhered to the same kind of stilted government pronouncements – no doubt selected with one eye on the practical needs of the Arabic speaking diplomats we were all supposedly to become. Just as, in the Latin textbooks of my childhood, Caesar had always seemed to be setting out next day *sine mora* to attack the hostile Belgians, so now it was invariably the director of this or that organization who was convening a conference, to discuss with government ministers how the general situation could be improved ...

What needed most improving was always clear enough: we needed more vocabulary. By June I had almost a shoebox full of the little white cards with which we memorized our way, page by page, through the MECAS book of ten selected word lists. The cards were about the size of a London tube-train ticket: on one side, we wrote the English and on the other its Arabic equivalent (with 'pl/v.n.' and 'imperf.' and an 'N.B.' for any unusual feature). Every afternoon saw another thirty squirrelled away in the box.

Sonic Booms and White Smoke

One afternoon was abruptly interrupted. It happened during the few weeks I spent word-listing on the flat roof of the house. The view from there was spectacular: the craggy, wooded hillsides of the Chouf fell away steeply below me, all the way down to the coast and the blue of the Mediterranean. On most days, I could pause every ten minutes to watch an MEA flight taxi into place at Beirut International Airport, take off down the shimmering runway and veer slowly out across the sea until it vanished.

There were days, though, when no planes moved on the airport tarmac. Then one listened only for the ominous sonic boom that meant Israeli F-15s were somewhere in the skies above Lebanon and no civil airliner could risk a take-off. Midway through one such afternoon, I saw an Israeli plane fall steeply down across the city and fly low along the coast before climbing back up into high clouds. Two minutes later it repeated the manoeuvre. This time, as it raced down the coast, there appeared in its wake a sudden blossoming of white smoke. A moment later, the air in Shemlan seemed to wobble and the sound of the bomb's explosion rippled across the Chouf.

Haatim Tye

Faced with events like that, there were aspects of the MECAS course that could sometimes seem better suited to a bygone era of Imperial Political Agents and client Gulf sheikhdoms than to the nasty business of modern Middle Eastern politics. After MECAS, we might still struggle to keep abreast of arguments in Arabic over armaments and UN resolutions; but we were seldom going to be stuck for a handy desert proverb.

Thus, we learned that Haste Comes From The Devil; we knew that it was vital that we Choose The Companion Before The Way, The Neighbour Before The House and we would not forget that He Who Takes His Clothes Off Gets Cold.

Best of all, though, we would have just the right words to cope, in the event of encountering an act of quite heroic kindness and generosity: 'Inte akram min Haatim Tye' – You are more generous than Haatim Tye. Sheikh Tye it was who slaughtered his prize stallion to serve it up as dinner for a hungry stranger arriving unannounced at his camp in the Syrian desert – only to discover too late that the stranger had travelled for weeks to offer him a fortune for the horse. If the Foreign Office ever needed a password for MECAS alumni – something instantly recognizable to them and no-one else – there could only be one choice: it would have to be Haatim Tye.

Impressions of the War

By now Christian Beirut was almost another country. We never strayed beyond the Chouf and West Beirut. Even there, a steady rise in the activities of the Arab Peacekeeping Force was prompting a new wariness as we made our way to and from evenings in the city.

Only rarely did I stay in the city overnight, at least between weekends. Late in June, though, I stayed because the evening's party had gone on far into the early hours and I was none too sure of the neighbourhood. Asleep on the sofa next morning, my waking dreams were filled with the roaring of an incredibly loud engine: it seemed to rev and rev for hours.

Suddenly awake, I rushed to the balcony. In the narrow street below was a stationary Syrian T-62, evidently inconvenienced by the fact that its route out of the street was blocked – and the obstacle in its way was my car. As the tank belched a great cloud of black diesel fumes and lurched forward, I had two flights of stairs to descend in a hurry. The tank and I reached the car more or less simultaneously, which thankfully was just in time. Syrian soldiers on the pavement waved and laughed, but it had almost been Pancake Day for the VW.

Explaining the loss of my car to Nouha would have been deeply embarrassing: though she would never have said so, it was plainly a mystery to her that anyone should want to trouble himself driving to Beirut more than once or twice a year. She would have much preferred to see me still sitting with all the men on her veranda each evening. I made a point of being there every Sunday for the best gathering of the week. Now that it was truly summer, the warmth and fragrancies of the evening were just a joy and made the harsh winter rains of January and February a distant memory.

Alas, though, things were about to change.

Fighting between the Peacekeeping Force and the Phalange had forced the port to close – a big setback for hopes of real peace (and personally disconcerting, since I had a cruise-ship berth to Athens booked for August). Worse, a heavy Syrian attack on the Christian militias in East Beirut had finally prompted street battles that looked much like those of 1976. A full resumption, in other words, of the civil war.

So the group that gathered together after church was unsurprisingly a little less lively than usual. After they had all taken their seats, but before Nouha had begun to serve the supper, the telephone rang and Salim went off to answer it. He returned as far as the kitchen, where there was a little cry from Nouha and much whispering. She came out to fetch the priest inside, at which point everyone fell silent. When the priest reappeared, it was to say that his brother (to whom he was very close) had been killed in that day's fighting.

He sat down and wept. All the guests gathered in a line and shook his hand one by one, offering what comfort they could. It was moving to see so much affection for the priest in his grief. I understood little of what was said over supper. It was plain to see, though, how the death of someone close to the village had been interpreted: everyone that evening clearly took it to mean the future would now be different. And so indeed it proved.

Murder in the Village

One afternoon in April, a British expatriate man living in the village – vaguely known to us, but hardly a familiar figure – was killed by a single rifle shot as he stood with a sundowner on the balcony of his house. This prompted a huge amount of village gossip: it was said the man had been deeply involved in arms sales to various militias around Beirut. It was clearly regarded as a serious incident by the school's Director and the staff. They assembled the students together next morning, to reassure us: the word from the embassy, said the Director, was that the murder was almost certainly premeditated and not a random shooting.

Still, the shock of a cold-blooded murder in the village did nothing to allay our wariness of anyone seen carrying a gun. Not that it was a common sight. Leaving aside those carried by the soldiers at road checkpoints – and of course the occasional morning sniper from our resident Syrian platoon, out in search of a bird – there was rarely a gun to be seen.

It was gunfire rather than guns that seemed by June to have become a part of normal life. In earlier months, I'd generally fallen asleep at night listening to Shemlan's resident colony of frogs: they croaked and burbled in a deep empty tank that was sunk into the ground almost opposite the Hittis' home. Now, I invariably fell asleep instead to the sound of machine guns ratter-tatt-tatting somewhere along the Chouf. That sounds more alarming than it was at the time: perhaps we were unduly complacent, but soon the machine guns hardly registered as any more threatening than the occasional sound of Israeli artillery had been in the spring.

The Heavy Fighting

Then came the heavy fighting of July, between the Syrians and the Christian militias in Beirut. By day, we could hear the constant shelling in the city and see great palls of smoke rising into the sky. And each evening, after darkness fell, the battles in East Beirut became a kind of appalling spectator sport.

Quite a crowd gathered on the Hittis' rooftop when the fighting seemed especially intense. Bassam and several of his teenage friends proudly paraded their weapons expertise, identifying this or that explosion as the work of a T-62 or an anti-tank gun or whatever. Most spectacular were the Katyusha rockets, small blobs of red light that moved through the darkness far less quickly than tracer and ended in a shocking ball of flame. On some nights, the gruesome grandstanding went on well into the early hours.

As had briefly happened back in May, the fighting made it dangerous to travel on many roads along the Chouf. A blackboard was put up at the front entrance to the school, and each morning the staff would list on it those roads that the embassy had advised them were closed by checkpoints, or simply too hazardous to use.

The list grew longer by the week. Before the end of July, we were regularly being advised not to try driving beyond Souq-El-Gharb, just a few miles down the road. I drove there one afternoon to make a telephone call to Chantal from the Post Office – all lines from Shemlan had been temporarily cut – and was dismayed to find several buildings in Souq-El-Gharb's main street protected by fresh sandbag defences.

Planning Departure

More than likely, I was calling Chantal for news about the port. It had been closed since July 1st, forcing the staff at Merzario's offices into a frenzy of rescheduling. Now it looked as though I might need to follow suit. My ferry to Piraeus was due to sail from Beirut on August 1st; but by mid-July it seemed most unlikely the port would be reopening at all that summer (and in the event, it didn't). The best alternative, said Chantal, might be a boat to Cyprus from Jounieh. But how certain could I be of finding the harbour open in Jounieh?

Most of the other students were booked to return home by air. The airport was still operating more or less normally most days, though no-one could be sure this would last. Suddenly everyone was obsessed with the latest transport problems, even while we prepared for our final exams on July 20 and 21. It was one measure of how quickly things seemed to be unravelling.

And it was now a clear possibility that the end of our term might also be the end of MECAS. The exams came and went, followed by our end-of-term dance on the school premises and our farewell visits round the village. These were tinged with a palpable sadness that must surely have been absent from the students' farewells in happier times.

Towards the end of the month, I was invited to lunch at their home in West Beirut by the head of Middle East Airlines, Assad Nasr, and his wife.

The lunch finally brought home to me that hoping for a miracle in the port was a waste of time. I had to face abandoning my car for a flight, or else make alternative plans to drive home. In retrospect it seems an odd decision, but I opted for the drive.

Chantal made enquiries and learned that most of the passenger ships out of Beirut were sailing instead to Cyprus – with just a few docking in Syria at the northern port of Latakia. This was a bit of a slog from Beirut: more than twice the distance inland to Damascus. But any Jounieh-Cyprus crossing would be fraught with uncertainties, while a definite booking was available from Latakia. Also, Chantal had two friends working as teachers in the Syrian port city who would put us up for a night or two if necessary. The next evening she and I sat in her parents' Manara apartment and plotted the trip to Latakia.

And so the day finally arrived, to bid farewell to Salim, Nouha and Bassam – and Amin and his wife, who had just become the proud parents of a baby girl. It was hard. My Arabic had been (just about) equal to the demands of the MECAS summer exams, but it was no-where near good enough to cope with such an emotional occasion.

In a useless gesture of thanks to Nouha, I had bought her a jewelled brooch in the Hamra. When the time came to leave, and Chantal (who'd been given a lift up from the city by a friend) was already waiting for me in the car below the house, I presented my tiny gift – and regretted it immediately. Nouha squealed with indignation, bending forwards and slapping her knees – I think it was the only time in seven months I had seen her just a tiny bit angry. But then we embraced warmly with tears in our eyes, and Salim silently led me down the steps to the road.

A Labour of Love

Riding shotgun for me to Latakia was a labour of love on Chantal's part. There can be few if any greyer, grubbier cities anywhere on the Mediterranean. She was convinced, though, that I would run into some sticky bureaucracy when I got there, and of course she was right.

It was a long day's drive, from Jounieh up the coastal highway via Jbail and Tripoli. We were exhausted when we arrived late in the evening, and it took us over an hour to find our way to her friends' home. A young married couple, they lived in a bungalow on a sprawling suburban estate that looked depressingly fly-blown even in the dark.

It must have intrigued them that Chantal should be going to so much trouble to say goodbye to me, but they were far too courteous to pry. Next day, Chantal and I set off alone to the port. I had booked a cabin to Piraeus on a Greek boat called the *Heraklion*, scheduled to sail at 3pm, but I still half-expected to find the sailing postponed for some reason that the shipping line had not seen fit to mention. Reaching the dockside by mid-morning, it was an enormous relief to find the *Heraklion* exactly where it was supposed to be, and already loading vehicles.

With a revived sense of optimism, we headed for the Customs building, ready to face one last test of nerve over those magic words 'INVALID FOR SYRIA'. They had caused no difficulty when we were entering Syria the day before. Was it too much to hope that I could now make an elegant exit?

The answer was a fair time coming. We had to sit and wait for the rest of the morning behind a line of the usual variety of garishly painted trucks that clog every route between Turkey and the Arab world. At long last, though, we were approached by a posse of uniformed men who waved us into a reception bay. And no sooner had I handed over all my papers, than the offending phrase grabbed the eye of one of these officials, whose name was Mustafa.

Mustafa evidently held the senior rank, and seemed instantly to regard the offending condition on my carnet as a personal affront. He launched into a tirade of hostile questions. Each (painstakingly polite) answer made him more sullen than before. Finally, sweeping aside all my protests, he insisted I would have to drive to the Duty-Free Zone to have my exit papers properly stamped. It was a matter of sublime indifference to him that the Zone, as Chantal immediately established with another official, was fully 30 kilometres from the port. Defiantly, he even scribbled a little note of introduction for us to his Duty-Free colleagues (which I carried in my passport for years after).

We now faced a horrible dilemma. Given the sailing time of 3pm, there were scarcely two hours remaining in which to make a return trip to the Zone, and to cope with all of the shenanigans this might involve. What to do?

We called Chantal's friends, who with great kindness insisted they would be our guides. Clinging to our last shreds of optimism, we set off to collect them and headed for the Zone. Before long, however, the four of us were locked in an awkward silence. Was it really worthwhile trying to beat the traffic jams out of the city? With over half-an-hour gone and no real progress made, I realised it was hopeless. Despairingly and apologetically, I turned the car around and we crawled agonisingly slowly back to the port.

Since my departure papers were virtually complete, I decided there had to be a sporting chance of catching the ship at the last moment without the final stamp supposedly only available at the Zone. It seemed to have been the right call, when we reached the boarding ramp: all other vehicles had already been embarked, and my VW was waved aboard immediately.

At which point, however, my papers were demanded again and returned to Mustafa in his lair. There followed a tense stand-off, with messages relayed down to me from the ship's captain every five minutes to say he could wait no longer. Meanwhile, of Mustafa or my papers there was no sign at all.

Eventually, with the tide about to turn, the captain ordered my car removed from his ship. Unless I wanted to see it dumped into the harbour, I had little choice but to drive it back onto the quayside. This I did, watched by scores of passengers who by now were lining the stern rails to watch the commotion below. It was not a good moment, and I had missed the boat.

As its stern pulled away from the quay, a man arrived from the

Customs shed and casually announced that my papers were ready to be collected.

With Chantal in tears and her friends haranguing the port officials on my behalf, it seemed the next step might well be a Syrian police station. And if Mustafa had reappeared on the dockside, we would probably have been facing a group charge of causing grievous bodily harm. Instead, a second emissary arrived from Customs – carrying my (stamped) departure papers in one hand ... and in the other an invitation to take tea with the Port Director.

Bemused, we were escorted in a convoy of cars to his offices. These occupied a former colonial mansion with a splendid view of the harbour. The Director's own room had probably been used for official receptions under the French mandate: it was vast, as was the Director's desk. He was standing behind it as we were ushered in, and he waved us into picking a sofa each from several that were clustered at the side of the room.

Then he stepped smartly round his desk to join us, clasping each of us by the hand and dropping any pretence of formality. It was suddenly apparent that he was genuinely and touchingly embarrassed.

'What can I say to you, my friends?' he asked us, in immaculate English. 'You will be familiar with the work of Kafka, I think? Well, I must work every day in his castle.' He rolled his eyes and gave a deep sigh. 'Kafka understood my world. *Yaa salaam!* What a wonderful writer.'

He was utterly charming. By the time trays arrived bearing glasses of mint tea and bowls with the usual huge chunks of sugar, it was already out of the question for us to mention anything so nit-picking as a missed boat. Our host plainly had to struggle every day at living with a whole nation that had missed the boat.

'You cannot imagine how hard it is, to live in a place where the simplest things go wrong every day', he explained, though not without a tired smile. '*Kull yawm!* But we must do what we can, and one day things will get better. *Inshallaah!*'

My unfortunate experience of his port was soon put behind us. (It transpired that Mustafa was locked in a bitter feud with one of his cousins, who also worked in Customs. The offending relative had criticised Mustafa for holding us up all morning in the truck line. Mustafa had therefore been determined to give us a tricky passage, regardless of any wording on my carnet.) We talked of English manners and Arab sensitivities for an hour or more. Then the Director embraced each of us warmly and invited me to return again later in the week if I still needed help to find another boat.

There was not a hint of self-pity in this invitation. One had to wonder, though, how many weeks or months would have to pass before he would host another tea-party conversation about Kafka and the dysfunctional bureaucracies of the Arab world – and he could see we were not overly eager to spend a day longer in Latakia if we had any alternative.

We stayed one more night with Chantal's friends. It was an uncomfortable evening, and I was determined not to repeat it. After a string of telephone calls, Chantal discovered that I would have to wait another full week for the next boat to Piraeus. There was, however, one alternative: I could drive to the container port of Mersine in the south-east corner of Turkey, and try to rendezvous with a Merzario container ship whose captain Chantal knew well. With any luck, I'd be able to hitch a berth for my VW to Italy, free of charge.

And so it happened that Chantal and I, having driven together to so many places over the past few months, shared one last drive – this time to the Syrian border with Turkey. It was a horrid way to say good-bye: all the frustrations of finding a ship made it hard for me to disguise my impatience to leave, yet she had no wish for us to be parting at all. She would be left only with a deflating journey back to Beirut after I was gone. When we would meet again, neither of us could be sure. We relied on a tape cassette to close the awkward space between us, and listened many times to Barbara singing L'Aigle Noir as the border grew closer.

Behind us, slightly comically, followed the husband from Latakia on a scooter. When finally we reached the border, there was an awful moment as the guards poked fun at me for leaving Chantal behind. But she wasted no time on sentimental gestures. She leapt aboard the pillion seat of the scooter and the next moment was waving behind her, as it sped back along the forested road into Syria.

Under other circumstances, the next stage of the journey would have been thoroughly enjoyable. I was totally unprepared for the fairy-tale landscape of Turkey's south-eastern corner, as stunningly beautiful as its towns were disappointing – all the more so, given names like Antioch, Iskanderun and Tarsus. As it was, I could think of little else but reaching Mersine safely and finding my Merzario captain.

We met on my second evening in the city, in a sleazy restaurant of his choice where half a dozen Polish waitresses endured the nightly attentions of scores of lascivious merchant seamen. It was a simple matter to confirm the arrangement that Chantal had already made with him: once all the containers and trucks had been loaded next day, my car would be hoisted aboard if there was any room to spare.

And mercifully, there was. The ship set sail late the next afternoon for Ravenna, on Italy's Adriatic coast. It was not quite the luxury cruise I'd planned. I slept on a bunk in a container, and took my meals with a crew of grunting Swedish sailors in a galley where hard-core porn movies played around the clock.

We reached Ravenna early on the fourth evening. I left the ship a couple of miles out to sea and went ashore on the pilot's launch. This at least allowed me to spend the night in a blissfully porn-free zone: I slept in a construction gang's unlocked caravan, parked on the dockside. My last abiding memory of a half-year in Lebanon is of waking soon after dawn, to see the massive shape of my container-ship's stern gliding slowly past the caravan's window above my head and into its berth. An hour later, my VW Beetle was yanked unceremoniously up from the hold and onto the quay, undamaged and ready for the long drive home to London.

Whether my Arabic ever really earned a penny for the bank that funded my studies, I rather doubt. Only on one occasion did I have the chance to deal with a senior figure who could speak no English: he was the head of Yemeni Airlines, and his European language was Italian. So we had a faltering conversation for half-an-hour in his office in Sana'a about the finances of aircraft leasing. It would have pleased my MECAS teachers and graced the pages of *The Way*

Prepared. But how much my Yemeni friend understood, I don't really know. And he'd certainly never heard of Haatim Tye.

Going Back

I subsequently visited Beirut several times as a *Financial Times* journalist – always seeing Chantal while she remained there, and once meeting up with her in Cyprus. She went on working for Merzario in the city until 1982 and then transferred to their offices in Italy. Eventually, she met and married an Italian, and sadly we lost touch.

It was a long time before I could bring myself to re-visit Shemlan. Of course I heard the news when the school was finally evacuated back to England for good, late in 1978, and I was concerned to hear about the evacuation of the village during the Israeli invasion of 1982 that cost Nabeel his life. After years away, though, I saw little point in trying to make contact again with the family. Perhaps I should have made more effort; but I was lazy and MECAS was a chapter of my life that had closed.

Then in 1998 I returned on a business trip to Beirut. My hosts, hearing that I had studied in Shemlan, insisted that I take a car and chauffeur for the afternoon to make the old familiar drive up to the village. I half-expected a shock and duly got one. No doubt like many other alumni before me, I was startled at the rundown state of the place. So many of the houses were boarded up and abandoned that it came as no surprise, by the time we reached it, to see the Hittis' house in the same condition. Three bullet holes in the wall marked the corner where my bedroom had been.

Duncan Campbell-Smith, then a banker, attended MECAS in 1978. He is now the Director of Communications for Rolls-Royce plc. These extracts are taken from a more detailed memoir of his time in Shemlan in 1978, which is placed in the context of the confused politics of the Lebanon at that time.

ONE OF THE FINAL BATCH 1978

Sherard Cowper-Coles

I was one of the last batch to go to MECAS proper, from September to November 1978. I still don't know whether I chose Arabic or Arabic chose me. I joined the FCO straight from reading Mods and Greats at Oxford, in August 1977. Within weeks of joining I was told that I was suited for hard language training, and could express a preference between Arabic, Chinese and Japanese. I chose Arabic because – I thought rather pretentiously – it completed my knowledge of the Mediterranean Basin, because Arab culture and history was more familiar to me than those of China or Japan and also because, being virtually tone deaf, I could not see myself succeeding with Chinese, whatever the examiners had said.

There followed much excitement about going to the legendary MECAS, which had been temporarily closed because of the Lebanese Civil War, but was due to reopen in September 1978. That summer, the Director, Julian Walker, briefed us in the old Palace Chambers, above Westminster Tube Station, on what we needed to know. I was to drive out, in my proudly acquired Mini, meeting Peter Collecott and James Watt in Turkey, and then completing a journey across Anatolia and Syria in convoy. I shall never forget that journey, or arriving in Shemlan over the mountains from Damascus.

The Syrian Army was everywhere, with checkpoints on every road. Christopher and Nina Prentice, Chris and Dianne Wilton and Richard Northern were among those who joined us in Shemlan.

Once at MECAS, the Chief Instructor, the irrepressible Douglas Galloway, soon had us galloping through *The Way Prepared*, and the MECAS grammar and word list, and familiarising ourselves with Hans Wehr. I still remember understanding that Arabic did not actually have as many verbs meaning to 'Look up alphabetically' as I had first thought, and came to appreciate the beauty of Wehr's wonderful feat of linguistic architecture. I remember from that period visiting Beirut, and seeing the devastation there, but also eating very well in a restaurant run by an aged Jean Pierre (I think) who had arrived in Lebanon from France in the 1930s, and was still cooking. I remember shopping in Hamra, and expeditions to Jisr al Qadi (including impromptu swimming in the river there) and the palace at Beiteddin, and above all the Rock (or Cliff House, as we called it) restaurant. I remember the MECAS bar, and the famous Line Book, which recorded my description of Douglas Galloway as an 'intellectual commando' whatever that meant. And there was a famous 'friendly' football match with the local *shebab*, which ended in fisticuffs.

And then the fighting broke out, with Syrian Katyushas flying over the hills from the valley behind, down on to Beirut. I remember the great clouds of black smoke rising up from the oil tanks down by the port. And, as is still the case today, hearing the sonic booms from the Israeli aircraft flying over to see what was going on.

Then came the bad news that we might have to leave, conveyed by the elegant Sir Peter Wakefield, Ambassador to Lebanon. We were very upset, and so were the teachers, almost all of whom came back to London.

We drove back at high speed in convoy across Syria and Turkey and then Greece, from Igoumenitsa to Brindisi, I think, and up to Ancona, over the Alps and Austria, through Germany and France and Belgium to the hovercraft and home. I still remember racing through Turkey at night in convoy behind Douglas Galloway seeing the sparks from his cigarette falling like the sparks from a steam engine at night.

And then we resumed, in Palace Chambers, London, returning twice to Syria for wonderful language breaks. At some stage we put on a Christmas show, which featured the 'MECAS Evacuation Suite', still on a cassette in my collection. And, after the Higher, I was lucky enough to be sent in April 1980 to spend four months at the University of Alexandria, living with an Egyptian family there, before joining Sir Michael Weir's Chancery in Cairo that summer.

And then in Cairo in 1981 I met, and in 1982 married, Bridget Elliott who, while reading Arabic at SOAS, had completed the MECAS Summer Course in 1975, and actually spent more time in Shemlan than I had. Which completed the circle.

Sir Sherard Cowper-Coles KCMG, LVO attended MECAS in 1978. He was appointed Ambassador to Israel 2001-03 and to Saudi Arabia in 2003.

CORRIGENDUM

THE ARABISTS OF SHEMLAN

Page 271 – Appendix A

In a last-minute re-arrangement of the Annexes, the list of Administration Officers of MECAS was omitted from the text:

Administration Officers

1944-52	K Barrance		1969-71	D A Wright
1952-54	J F Taylor		1971-73	L Banks
1954-57	M W P Cronly-Dillon		1973-75	D G Tunstall
1957-60	J Greaves		1975-76	G Kirby
1960-64	D Pragnell		1977-78	J R Archer
1964-68	R Willcocks			

APPENDIX A

Directors, Instructors and Administration Officers
of MECAS

Directors

1944-48	B Thomas	1965-69	A R Walmsley
1948-53	T V Brenan	1969-73	D C Carden
1953-56	A C Trott	1973-75	J C Moberly
1956-60	D J D Maitland	1975-76	B R Pridham
1960-65	A J Wilton	1977-78	J F Walker

Principal Instructors

1944-46	A Eban	1962-63	A Jones
1946-47	G Kirk	1963-64	H B Walker
1948-54	N N Lewis	1964-65	D Cowan
1955-58	A J M Craig	1965-68	L McLoughlin
1958	H D Michell	1968-70	J Hopkins
1958-59	W Kensdale	1970-75	L McLoughlin
1959-60	D Cowan	1975-76	D Harvey
1960-61	J Hopkins	1976-77	E H Noble
1961-62	M C Lyons	1977-78	D Galloway

Arab Instructors of MECAS

(P – Palestinian; L – Lebanese)

1944-47	Mr Sa'ad (P)		1961-65	Fawzi Khoury (P)
1944-48	Mr Haddad (P)		1962-78	Selim Nader (L)
1944-60	Tawfiq Farah (P)		1962-74	Ibrahim Matar (P)
1945-76	Wadi' Khoury (P)		1962-70	Michel Khoury (P)
1946-75	Constantine Theodory (P)		1962-74	Badi' Massouh (L)
1947-48	Mr Jabri (L)		1965-78	Daoud Dallal (P)
1954-57	Selim Nasr (P)		1968-78	Farid Tabib (L)
1954- ?68	Emile Hitti (L)		1968-71	Shahin Nimr (L)
1957-68	Khalil Khoury (P)		1970-72	George Dabaghi (L)
1957- ?	Isbir Maqdisi (L)		1970-78	William Haddad (L)
1957-78	Michel Khammar (L)		1970-72	George Sayigh (P)
1957-64	Yusuf al-Khadra (P)		1972-74	Khalid al-Sayyid (P)
1957- ?	Najib Germanus (L)		1973-75	Nadim Khuri (P)
1958-78	Talaat Dajani (P)		1974-76	Raja Assad (L)
1958-72	Ibrahim Dallal (P)		1974-78	Salim Afyouny (L)
1960-66	Tawfiq Qustandi (P)		1974-75	Mr Shoueiri (L)
1960-78	Ahmed Moumneh (L)		1975-78	Michel Abu Jaoudeh (L)
1960-78	Fadl Shana'a (P)		1977-78	Leila Haddad (L)
1960-61	Daoud Dallal (P)		1977-78	Mrs Dawaanee (P)

APPENDIX B

The MECAS Verb
Research by Professor Alan Jones

makasa yamkisu maks	to cheat, defraud; +*fi* to involve oneself in (something onerous)
makisa yamkasu makas	to be a language student; to be crammed; to be in the habit of learning 19 words a day
makkasa	to collect taxes; to teach in a language school
makasa	to bargain, haggle; to offer a language allowance to
amkasa	to go to MECAS; to sweat five nights a week
tamakkasa	to win a scholarship to MECAS; to feed on camel-thorn or starch
tamakasa	to form a syndicate; + *ma'a* to discuss local scandal with
immakasa	to engage in espionage while pretending to study a foreign language; to learn to drive in Beirut
imtakasa	to undergo a word-test or examination: + *bi* to participate in a drunken orgy

imkassa	to cease (pain); to graduate from MECAS
istamkasa	to wish to go to MECAS; to preach the harmlessness of language training
imkassa	to become accidentally red on the face and neck; to go skiing on alternate weekends
imkawkasa	to be green or blue with crimson and silver marks (of striped Yemeni cloth)
imkawwasa	to last long (of a hangover); to become long (of a beard)
imkansasa	to become round-shouldered, dim-sighted or drooling
imkansa	to be hard or difficult (of obscure vocabulary)
makasi	this fossilized imperative appears to be an imprecation meaning 'get lost' or words to that effect.

Alan Jones was Principal Instructor at MECAS 1962-3. He taught at Oxford from 1957-2000, being successively University Lecturer in Arabic, Turkish and Islamic Studies, Reader in Classical Arabic, and finally Professor of Classical Arabic. He is Emeritus Fellow of both Pembroke College and St. Cross College. His research has been mainly in Arabic language from the earliest times to the present day, pre-Islamic Arabian poetry, the Quran, and Andalusian Arabic literature. Since 1967 he has also worked on the application of computers to texts in Arabic-based scripts.

APPENDIX C

The MECAS Association

General Commitee

President	Sir James Craig GCMG
Past-President	Sir Harold Walker KCMG
Secretary	Patrick de Courcy-Ireland CVO
Treasurer	Brian Constant MBE
Membership Secretary	Richard Owens MBE

Membership

At 31st December 2005, there were 471 active members.

The MECAS Archive

Editorial Panel:	Sir James Craig GCMG
	Sir Donald Maitland GCMG OBE
	Paul Tempest
Archivist:	Larry Banks OBE
Editor:	Paul Tempest